Putting Jesus in His Place

A Radical Vision of Household and Kingdom

Halvor Moxnes

Westminster John Knox Press
LOUISVILLE • LONDON

Scripture quotations from the Revised Standard Version of the Bible are copyright © 1946, 1952, 1971, and 1973 by the Division of Christian Education of the National Council of the Churches of Christ in the U.S.A. and are used by permission.

Scripture quotations from the New Revised Standard Version of the Bible are copyright © 1989 by the Division of Christian Education of the National Council of the Churches of Christ in the U.S.A. and are used by permission.

Scripture quotations marked TEV are from the *Good News Bible*—Old Testament: Copyright © American Bible Society 1976; New Testament: Copyright © American Bible Society 1966, 1971, 1976.

Book design by Sharon Adams
Cover design by Mark Abrams
On the cover: *The Youth of Our Lord* (oil on canvas) by John Rogers Herbert (1810–90).

First edition
Published by Westminster John Knox Press
Louisville, Kentucky

This book is printed on acid-free paper that meets the American National Standards Institute Z39.48 standard. ∞

PRINTED IN THE UNITED STATES OF AMERICA

03 04 05 06 07 08 09 10 11 12 — 10 9 8 7 6 5 4 3 2 1

Library of Congress Cataloging-in-Publication Data

Moxnes, Halvor.
    Putting Jesus in his place : a radical vision of household and kingdom / Halvor Moxnes.
      p. cm.
    Includes bibliographical references and index.
    ISBN 0-664-22310-9 (alk. paper)
    1. Jesus Christ—Homes and haunts—Israel—Galilee.   2. Galilee (Israel)—Social life and customs.   I. Title.

BT303.9.M69 2003
232.9'08—dc21
                                          2003047902

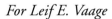

For Leif E. Vaage

Contents

Acknowledgments

This book has a long history and a long list of colleagues and friends who have helped in the process. Thanks are first due to Dale B. Martin, who challenged me to think about place and theory, to Elizabeth A. Clark who inspired me to read early Christian writers, and to Eric M. Meyers who introduced me to the archaeology and history of Galilee. The spring semester in 1997 at Duke University was an exciting period, with a seminar with Eric Meyers and his students, and the theory group with Dale and Liz and, not least, a number of graduate students who have gone on to become inspiring colleagues and friends. But these ideas and the work done then would not have matured into this book without the never-ending conversations with Leif E. Vaage at Emmanuel College in Toronto in two spring terms, 1999 and 2001. Leif introduced me to Q studies, but more importantly he is an unsurpassed conversation partner and a better reader of my texts than I am myself. As a small token of thanks the book is dedicated to him. Also other colleagues at Emmanuel and the University of Toronto, especially Peter Richardson, provided support and encouraged curiosity. Thanks are due to Dale and Liz, who read parts of the manuscript, to Troels Engberg Pedersen, who read the whole; and in particular to Leif, who read chapters along the way, and in the end also the final version. My editor at Westminster John Knox, Carey Newman, showed an energetic interest in the project and pushed me toward writing in a way that could both communicate my ideas and communicate with my readers. I hope he has had some success; shortcomings in this and other areas are utterly my responsibility.

The hospitality of scholarly institutions is one of the true gifts of academic life. It has been generously provided by the Department of Religious Studies, Duke University, and by Emmanuel College, Victoria University in the University of Toronto. And the libraries of these institutions became home places that opened up their resources and provided assistance, which is also true of the library of my own Faculty of Theology at the University of Oslo. I am also grateful to the Faculty of Theology for a good system of sabbaticals and economic support for travels that made my research periods possible. "The Formation of Christian Identity in Antiquity," a project financially supported by the Norwegian Research Council, has provided financial support, and colleagues and graduate students in the project, from biblical and early Christian studies, history of religion and classical studies, have provided a challenging and friendly environment for my work.

Along the way, earlier versions of the book have been given as guest lectures or presentations at the universities of Aarhus, Copenhagen, Uppsala, Bologna, and Toronto, or as papers at the Society of Biblical Literature and the Society for New Testament Studies; and I am grateful for discussions and critical questions. The Context group has as always been an important environment of intellectual and social stimulus, easily recognizable in the book.

A book about home and household has made me extremely aware also of my personal needs for these institutions. Dale and Liz helped me find housing and became family at Duke; Lynne and Paul Stott gave me a home away from home in Toronto; Leif Vaage and his family included me in their extended household, and others became family of friends, like Luigi, David and Rob, John and Chunha. And, as always, Arnfinn is home; he has been my daily discussion partner on all aspects of place and home and, not least, has kept the project on track. Thanks to all of you!

Finally, sincere thanks are due to my editors, Carey Newman who initiated the project and expertly guided it along, Gregory L. Glover who took it over at its final stage, and the rest of the efficient and helpful staff at Westminster John Knox! Thanks also to Vemund Blomkvist who helped me with proofreading.

Chapter 1

What Is in a Place?

"Where do you come from?" This is an old conversation starter, known from Homer on. I have wondered why this is such a popular question, especially in many traditional societies. One reason may be that in such societies many people lived in small and isolated communities, and until recently they did not travel or move much. Thus, place of origin took on a special importance. For instance, in the Old Norse sagas people were named after their homesteads. There was a sense of "rootedness" in the place of origin. This seems still to be the case for many when they ask, "Where do you come from?" But where do I come from? In my youth my family moved several times, so it is not easy to find any one place that will answer the question. And it seems strange that a place where I lived my first few years should hold more information about who I am than other places where I have afterward chosen to live and to form important relationships.

The question "Where do you come from?" which seems so simple, hides a number of assumptions and presuppositions about relations between an individual and her/his place of origin or residence. We tend to think that if we know the place that people come from, we know something about them. But what we think about that specific relation between place and people, and what importance we ascribe to it, differs much in various cultures.

1

"Where do you come from?" was also a question that was addressed to Jesus and much discussed in the traditions about him. It is reflected in the comment ascribed to Nathanael in John 1:46: "Can anything good come out of Nazareth?" Here the same presupposition is at work—that there is a relationship between place of origin and the character of the person. In his lifetime Jesus was known as Jesus from Nazareth. But Jesus left Nazareth. Most of his public career took place outside of his home village, in other parts of Galilee, and he and his followers were also known as Galileans. He died in a fateful encounter with another place, Jerusalem. He was not just formed by his place of origin, but actively engaged in forming a life and shaping other people's lives in other places. Thus, the relation between place and identity is also a matter of places of choice. It is John's Gospel that most insistently asks questions about place and the identity of Jesus: "Where are you staying?" (John 1:38) "Where are you going?" (John 13:36). In many ways John's Gospel is "modern" in the way it poses questions of identity in terms of *place*. And it is these sorts of questions I want to raise in this book: Where did Jesus come from? What did his place of origin mean? But even more, I shall ask how he actively shaped and challenged those places that were part of people's identity.

PLACING THE BOOK

The purpose of this book is to see the activities and words of Jesus in terms of their position and function in *place*. The goal is to uncover the *spatial dimensions* of the historical Jesus. My starting point is that identities are located, developed, and sustained in place. I shall therefore look at the house with household, the village and the larger area, and Galilee itself as important locations of identities. But to be in a place, to be "placed," does not just imply geographical location; we may also, for instance, speak of social, ideological, or mental places in terms of gender, ideology, or power. To say that Jesus and his followers were placed in a house or a village also indicated that they were placed in a system of social and gender positions. But Jesus left his own household and dislocated his would-be-followers from their households, and established the possibility of a new place as basis for identity. This view of the spatial dimension of Jesus' activities is consciously chosen. It has so far been neglected in studies of the historical Jesus, and therefore I want to highlight it.

Thus, this is a book on the historical Jesus viewed from a particular perspective, not a biography or a life of Jesus. Consequently, it does not and will not cover all aspects necessary for a biography. As a study of the place of Jesus, it consciously focuses on his beginnings in Galilee and the primary places for socialization, and his break with those places. That sets this study apart from other studies, which center on the end of Jesus' life, his death and crucifixion, with a focus on Jerusalem as the place for the final events.[1] Their goal is to tell the story of Jesus in such a way that it leads up to and explains that end. This book is different. In speaking about Jesus' position in relation to places in Galilee, it points toward Jesus' breaks with and challenges to other places of power and symbolic order. When we have noticed how Jesus chose a place on the margins in Galilee, his death outside Jerusalem at the absolute margin, Golgotha, comes as no surprise. But it is beyond the scope of this book to tell how that happened and to point to differences or similarities between Galilee and Jerusalem.[2]

Likewise, this new perspective means that the study does not survey all the other discussions that have dominated the study of the historical Jesus in various phases of previous scholarship. This means, for instance, that we do not examine in depth Jesus' relation to Judaism, a central topic in most studies of the historical Jesus in the so-called "Third Quest."[3] In this study, with its focus on the spatial dimension of human life and human practice, Jewish practices and structures of order are relevant, but this is not a study of Judaism as an ideology within the context of the history of religious ideas, within which so many of the studies of Jesus and Judaism are undertaken. Nor will this study discuss another topic that has caused much discussion in recent scholarship: whether Jesus was an apocalyptic figure or not. That was a question influenced by the modern focus on time. Some of the texts on the kingdom of God that are used in this study have been central to that discussion, but here they will be read from the perspective of place. This study should be judged for what it accomplishes, not whether it answers the questions posed by these other interests.

The Place of the Reader

If we ask about the place of Jesus, we must also ask about the place of the reader. That we all read from our own particular places is an insight that has become more widely recognized.[4] Therefore, our studies should also demonstrate an awareness of the place of the authors, from which we construct our scripts.

The first place that I must consider is my own place as a reader, how my questions and the way I read are informed by the places that I have inhabited. Second, I must consider the larger context of interpretations with which I interact, that is, the geographical, social, and ideological place of earlier interpreters that have shaped the way in which Jesus has been placed. And then, finally and foremost, it is the place of Jesus in his context, which is the primary goal of this book. Let us have a look at each of these in turn.

Starting with my own life, it is obvious that my experience with places has shaped not only an interest in places, but also the particular aspects and perspectives of place that I find fascinating in a study of Jesus. I indicated above that I was unsatisfied being defined by a place that I had not chosen. As many other youngsters growing up in small places on the periphery along the western coastline of Norway, I wanted to get away to other places that gave more opportunities. I know that my experience of living at the geographical periphery of Norway in the twentieth century is not the same as living in Galilee in the first century or in Sinai today (see chapter 3), but at least it makes me ask the question: What was it like to live at the periphery and to leave that place?[5] From my own experience I know also that place and periphery refer not only to geographical, but also to social, cultural, and ideological places. After leaving my childhood's periphery, I eventually attended the University of Oslo, centrally located in Norway. But in other ways I could not escape the periphery. I was still outside the dominant places of power, of masculinity, and of heterosexuality. Being a gay New Testament scholar has put me in an interesting place, situated between traditional "male stream" theology and a minority position. It has made me aware that the gender system represents a place in households and in society at large that determines the power structures of those places. Systems of gender and sexuality are ways of "putting people in their places." To break with these systems or to blur the boundaries of these places makes free but also puts one in a precarious position.

Traveling is another way to become aware of the dynamics of boundaries between places. Especially during my periods of study in the United States in the 1970s, I became intrigued by the cultural complexities involved in understanding places that at first sight appeared to be similar to those I knew from Europe. I think it was this curiosity that helped me write the "travelogue" from Galilee (chapter 8), a place that I believed I knew well from the religious education of my childhood. In recent years, working together with colleagues and students in a network of theological schools in Africa, Asia, Latin America, and Europe has brought me to see other places than my own, and in small ways also to see from other places. This has made me more aware of the power of places to create hegemonies of reading and interpretation. Europe and North America have been and remain privileged places from which to read. Centuries of hegemony of colonial power and domination defined the rest of the world as places that were "other." Jesus, too, was read from this colonial perspective, which is slowly changing in a postcolonial world.[6]

In a study of the historical Jesus it is also necessary to emphasize another aspect of hegemony and colonialism, the patriarchy and male dominance in biblical scholarship. Jesus has been discussed and presented from male place almost exclusively, both in terms of those who have undertaken this type of study and in terms of perspectives and presuppositions. Elisabeth Schüssler Fiorenza, who has herself made important contributions to a reconstruction of the Jesus movement from a feminist perspective, has rightly and insistently pointed out how scholarship on Jesus has been located at the intersection of male power and hierarchy.[7]

In this book I have tried to uncover and discuss some of the presuppositions in thinking about Jesus and place that are rooted in the biblical scholarship of the nineteenth and twentieth centuries, dominated by male, European, and North American scholars. There is now a growing interest in the place of this scholarship within social, ideological, and political structures.[8] The position of these scholars within these structures greatly influenced the way they were thinking of home, family, masculinity, kingdom of God, even Galilee—places that are central to this book. From the nineteenth century onward, centrally placed New Testament scholars created a hegemonic discourse on these places, a discourse that has been taken for granted, ingrained in the dominant, bourgeois culture of its time.[9]

I have now sketched how an awareness of place informs the way we read, based on my own place and that of the history and interpretation by other scholars. That does not make me despair of the task of this book. First and of foremost importance is the study of Jesus in relation to place, and the use of place as a heuristic tool to understand Jesus.

Jesus in a Queer Place

We understand persons with the help of some category by which we may characterize them. In historical Jesus research, this search for terms to describe Jesus usually takes one of two forms.[10] We may use ancient categories like prophet, Cynic, or Hasid. On the other hand, we may use modern categories, for instance, charismatic, ascetic, social revolutionary.[11] These latter categories are obviously anachronistic. But they do help us to explain what type of person we may imagine Jesus to have been. When I suggest the term "queer" to characterize Jesus, that is clearly anachronistic; the purpose is to find a name that can help indicate to modern readers what I find characteristic of Jesus. I use "queer" not in a limited meaning referring exclusively to sexual identity. This book is not a discussion of Jesus' sexuality. I use "queer" to mean a questioning of settled or fixed categories of identity, not accepting the given orders or structures of the places that people inhabit. I arrive at this understanding of Jesus by employing queer theory, a critical analysis of power structures and deconstruction of all that claims to be "normal."[12]

In this book I study how normality and power are expressed through place. It was literary critic Lee Edelman's essay on the rhetoric of the Queer movement in the United States in its protest against the social, cultural, and political discrimination of gays and lesbians in the wake of AIDS that made me interested in studying Jesus in relation to place. The Queer movement, Edelman says, does not choose a consistent and strategic form of politics; rather, "its vigorous and unmethodical dislocations of 'identity' create . . . a zone of possibilities in which the embodiment of the subject might be experienced otherwise."[13]

Edelman's vocabulary of place and spatiality caught my attention. To speak of "dislocations of identity" means that identity has a place, a locality, from which it can be dislocated. And this process of dislocation creates another place, a "zone of possibilities" for "the embodiment of the subject." This suggests that the subject and its identity are embodied; it is not just an idea, a consciousness, but a body. And a change in identity is indicated by a new place in which the subject is embodied, that is, place and body belong together. In this statement by Edelman I recognized a similarity to the Christian idea of conversion, but I realized that I had always considered this form of change of identity with the categories of *time*. That is the way in which the Pauline letters speak about conversion, as a contrast between "before" and "now."[14] In contrast, Edelman describes the transition in categories of *place;* it is a new experience of the relations between body and place that expresses a change in identity.

What if I were to substitute Jesus as the agent in this quotation? Would it make sense to say of Jesus' activities in Palestine in the first century C.E. that "his vigorous and unmethodical dislocations of 'identity' created . . . a zone of possibilities in which the embodiment of the subject might be experienced otherwise"? Did Jesus call people to leave one place and go to another one, or did he invite them to leave an old era (then) in favor of a new (now)?

It is this unsettling dislocation that I have tried to follow in the various chapters of this book. House and household were the central institutions of ancient Israel, and they also shaped and influenced Jesus. His break with these institutions represented a questioning of identity (chapters 3–5), but, strangely enough, Jesus did not establish a fixed place of new identity. He broke with his household of origin, but he did not stop speaking of house and family. Rather, his image of household represented a contrast to that of the traditional family. Moreover, Jesus himself did not occupy the traditional male role in the household; and he also called followers away from that position into an ambiguous male role. Finally, he presented the kingdom of God (a new place) not in majestic power, but with a strange combination of ambitious statements and pictures drawn from the simple life of Galilean households.

Thus, I suggest that "queer" is the best term to characterize Jesus. To use the term "queer" of Jesus describes the unsettling quality about him. The term queer describes a position over against something; it is not a definition of an identity. It follows that this book will not "put Jesus in his place" once and for all. It is, rather, an attempt to use the discourse of place to see how Jesus destabilizes places—potentially also those of the present readers. In the following section I have tried to outline the theoretical place I inhabit: an attempt to move from the hegemony of time, which has determined so much of Jesus scholarship, to the questions of place.

TIME, PLACE, AND HISTORICAL JESUS STUDIES

Time and Modernity

My own interest in seeing Jesus within place is part of a renewed focus on the relation between place, identity, and meaning. But why did this perspective have to be brought back into focus? Why was it, so to speak, forgotten in academic and also in theological discourse? In one sense, the importance of place is obvious. Nothing exists without place; we all live our lives, at every moment, in place. We orient ourselves in place all the time. We need only think of how often we use terms like "up" and "down," "in front of," "behind," "near," and "far off." Place has also given rise to many metaphors. We often use expressions like to be "in place" or "out of place," "everything has its place," and the like. Place has been important all along, but it has been taken for granted. So much has it been taken for granted that the philosophical discussion of the importance of place has been all but forgotten and has been little studied.[15] Although, or just because, we are "in place" from the very beginning of our life, we have not thought very much about this basic fact.

But it is not simply a matter of overlooking what is so simple that we take it for granted. It is also a question of specific reasons that attention to place was lost. Identity has been discussed in relation to the concepts of time and of place. In the modern period, priority has been given to time.[16] There seems to be a connection between this emphasis on the connection between time and identity and the establishing of history as a modern, scholarly discipline. History was a true child of modernism, in that it focused on change and progress as the processes of modernism.[17] During the Enlightenment there were changes in the understanding of time and of the development of history. Traditionally, the Christian perspective on history had been one of a decline of the human condition since the fall in the garden of Eden. Within the new scholarly history this perspective was displaced by a more secular one, which focused on the idea of human progress.

There was a loss of concern for place within philosophy concurrent with the rise of modern history, although it had its roots much earlier. Edward S. Casey[18] has traced how interest in place disappeared not only from philosophy, but from general consciousness as well. Casey has argued for the necessity of returning to an explicit reflection and discourse on place. One of Casey's specific contributions is to distinguish between "space" and "place." He holds that "space" is a cosmic category in contrast to "place," which is local. Moreover, space is more closely associated with time. The transition from preoccupation with place to emphasis on time and space happened over a long span of time, from about 400 B.C.E. (Aristotle) to 1900 C.E. Casey contrasts place and space to indicate the significance of this change: "While place solicits questions of limit and boundary, and of location and surrounding, space sets these questions aside in favor of a concern with the absolute and the infinite, the immense and the indefinitely extended."[19]

This transition from the local to the cosmic appears to be influenced by Christianity and the development of a particular theological worldview: within theology there was an emphasis on the infinity of space. It followed from the idea that God was limitless in his power that his presence in the universe at large was also unlimited. There were close contacts between this theological worldview and natural sciences, especially physics, in their concern with the spatial infinity of the physical universe. Thus, in both instances, the idea of universal space was substituted for the sense of place, the local.

The transition from place to time and space also had consequences for politics. The ascendancy of the idea of unlimited space and unlimited God went parallel with the age of exploration in the fifteenth century. That was an era "in which the domination of native peoples was accomplished by their deplacialization: the systematic destruction of regional landscapes that served as the concrete settings for local cultures."[20] The transition from interest in place itself to place only as a site determined within space also had consequences for representations of place in cartography. Early maps were often based on routes of itineraries between places. The seventeenth century saw the creation of metrically precise maps. These maps presented the earth as "a global scene for sites of discovery and exploitation."[21]

The universal sense of time was also "ideally suited to the new age of European imperialism. It gave the West a civilizing mission based on modernization—a process that came to mean making everyone else like the West."[22] This focus on time emphasized progress and development as signs of modernization. Progress was above all associated with the advance of modern technology, which was also viewed as a sign of advanced political and social organization. It was Europe and North America that were in the forefront of this progress, and that created a mentality of superiority and right to leadership vis-à-vis the rest of the world. This also provided a justification for military, economic, and colonial expansion. The colonization of Asia, Africa, and Latin America was defended with concepts of progress and modernization: "progress entails the conquest of place, the tearing down of all spatial barriers, and the ultimate annihilation of space through time. The reduction of space to a contingent category is implied in the notion of progress itself."[23]

Focus on time and progress characterized the modern period, particularly in the West. Moreover, the contrast between "time" and "place" was part of a larger dichotomy that included notions of developed and underdeveloped. This dichotomy was also gendered, in the contrast between culture and nature. Masculine and feminine followed a similar pattern, and were strongly associated with the other pairs of contrast.[24]

A Return to Place

In recent years we have witnessed a new interest in place in many areas of study. We described above the important role of history within modernism, with its emphasis on time, progress, and development. One of the protests against this hegemonic history writing in the 1960s came from the social and spatial margins. Politically, the most important impulse was the decolonization of Africa and Asia. This was also a period when democratization of higher education in Europe and North America brought many more women, working-class, and minority students into the universities. Partly for this reason there was a growth in interest in social history, especially histories of local communities, groups, or regions. By bringing out diversity based on local places, such studies both fragmented a unified view of history and challenged traditional pictures of development and progress. For instance, in the United States such writings challenged the hegemonic view of a continuous development from the founding fathers to the present-day political system.[25] This reaction against the large schemes of a master narrative from the position of local places, local communities, and ordinary people corresponds to a larger shift of perspectives and values implied in the term postmodernism, especially in terms of intellectual paradigms and hierarchies.

We find this tendency within a wide range of studies: for example, geography, anthropology, sociology, history, philosophy, and religion. Central to all of them is the perspective that place is a key factor for systems of meaning and identity. The same criticism from a local place against a hegemonic, universal history is repeated in protests against other forms of globalization. Typical examples of the global culture are places formed for certain ends, like transport, transit, commerce, and leisure (for instance, airports, shopping malls, and entertainment parks). These places are characterized by a sameness that makes it almost impossible to say whether we are in Singapore, Minneapolis, or London. They are based on some common elements without relation to any specific place, as well as a mixture of elements taken from many different places. They are lacking those qualities that characterize places. They do not put people in relational structures, they do not integrate history, and they are not concerned with identity.[26]

Many people find these types of places, which are a part of life for most people in modern societies, familiar. People thrive on combining and mixing many elements, walking in and out of diverse identities. But another reaction is also very common, and that is to look for a secure place in a shifting world. David Harvey puts this well: "Place-identity, in this collage of superimposed spatial images that implodes in upon us, becomes an important issue, because everyone occupies a space of individuation (a body, a room, a home, a shaping community, a nation), and how we individuate ourselves shapes identity. Furthermore, if no one 'knows their place' in this shifting collage world, how can a secure social order be fashioned or sustained?"[27] Thus, for many the search for a place to secure identity is first of all a personal, individual desire, associated with the different types of places one occupies. But it is also a larger, communal concern. This latter aspect has become increasingly important in the last decades.

In contrast to rapid changes technologically, socially, and economically, many look for a place to give some continuity and stability. The German philosopher Heidegger was an early and prominent representative of this position in the first part of the twentieth century. His philosophy, however, also shows the problems that may accompany such an emphasis on fixed place as the basis for identity. It was no accident that Heidegger's philosophy of place, with the importance of being rooted in a place, was an integral part of his Nazi ideology. It was part of a reactionary cultural and political criticism. In a similar way, a focus on identity localized in place and combined with language and mythical history is used politically in many of the ugly forms of present-day nationalism. Nationalistic groups tend to describe themselves as based on age-old traditions. More often, however, they represent a modern phenomenon, as, for example, a reaction to social and political changes in the former Soviet Union and Eastern Europe. Characteristically, they make exclusive claims to place, enclose particular places, and endow them with fixed identities.[28]

So, although we might see a return to place against the threat of globalization in a positive light, I think there is also reason for caution. We are reminded that place is no neutral category. It is always constructed and used ideologically. The search for a place that can provide a secure identity may be a search for an illusion if it rests on a view of place as bounded, as singularly fixed and unproblematic in its identity.[29]

Jesus and the History of Progress

It was no coincidence that studies of the historical Jesus were part of a European enterprise and became inscribed in the history of modernism. The very idea of a historical Jesus is linked to the rise of historical studies and the establishment of history as a modern scholarly discipline in the period of the Enlightenment. The perspectives and interests in the study of the historical Jesus were determined by the larger cultural context of the rise of modernity.[30] In much of the Jesus literature of the nineteenth century, Jesus was represented as the model of the "modern," or Western, man. For instance, the nineteenth-century French scholar Ernest Renan in his immensely popular *Vie de Jésus*[31] represented Jesus as breaking with the boundaries of family and race. He did not represent a parochial position of any particular, that is, Jewish, race and religion, but was the founder of a religion of humanity. Likewise, in the first part of the nineteenth century the influential German theologian Friedrich Schleiermacher portrayed Jesus as someone who was not bound by the local boundaries of Palestinian regions, but was concerned with the larger *Land* and *Volk* (people).[32] Part of this master narrative was a distinction between higher and lower degrees of progress and modernization. Thus, Jesus was presented in contrast to his opponents, the Jewish leaders in Palestine. They represented the narrower, localized traditions, very concerned with boundaries, and thus they were portrayed as belonging to a lower place in the hierarchy of progress. We find a similar attitude in a prevalent view of early Christianity as progress compared to Judaism. One of the differences between Judaism and Christianity was held to be the universalism of Christianity versus the particularity of Judaism (for example, the presumed break by Christianity with the orientation toward place and land that was presumed central to Judaism).[33]

This focus on time and progress was characteristic also of the perspectives in the so-called Second Quest for the historical Jesus from the 1950s onward. One of the earliest books on the historical Jesus from this period was *Jesus of Nazareth*, by one of the pupils of Bultmann, Günther Bornkamm.[34] In a chapter bearing the same title, Bornkamm attempts to see Jesus "in the setting of his own world."[35] This is part of an effort to describe the identity of Jesus within the context of the Jewish people. Bornkamm speaks of "its life and its character." But Bornkamm describes this world completely in terms of time and history:

> As we saw, time and history, the past and the future, determine in a unique way the thought, experience and hopes of the Jewish people. This people finds its God and itself in the past, in which its life and character was given to it; and in the future, in which its life and its character are to be restored to it. . . . Thus the world in which Jesus appears is a world between past and future; . . . the immediate present is practically non-existent.[36]

It is into this void of an almost "empty" present that Jesus enters with an "unmistakable otherness." He represents "the present" with his teaching, of which Bornkamm says: "The reality of God and the authority of his will are always directly present, and are fulfilled in him."[37] This presentation of the historical Jesus from the Second Quest illustrates the point I made above about the focus on time in modernist history writing. Bornkamm's Jesus belongs within the history project of modernism with its emphasis on progress and development. The negative view of Judaism in Bornkamm's book is based on the idea that Christianity is superior. Within this paradigm Jesus and Christianity represent progress over against a Judaism that has lost God's presence. People are pictured within a time frame, not located in place. The physical location and the material existence become less important than the words that articulate meaning. It is typical that neither the miracles nor other acts of Jesus play any significant role in Bornkamm's presentation. It is his proclamation of the kingdom and of the will of God that take up the main sections of the book. The result is a focus on Jesus as the unique personality, who represents an "unmistakable otherness." This image of the unique and solitary personality is in line with cultural and theological ideals of the heroic male individual from the late nineteenth century, which to a large degree has influenced Jesus studies.

This historical perspective on progress was combined with a hermeneutical perspective. The Second Quest was concerned with the continuity between Jesus and modern believers within a time frame. This led to a separation of religion from its integration in a spatial and social system. The result was an exclusively abstract interpretation of terms like "proclamation of the kingdom" and "the will of God." The association between time and ideas is visible in presentations of Jesus that put all emphasis on ideas, and not on the local, spatial context.[38]

What Brought Jesus Back into Place?

The so-called Second Quest showed little interest in Galilee or in Palestine as a local entity. But within the last twenty years there has been a steadily growing interest in Galilee as the local context for many of Jesus' activities. There are three trends in particular that represent this interest in place. First, the Third Quest of historical Jesus studies is concerned with historical questions more than with theological issues. Therefore, in line with developments within recent historical studies in other fields, it is concerned with local and social history, not only with the history of ideas. Therefore, the specific Palestinian context for Jesus, questions of social and economic situation, of gender and household, play a much larger role than in earlier studies. Second, there has been a rapid development of archaeological excavations and historical studies of ancient Palestine, above all in Galilee. This has provided very specific information about many places that are of direct relevance for the study of the historical Jesus.

The third aspect is of a somewhat different character. It concerns the question of the relevance and meaning of studying the historical Jesus, and it is related to the growing interest in the place of the reader that I mentioned above. In contrast to the mostly academic study of the historical Jesus, this perspective originated outside traditional historical studies in European and American academic communities. Many ordinary Christians as well as some theologians in Latin America and in other poor areas of the world have focused on the similarity between the places in which Jesus lived and their own place, socially and politically.[39] They recognize in the gospel stories how Jesus lived and worked among a poor peasant population, dominated by outside lords. Their interpretation focuses on how Jesus identified with these poor people and empowered them to restore their dignity and humanity. In this way the poor recognize Jesus in their own place.

Thus, there are clear interests in the place of Jesus in the Third Quest, mostly the geographical places themselves, but also in the hermeneutical function of place. What is lacking, however, is a more systematic approach to the importance of place for understanding Jesus. A systematic approach will also use theoretical perspectives from place studies to answer the question "What is in a place?"

WHAT IS IN A PLACE?

Place and Social Structures

It is not easy to explain in a simple way what I mean by "place." Place is not a simple or a one-dimensional category. It is first a spatial locality. Often when we think of "place," we think of a specific locality, with a distinct character. This spatial locality is identified by the community and the social relations that are played out in that place. A place is determined and organized by social structures and forces, and we know that various forces and groups often contest the right to a place. Moreover, a place is also imbued with meaning from history and tradition. Place is also associated and identified with order and structure, as in "everything has its place." Thus, place is a multifaceted term, and also a contested term. Therefore, we will not view place as "fixed" in its identity, as bounded, and as the site of a normative authenticity. It is more appropriate to see places and their identities as "always unfixed, contested and multiple."[40] Instead of seeing places as bounded enclosures, we should see their identities as formed in interactions with the outside and with others.[41]

This perspective has important consequences for a study of Jesus and place. We shall not try to find the right place for Jesus, as if there were only one fixed position and category to put him into. Rather, we will see Jesus and his activity as engaged in a contest over places in Galilee in the first century. These were places of people's lives in production and human interaction, houses and households, village and larger area. People's position in these places also placed them in normative structures that reflected the cosmologies and traditions of Jewish Galilee.

When we try to situate Jesus in place, rather than in religious ideas, we always see him in a social context, and engaged in the social relations of the village or the larger area. Therefore it is important to grasp the character of the interrelationship between place and social structures. David Harvey says, "Command over space is a fundamental and all pervasive source of social power in and over everyday life."[42] We noticed above how the philosopher Edward Casey made a careful distinction between space as a cosmic category and place as a local category. Harvey does not make this distinction, and uses, as in this quotation, space with a meaning that is close to Casey's place, about locations for everyday life.[43]

Inspired by the French philosopher Henri Lefebvre,[44] Harvey has suggested a "grid of spatial practices" as a way to analyze the relations between cultural and material forces in a social interaction in place. I shall use a simplified version of his model to look at Palestine at the time of Jesus and to understand Jesus within that particular place.[45] Two (out of the four) modes of social practice that Harvey outlines are particularly helpful for analyzing Palestine under the rule of the Herods. The first is "appropriation and use of space." It examines "the way in which space is occupied by objects . . . , activities (land uses), individuals, classes and other social groupings."[46] Here we may think of life and activities on farms, in households, and in villages in Palestine as they are reflected in the parables of Jesus and in narratives about him. This is the local scene, with villagers who are on a relatively equal social footing. The second perspective is "domination and control of space." It reflects "how individuals and powerful groups dominate the organization and production of space."[47] In the setting of first-century Palestine, these powerful groups were Herod and his sons and their families, the elite and wealthy landowners, the temple in Jerusalem and the priestly elite, and the Roman authorities. Their domination took the form of taxes, conscriptions of forced labor, tithes, and the like.

The most innovative part of the theory is the way in which Harvey relates these spatial practices to three analytical dimensions. Here Harvey adapts Lefebvre's discussion of spatial experience, perception, and imagination. The first is "material spatial practices," in Lefebvre's terms "spatial experience." Material spatial practices refer to physical and material flows of goods, money, and people in and across space to assure production and social reproduction. This is what actually goes on in the "use of space" and in the "control of space." In first-century Palestine we may think of agricultural production, for example, of grain, wine, and oil, produced by work on the farms, that secures sustenance for the household. But we may also think of the way in which a surplus of this production is extracted through taxation and tithing, that is, expressions of the domination and control of space.

With the second dimension, we move from the material practice to the cultural or ideological level. How does one think and speak about this material practice, how is it presented and justified? Harvey speaks of this cultural level as "representations of space." Representations "encompass all the signs and significations, codes and knowledge, that allow such material practices to be talked about and understood." This is what Lefebvre speaks of as perception.[48] With this term Lefebvre and Harvey think of the ideological underpinning of the power behind the spatial practice. The ideology of the powerful represents this practice (or perception) as "the order of things," as "natural." It is often taken so much for granted that it is not even discussed. In Palestine we might think of the way in which the Torah and oral tradition regulated agriculture, family structures, temple offerings, and purity systems. Attributing divine authority to Torah and oral tradition defended the specific structures of the system. Therefore, Harvey argues, such representations are above all created by the perceptions of the elite, but often their power rests on their being generally accepted as "the way things are" also by those who are exploited or suffer from the system.

But what if these groups protest, or start to criticize the system, or to present alternatives? This is the possibility that Lefebvre and Harvey introduce as the third dimension. Harvey speaks of this dimension as "spaces of representation" or "imagination." In order to distinguish this dimension more easily from the second dimension ("representations of space"), I shall use the term "imagined places." These places represent ways in which new meanings and possibilities for spatial practice, as in the form of utopian plans, can be imagined. They "are mental inventions (codes, signs, 'spatial discourses,' utopian plans, imaginary landscapes, and even material constructs such as symbolic spaces, particular built environments, paintings, museums and the like) that imagine new meanings or possibilities for spatial practices."[49] They include the opposition to aspects of spatial practice from a different perspective, from a nonelite position. Lefebvre speaks of the representations by the elite (above) as "frontal relations," which indicate their visibility and power. The imaginations of the nonelite embody "complex symbolisms . . . , linked to the clandestine or underground side of social life."[50] We may think of various first-century movements in Galilee that built their protest on traditions found in the Torah. In the Jesus material such protest includes many of Jesus' parables and his teachings on the kingdom, which outlined a different way of structuring society and use of the resources of the land.

It is the combination of these aspects that makes Harvey's grid so comprehensive in an analysis of a specific context. I find Harvey's and Lefebvre's third dimension, which I have called "imagined places," especially significant in that it gives the nonelite an active role in shaping their own place.[51] Thus, it deconstructs an understanding of power as an essence, resting with the elite only, and points instead to power as a relation. This perspective will therefore suggest that we can study Jesus not just as a passive object for the elite's control of and presentation of place, but also as an agent.

Struggle over Places

It is my thesis that the conflicts in which Jesus was involved in Galilee can best be understood as conflicts over the use and understanding of place. This thesis takes some explanation. Most often, the conflicts of Jesus with Jewish leaders have been described in terms of disagreements over the interpretation and use of the

Torah. And more recently, scholars like E. P. Sanders and G. Vermes have argued that there was no such conflict, because Jesus did not represent a principled break with the Torah.[52] From this viewpoint, the conflicts between Jesus and Jewish groups must be ascribed to a later period, to conflicts between the followers of Jesus and the synagogue leadership. But the result is that Jesus' conflicts with his Jewish environment—which we must presuppose since Jesus was actually executed—become difficult to understand if the Romans were not the sole initiators of the process against Jesus. Therefore, I think that we should consider other reasons for conflicts between Jesus and his environment, also in Galilee. I suggest that these reasons are to be found in Jesus' conflict with traditional life in the household and villages of Galilee. This life that had land as its basis for sustenance and community was threatened by economic changes that benefited the elite in the first century. I think that Jesus with his movement challenged this life that was bound to the traditions and values of society, not with discussions over the law, but simply by breaking away from this life on the land.

Jesus' conflicts with village communities and leaders are further explained in light of the perspectives in Tim Cresswell's *In Place, out of Place*.[53] Cresswell's interest is the way in which transgression is related to place, and consequently, to the ideological function of place. Place plays a role in the constitution of ideology, especially in defining "what is good, just and appropriate and what is not."[54] This expression draws attention to the commonsense and everyday nature of ideology.[55] Moreover, this commonsense aspect of ideology creates its "naturalness." Such unarticulated classifications are very strong, and they result in internalization of ideology expressed in terms like "knowing one's place" and having a "sense of limits." Through this commonsense nature of ideology a group can become dominant, so that dominated groups become convinced that this ideology will also benefit them. Social struggle, to be effective, must question this commonsense nature of ideology. By questioning commonsense notions, dominated groups force the establishment to clarify the commonsense categories and to produce official categories with "official boundaries."

Cresswell claims that space and place are used to structure a normative landscape, "ideas about what is right, just and appropriate are transmitted through space and place."[56] However, these values are not inherent in the place. They are created, and must be formulated and defended from heresy. That is why there emerges a "normative landscape." Transgressions of space put this normative geography into question, challenge it, and make visible what has formerly been taken for granted. Transgressions do not substitute one normative understanding of place and boundaries with another. What is questioned is simply a view of place as bounded, as fixed in its identity. Transgressions present a position in which identities of places are unfixed, where they are always contested, where there are multiple meanings. This is a perspective that helps us see Jesus contesting the meaning of places like Galilee and Jerusalem. However, places are not just an empty topography for the social conflicts that play themselves out; they are part of that which is contested.[57]

Place and Gender

Jesus grew up and lived in a gendered place. This is an obvious statement, which nevertheless must be stated and its meaning explored. Gender has most often been studied only in terms of social relations and not in its spatial dimension. Some aspects of the relations between place and gender nevertheless come out in everyday language, as, for instance, in a saying that was popular wisdom a generation or two ago: "A woman's place is in the kitchen." In this saying there was an association between gender and place in the way that certain places were coded feminine. "Home" and "kitchen" were associated with women and mothers, and they therefore took on meanings of authenticity and nostalgic desire. This expression about a woman's place also said something about a hierarchy of places, a relationship between kitchen as a woman's place and other places, such as factories, offices, or pulpits, which were places for men. But this expression says something more than that the kitchen is coded feminine, as a place associated with women. To speak of "a woman's place" implies that a woman has a place around her, something that need not be physical or geographical, but that can be social, mental, and ideological. This we might speak of as "a place of her own," or perhaps better, a "space of her own," something that is not so local and specific as place, but more conceptual and general.

It is this double aspect of place and space that I want to explore in a study of Jesus and his first male followers. Not only is place gendered, gender is also spatial. This means that gender roles are played out in place. To be a man is to occupy a certain place, not only in terms of location, but also in terms of social hierarchies, mental presuppositions, ideological expectations, and traditions. All these aspects make up a space that we may call "male space." In this study our task is not to work with an abstract image of "male space" based on modern, Western notions of masculinity, but to use it as a heuristic tool to study masculinity in Jesus' context.

It is no accident that the example I chose was about a woman and women's place. Although geography traditionally has been a man's discipline, or maybe because of that, places that are local, specific, and concrete are mostly coded feminine. Male geographers have placed themselves outside places. They look at places and describe them. On the other hand, so feminist geographers argue, an emphasis on boundaries and an identity that is fixed and distinguished from another is culturally coded as masculine.[58]

In contrast to this position, Doreen Massey argues that the meaning of place is not something static that is fixed forever, but instead something that is shaped by the particular social interrelations that take place in specific locations.[59] The advantage with this position is that it brings the importance of gender for place up into the open. Gender is now explicitly present. This opens up a flexible discussion, so that the gender aspects of social interrelations and the specific relations between place and gender in each instance are discussed. Thus, we must take into consideration that Jesus' context in first-century Palestine was culturally different from that of the modern Western world. Some of these differences will become apparent when we discuss the culturally specific meaning of "home" in chapter 2.

PLACING JESUS IN THE GOSPELS AND IN GALILEE

Place in the Earliest Jesus Tradition

A reading of the source material about Jesus with a view to the importance of place will give more prominence to a group of Gospel texts that are related to household and to conflicts within households. In each chapter I have chosen key sayings of Jesus about place and have used those to establish a position on the issue under discussion. These sayings are selected from the very earliest parts of the Jesus tradition. In a second section or in the following chapter, I give a rapid survey of material from the broader gospel tradition in light of the earlier material. In this way I try to combine a reasoned judgment of what is the earliest Jesus tradition with the collected witness of the gospels.[60]

Texts that are related to house, household, and conflicts within households belong mostly to the sayings material of Jesus. The main sources are the sayings in Q and in *Gospel of Thomas,* as well as sayings material in Mark.[61] This material has little information about the specific location and geographical setting of sayings of Jesus and his activities. These sayings are more concerned with general or typical places.[62] For instance, at the center of the worldview of the Q material is the house and household.[63] We find the same perspective in another group of ancient Jesus material, the parables. They represent a localized presentation of a worldview, centered around home and household, village, and the distant city, and finally the world beyond.[64] In many sayings in Q and the *Gospel of Thomas* this worldview is not made explicit. Rather, it is presupposed in the way in which persons are placed in relation to each other. Thus, "place" is also a social and mental category that underlies these texts.

There is a great deal of overlap in the sayings of Q, Mark, and the *Gospel of Thomas* with regard to place and especially about leaving household and family.[65] The sayings material in these texts will take us back to the earliest layers of the Jesus tradition. The material has to be sifted with regard to redactional material, framings, later additions, and so on, but it is possible to sort out the oldest layers of tradition.[66] It is generally accepted that Q and Mark represent the earliest level of the Jesus material (probably due to their use of a common oral tradition).[67] However, there are also good reasons to think that at least some of the sayings in the *Gospel of Thomas* represent a Jesus tradition that is old and independent of the synoptic gospels.[68]

To say that this material will take us back to the earliest layers of the Jesus tradition means that this is as far as we can come. We are not attempting to find the "real" historical Jesus, independent of any context. There is always an interplay

between the tradition from Jesus and the use of that tradition, its contextualiza-
tion among the hearers. The early material in Q, Mark, and the *Gospel of Thomas*
is important also in that it brings us back to early groups of followers, presumably sharing a similar context and situation with the followers of Jesus.[69] This
does not mean that such early material cannot be found in other sources; in chapter 4, for instance, I will use the eunuch saying in Matt. 19:12, accepting the
arguments that this saying probably goes back to the earliest Jesus tradition.

These are the primary texts for this study:[70]

> Q: 6:20–23; 9:58; 9:59–60; 11:2–4, 9–10, 11–13; 11:14–23; 12:22–31;
> 12:51–53;
>
> Mark: 1:16–20; 3:31–35; 4:30–32; 6:4; 10:28–30;
>
> *Gos. Thom.* 16; 20; 31; 55; 86; 99; 101;
>
> Matt. 19:12

Supporting evidence is drawn from a broader textual basis, for example, parables, the infancy narratives in Matt. 1–2 and Luke 1–2, sayings that are thematically associated with the above sayings, and narrative developments in the gospels.

Jesus and Place in the Gospels

Different from the sayings sources, the synoptic gospels and John have often
framed sayings referring to place with narrative material that makes the spatial
and even geographical references explicit. They have also structured their narratives within a spatial framework. Thus, beginning with Mark's Gospel, the synoptic gospels have constructed both a time span and a place frame. The Jesus story
is developed as a biography, consisting of one journey from the beginning of his
proclamation until his death and resurrection. In spatial terms, this journey leads
from Galilee to Jerusalem. John's Gospel has a different time span as well as a different geographical framework. His time span includes more journeys over an
extended period of time, accompanied by several shifts in location between
Jerusalem and Galilee.

This spatial framework of the gospels has been discussed, particularly for
Mark's Gospel, as early as the 1930s.[71] The author of Mark's Gospel uses the contrast between Galilee and Jerusalem to structure the Gospel into two geographical entities. These entities are also reflected theologically in different attitudes and
responses to Jesus, positive in Galilee and negative in Jerusalem. More recently,
Mark's Gospel has been studied primarily as a literary document, and place and
space have been studied as parts of the narrative structure of the gospel. For
instance, the Sea of Galilee has a prominent role in the narrative; Jesus travels
back and forth across the sea, which takes on a mythic meaning in the gospel.[72]

Luke and Matthew by and large follow Mark's structure in dividing Jesus'
activities into two periods that are also divided spatially between Galilee and

Jerusalem, although the division is not so clear-cut or elaborated. For instance, between the two sections Luke introduces a long journey from Galilee to Jerusalem, spanning over ten chapters (9:51–19:27). Thus, "the way" becomes the most important spatial metaphor in Luke's Gospel as well as in Acts. Here the Christians are spoken of simply as those who follow "the way" (9:2; 22:4; 24:14). Luke is also concerned with the "power of place." The contrast between the rich and the poor in his gospel is expressed in spatial categories. It is, for instance, expressed in Jesus' proclamation of a kingdom in which the power of place is differently structured than in the daily world of Galilean small farmers. One of the characteristics of Matthew's Gospel is the infancy narrative (Matt. 1–2), which serves as an introduction to Jesus' adult activity as a Galilean prophet. Matthew is concerned to show how Jesus' transition from place to place was part of the plans and providence of God. Matthew proves this by quotations from the Bible that link places in Jesus' life to history and God's election. Thus, places and landscapes are inscribed in a tradition of "sacred memory." Finally, John's Gospel has a special combination of "time" and "place," in which the spatial and the temporal aspects supplement and interpret one another.[73] For instance, John uses categories like "before" and "now," and also spatial categories like "above" and "below." That which is "above" is also distant, far away.

In the gospels there is a conscious use of place, which provides both information and perspective. It is part of a theological and literary redaction, and it shows the importance of place for constructions of identity in the cultures of Mediterranean antiquity.

Galilee as the Place of Jesus

The importance that many sources attach to Galilee as the home place for Jesus, and on his activity in or near Galilee, makes it necessary also to study what sort of place Galilee was in the first century. Or we may pose the question in a somewhat different way: How have scholars constructed Galilee as a place for the historical Jesus?[74] It is only in recent years that Galilee has come into center stage as the specific social and cultural world that shaped Jesus.[75] When Sean Freyne wrote the first major study of Galilee in 1980, it was an obscure topic,[76] of little interest to students of the historical Jesus during the Second Quest. Since then an extensive program of excavations in Galilee has opened up new vistas and has contributed to new knowledge about Galilee in antiquity. The last twenty years of excavations in Galilee have brought to light material remains that cover almost every aspect of life in Galilee from Roman and Byzantine periods: villages and towns, with houses of a large variety of types and sizes, palaces, synagogues, aqueducts, roads, and of course all sorts of pottery, housewares, mosaics, tools—even a fishing boat from the Sea of Galilee! Whole towns have been brought to life, with the most extraordinary findings probably in Herod Antipas's city of Sepphoris.[77] It is fortunate that these excavations have happened in a period with great changes in the discipline of archaeology. Focus has shifted from collections of artifacts of a religious or artistic nature and major architectural works, toward more interest in everyday structures, village houses, farms, shops, and the like, as well as remains of production and industry. Examples of the latter are winepresses and developments of farm structure, as in the form of terracing and water systems. The result is studies of daily life and culture, and an intriguing possibility of coordinating literary and archaeological texts.[78]

Thus, we probably now know more about Galilee than ever before, and will continue to acquire new knowledge. This does not necessarily mean that there is greater consensus about what it meant that Jesus was a Galilean. There are still many unresolved questions. First of all, with regard to Jesus it is a problem that most of the archaeological finds are from the Roman period, from the second century C.E. and later. There is (still) little that can be securely dated to the first century C.E. or earlier, and it is risky to extrapolate from a later period to an earlier. Furthermore, no less than literary texts, archaeological material must be interpreted, and this interpretation is presently much debated.

The interpretation must be based on an understanding of ancient agrarian societies in the Mediterranean. These were societies of a type that were distinctively different from modern industrial or postindustrial societies, and we must therefore attempt to grasp the structure of these societies.[79] A key to understanding these types of societies is to realize the importance of the family or household as the dominant social institution. In a society with few of what we would call public institutions, houses (as places for the domestic group) played an important role. But households were related to each other through systems of power, ruled by elites, sometimes with rulers (kings) and/or institutions like temples. We may speak of the first type of institutions as domestic, the others as political. Other areas of life and society, such as religion and economy, were basically subsumed under these institutions, so that we may speak of domestic and political religion and economy. Thus, the two institutions, domestic and political, were both related to and partly contrasted to each other. A general model to understand ancient agrarian societies, this will be helpful also to interpret the material from Galilee and to understand Galilean society.

OUTLINE OF THIS STUDY

With what we have read serving as an introduction, chapter 2 starts with placing Jesus in the central institution of ancient Galilee, the household. Since this has been a neglected aspect of Jesus studies, it is necessary to discuss the cultural presuppositions of modern readers when we encounter this material, and to get a picture of the cultural construction of household and family as it is presented in the gospels.

The chapters that follow this focus on the leave-taking of this central institution by Jesus and at least some of his followers. Chapter 3 gathers the sayings by Jesus on leaving household, and establishes that they appear to call people to follow him, but with no clear direction of a new location to which to go. These sayings seemed to be directed primarily at young men in the households. The finding that young men were the primary addressees for Jesus' sayings necessitated further explorations. Chapter 4 investigates the relation between masculinity and household. What did it mean for young men to leave their places as male members of the household—that is, how did leaving a "male space" affect their masculinity? And since all places are gendered, in what way was the place of Jesus' community gendered, and in what way was it a place where men and women could be integrated? This is the topic under discussion in chapter 5.

Chapters 6 and 7 take up some of the most central aspects of Jesus' activities and attempt to read them within a spatial perspective. In chapter 6, Jesus' sayings about the kingdom of God are discussed in terms of their function vis-à-vis his followers, as ways to create a new place within which they could be integrated after they had left their own households. Jesus' exorcisms also had a spatial dimension. Chapter 7 addresses the way exorcisms are described and suggests that it is with a discourse of spatial power, of God's kingdom over Galilee in opposition to the political power. This leads directly to chapter 8, which situates Jesus in Galilee, with Jesus actively engaged in shaping Galilee. Jesus' call to leave home is placed within the context of Galilee and contrasted with the thesis that it was Jesus' purpose to renew local communities. Finally, his teaching of the kingdom is put up against Herod Antipas's program to construct Galilee according to a Hellenistic economic and political program.

Chapter 2

Home Is the Beginning of Place

Jesus in the Context of House and Household

The starting point for definitions of place is often that most familiar place of all, the *home place*.[1] In this sense we may say that home is the beginning of place. Therefore, in order to understand Jesus we must start with his home place. But here we come up against two difficulties, which put us in a dilemma. The first one is that this is not a question that historical Jesus research has shown much interest in. Why has it not been regarded as important enough to discuss? I suppose that this is not simply due to scarcity of material, but also to implicit conceptions about Jesus as "the single hero." We simply do not want to implicate him in the domesticity of home place. But if we try to understand Jesus in his historical context, we obviously must start with his local context, and that means first and foremost his home place. This has historical significance, but it is also important for a faith perspective that confesses Jesus as "truly human." Therefore we should attempt to understand Jesus in the specific context of a home in Galilee in the first century.

But here we encounter another difficulty, which concerns our ideas about "home." Although we may think that home as "the beginning of place" is a universal idea, this might not be so. One author asks rather pointedly: "Are we, in fact, convinced that the perception of home and place, indigenous to our culture, can be so readily generalized?"[2] There is a linguistic problem in that the English term "home" is untranslatable into many other languages.[3] So, even when we try to understand the identity of Jesus in light of his home place, we may think about that home in ways that are uniquely modern and that belong to a specific cultural domain.

I therefore suggest the following procedure when we try to describe the home place of Jesus. First, we must discover what concepts to use and what mental pictures we can draw to understand what Jesus' home place was like. Since the English term "home" carries with it a lot of ideological baggage and cultural presuppositions that are anachronistic in relation to the first century C.E., we must try to find other categories. I suggest that the most telling concepts are those of house and household. They are the closest translations of the Greek terminology used in the gospels; moreover, they are concepts used in studies of social groups, particularly by sociologists and anthropologists. Second, we must try to find out what attempts there were in Jesus' environment to define the places called house and household. The birth narratives in Matthew and Luke are generally not regarded as giving reliable historical information about the early years of Jesus. Nonetheless, they may be mined for the information they give regarding household ideology, especially gender roles, from the point of view of two male authors. Third, I will draw on modern archaeology to study the interaction between social relations and specific locations, especially the house, in Galilee around the time of Jesus. Historical studies of that period indicate that there were external forces and pressures that affected households negatively. Finally, we must ask what specific information we can find about home place in the life of Jesus. Granted that there is little specific information about his childhood home in Nazareth; the most important source is the use of household images and examples in Jesus' sayings and parables. This sort of material will give us an impression of what place house and household held in Jesus' mental map and how he located himself within that map.

JESUS—MAN WITHOUT FAMILY?

Recently there has been a growing interest in the study of Jewish and early Christian families,[4] but the household as the primary location for Jesus' first socialization has received remarkably little attention. In most studies of the historical Jesus it is his public career that is described. Moreover, in presentations of the central aspects of his message, he appears primarily as an individual who speaks to and acts toward the larger public. His origin in terms of place and household has not evoked much interest. The question of his family is mostly relegated to a less important biographical interest.[5] In a similar manner his critical statements about family and household, and about leaving family, become just a topic, and not a very important one, in the overall picture of Jesus' message. This seems to be typical of recent Christian scholarship on Jesus.[6]

The situation is somewhat different among Jewish scholars. Many of them emphasize Jesus' relations to his family and his subsequent break with the family.[7] Does this reflect a more traditional emphasis on family among modern Jews than among modern Protestants? John P. Meier, who is Roman Catholic, is one of the few Christian scholars to treat the topic of Jesus and his family at any length, in his massive study of the historical Jesus.[8] But he does not discuss what "family" was at that time in Palestine. He speaks of family primarily in terms of Jesus' relatives, not in terms of place or household. The result is that his readers are left with the impression that families in first-century Palestine were the "same" as they are today, that is, that they correspond to whatever families mean to the various readers of Meier's book. And presumably these readers have many different experiences and notions of families.

There may be many reasons for this general neglect. It could be that there is little material in the sources on the question of Jesus' relations to his family. But I think it is more likely that the question of his home place is judged to be of little interest in efforts to describe the identity of Jesus. Such a judgment may be based on the presupposition that the identity of Jesus is determined by his words and works in his public career, not by his primary human, social relations. This seems to be a cultural presupposition, central to Western societies, which focuses almost exclusively on the individual person and on personal characteristics. The main focus in studies of the historical Jesus has been on Jesus as an individual, and his formative relations have played a much smaller role. In much of the study of the historical Jesus from the nineteenth century onward, it has been Jesus as the individual hero that has been at the center of interest. This corresponds to the picture of the unique personality as an ideal within liberal, middle-class groups in the nineteenth and twentieth centuries.[9]

Studies from the New Quest after World War II—for instance, Bornkamm's *Jesus from Nazareth*—provide examples of this emphasis on the individuality of Jesus. A focus on the individual person of Jesus corresponded to a primary interest in Christology and to the relation between the Jesus of history and the Christ of faith. In contrast, the Third Quest, with an interest in sociohistorical and sociological perspectives, has focused more on the social relationships of Jesus, in particular the relations between Jesus as a leader and his following.[10] But even so, the question of Jesus' relations to his family and place of origin have not been fully integrated with studies of his relations with his followers.[11]

Thus, I think it is both historically and hermeneutically appropriate to raise the question of Jesus' place within a household structure. Historically it is a matter of the context within which we can best understand Jesus. And hermeneutically it is a question of understanding Jesus in his social humanity, not as a christological metaphor modeled after a modern individualist. My interest in this is not the individual psychology of Jesus, but rather his place within the social and cultural setting of his time. Thus, we must attempt to imagine his place, first within a household, and second within the social structures and spatial locations to which households in Galilee in the first-century C.E. belonged.

HOME AND THE MODERN INDIVIDUAL

Before we attempt to put Jesus "in place" in the context of his family in first-century Palestine, we need to reflect on our own perspectives. When we think of the relation between family as social group and its location, we immediately think not only of "home," as the dwelling place for the family, but also of "home place," as the town or village where a person once grew up or now lives. But this understanding of home might have notions that take us in the wrong direction when we study Jesus' "home place" in Galilee. To say that "home is the beginning of place" points to the important role that home has when we speak of place. If we are asked to name a place that is important and filled with meaning for us, many of us will speak of home. Home place is associated with stability, safety, and support, often in contrast to workplace or foreign places. Thus, home is associated with ideals, often filled with nostalgic emotions. Many will think that the ideas associated with home are universal. Since they are so important to us, we automatically presuppose that they must have been the same for people in previous times and in different places as well. But that is not so. Many of the ideas that Western, middle-class readers now associate with their homes are in fact quite recent.[12]

In the medieval period and in the early modern period, Christians had viewed life as a pilgrimage toward a heavenly home. It was heaven that was spoken of as "home." Home did not play an important role in describing their earthly dwelling. The terminology used for that was "house" and "household." This terminology indicated a social order based on obedience to the head of the household, in most instances the housefather. Household was also the main metaphor for all other social arrangements. The king was spoken of as head of a house that comprised not only the royal household—the king was also regarded as a father for his subjects. Revolutions and the rise of nationalism in the eighteenth and nineteenth centuries brought changes in the use of political metaphors. The old order was based on the king's sovereignty because he was at the top of the hierarchy. He ruled areas that belonged to his house. Nationalism introduced a new idea, the nation-state, based on spatial boundaries and particular territories, and often on common languages. But this novelty needed a new symbolic form to be understood. That symbolic form was found in the metaphor of home and homeland, which turned this new reality into a familiar place.[13]

The metaphor was extended to the local level. "Home" became the center of a family life that had changed character from the previous model of house and household. As a result of social and economic changes in Europe and North America in the nineteenth century, home became for the middle classes a haven away from work and noise, away from the world and its pressures. Many Christians in the "modernized" parts of the world started to see their homes as a place of refuge in an alienating world. Consequently, "home" became a symbol of the unity and harmony of the family. It was a retreat where the family was alone, sheltered from outside pressures. In this way home became associated with the nuclear family. Home became the main image of the private sector, in contrast to work and public life. The image of home was part of the split between public and private that made the individual role central. This individual role was first and foremost a male role, and it was combined with the idea of a wife and home in a supporting, but subordinate, role. Thus, the public arena was associated with male space, and the private area was thought of as female space.

These changes in cultural presuppositions in the transition from "house" to "home" are reflected in similar changes in biblical language. The transition becomes visible in the way English Bibles translate the Greek terms for house, *oikos/oikia*, as they are used in the synoptic gospels. The seventeenth-century King James Version (KJV) translates these terms almost exclusively with "house." The KJV has only four instances of "home" (Matt. 8:6; Mark 5:19; Luke 9:61; 15:6). In translations from the nineteenth and twentieth centuries there is a steady increase in the use of "home." The Revised Standard Version of 1901 had 21, the New Revised Standard Version (NRSV, 1977) has 24, the *New American Bible* (NAB, 1970) has 43, and the *Good News Bible* (TEV, 1976) has as many as 62.

The *Good News Bible* is especially illuminating for the development that has taken place. Not all uses of "home" are actually translations of *oikos/oikia*. In many instances "home" is added, apparently with the purpose of clarifying the meaning of an expression, as, for example, to go "back home" (Luke 2:43; 12:43; 15:27, 30; 19:12; 23:48, 56). In many instances this gives a "homey" feeling—it reflects a modern, stereotypical use of "home" even when it is not appropriate. For instance, in Luke 23:56 the women from Galilee, who had followed Jesus all the way to his grave to see where he was buried, are said to go "back home." But this does not refer to their own houses in Galilee, but rather to Jerusalem, presumably to the acquaintances with whom they stayed. In narratives about hospitality "home" is used for *oikos* when Martha, the rich Pharisee, and the rich tax collector Zacchaeus are said to receive Jesus "in [their] home" (Luke 10:38; 14:1; 19:7 ["home" added TEV]). This use of "home" gives an impression of a secluded, private area in line with modern, Western attitudes, instead of the more public space of a house in first-century Palestine. Likewise, when it is said about the Gerasene who was possessed by demons that he "would not stay at home, but spent his time in the burial caves" (Luke 8:27), it gives an impression of a contrast that is privatized. It simply does not convey the contrast that is preserved in an earlier translation: "he lived not in a house but among the tombs" (RSV). The RSV in this way signals a contrast between the civilized, cultured way of life in houses in the town and life among the tombs outside the town limits, in an area that was regarded as impure. In many ways the associations of place implied in "house" are lost when "home" is substituted with its stronger meaning of "private" in contrast to "public."

This understanding of home as belonging to the "private sector" of society corresponded with changes in family structures in Western Europe, especially in the nineteenth century. There was a transition from larger households, which might include others than family members, to smaller, nuclear families consisting of father, mother, and children. These changes continued in the twentieth century, especially with the growing importance of individualism and autonomy. In modern societies individuals constitute family relations. The modern ideal is that marriage is based on love between two individuals, not on negotiations and alliances between families.[14] Consequently, relations between the two partners in a marriage are supposed to be grounded in equality, not on patriarchy.[15] That has led to an understanding of marriage partners as friends, sharing an equal relationship. Moreover, from this perspective relationships between persons of the same sex may be seen as examples of this ideal of equality.[16] In contrast, if they are viewed from the perspective of the patriarchal, heterosexual marriage as an ideal, they are regarded as examples of deviant behavior.

Modern societies focus their interest on the nuclear family and the changes that happen within it. Within welfare-state societies this family type has been at the center of interest for obvious reasons: it is the nuclear family, in the stage before the children have left home, that is of primary concern for welfare-state policies concerning the family. The focus on children has become increasingly important. This is partly because children's rights have become a more prominent moral and legal issue, but also because it is the family as a place for the upbringing and socialization of children that is of primary concern for society. This nuclear family type is typical of modern, Western societies, and in many of these societies it is combined with a high degree of individualism. For instance, an individual or nuclear family relates to society in a nonpersonal way through a bureaucracy. There is also a distinction between the public, or work, life of most people and the private life of the family, concerned with procreation, consumption, and housework.

It is, of course, not possible here to give even a sketch of the role of family, home, and individual in modern societies,[17] or of the often glaring conflicts between ideas and ideologies on the one hand and practical realities on the other. The idea of equality in marriage often coexists with the reality of a woman's heavier load at home. Moreover, there are variations based on social, cultural, and economic differences. "Modern societies" is also a very vague term that may conceal large differences, as anyone knows who has traveled outside one's own home place. Many states encourage changes in relations between marriage partners as an important part of the road toward modernization. I noticed one example of that in Cairo during a visit to Egypt. TV monitors at the subway stations showed brief educational movies of husband-and-wife relations in a traditional versus a modern marriage. The pictures from a traditional marriage showed examples of a husband who watched while his wife struggled alone with her work in the house. In the pictures from a modern marriage the husband assisted his wife with household chores and supported her when she was ill. My purpose of pointing out some of these changes to patriarchal concepts of families, and the present varieties, is to make us aware of our own presuppositions when we hear or use words like family and home. It is to be hoped that such awareness will make us realize that social relations like family and home may be different in other places and at other times. To think and to understand differently requires a conscious effort. Let us now make an effort to understand Jesus within the location of a household in Galilee in the first century C.E.

WHAT IS FAMILY?

I argued in the previous section that the modern perspectives on home and the nuclear family are not adequate to study sources from antiquity. It is well known that Greek, Latin, and Hebrew do not have terms for our word "family," meaning the nuclear family. But among the terms in use they all have words that reflect the relationship between the social group and its place of domicile: in Greek *oikos*, *oikia*, in Latin *domus,* and in Hebrew *beth*. These words that in their most direct meaning concern a building, a house, are also used of the household, the group that inhabits the house. In a broader sense they could also be used of the descent group. But in every meaning these terms point to the centrality of the place, the house, for the group associated with it. In modern European languages these ancient words are translated with various terms that indicate different perspectives on the groups that are associated with a house. Moreover, we find some of the same differences between various academic disciplines and their particular focuses for these terms, as the following outline will show.[18]

Household

"Household" is the term that most directly signals an association with a location, a house. A household is a group of people who share a residence, and who also share work and resources. A household is most often under the leadership of a "housefather" as head of the household. Included in this group are husband and wife, children, sometimes other relatives, servants, and other dependents living in the house. When we speak of a household, the emphasis is mostly on the economic and functional aspects of the common life of its members.

Family

A "family" is not necessarily the same as a household. The family may be both smaller and larger than the household group. On the one hand, all household members do not always belong to the same family. On the other hand, family members do not necessarily share the same household. A family is established by marriage, is upheld by procreation, and continues through inheritance. Studies of families often focus on the affective qualities of the relations between various members of the family, for instance, between husband and wife, parents and children, and siblings. Families form the most important area of study for sociologists. They have been most interested in social relations, and have paid little attention to the importance of house as a place for the family. The symbols, values, and meanings attached to families, the cultural importance of families (so to speak), have also been much studied.

Kinship

Finally, "kinship" studies see families and households as part of larger structures like tribes and clans.[19] Kinship studies have traditionally been central to anthropologists in their studies of "traditional" (earlier "primitive") societies. Here history in the form of lineage and genealogy plays an important part. These are groupings that in traditional societies relate individuals and families to the system of power in that society. Kinship is an important category in societies that are not organized on the basis of the individual. Larger kinship groups may provide a support system for the smaller family unit in times of need. Kinship also provides support of a different kind, for example, in terms of security about identity and of belonging to a large structure through preservation of genealogies and histories about ancestors. In ancient Israel and consequently in Jewish tradition kinship played a large role, both as a social system and as an idea.

Terms like family, household, and kinship are not objective facts; they are cultural constructions, ways to make sense of often complicated social systems. Within all studies of such groups, be they called "families," "kinships," or "households," it is imperative that they be studied within the context of their particular society, with respect to their economic and social function, as well as to their cultural meaning. Such groups are not just a social reality; they also serve as metaphors. Thereby they reveal culturally constructed notions about family, household, and kinship. Often they serve as metaphors for the larger community or society itself, and thus these groups are linked to society not just in practical ways, but as ideological constructions. Often the term family is used in a very broad and general sense for all these perspectives. The problem with that, as we discussed above, is that family is understood in light of what is the predominant social form in modern societies, namely, the nuclear family consisting of individuals.

In this study I shall use the terms "house" and "household" when I discuss what is often spoken of as "family" in the gospel material. I choose these terms partly because they make us aware that these groups were not identical with present-day families. Moreover, it is the household group and the house that I want to study. The purpose of this study is to see how the household was rooted in place, and how it interacted with the broader community of kinship, neighborhood, and village. The study of household units focuses on the household not so much as an emotional unit, but as a group that lives together, and that shares tasks that are necessary for the support and upkeep of the group. Consequently, there is a strong emphasis on the *place* in which they live—the *house* as a spatial arrangement—which makes it preferable to use the term "household."

JESUS IN A HOUSEHOLD

We will now look at the material in the gospels to find out what we can know about households in Galilee at the time of Jesus. There is little information specifically about Jesus' household of origin. There are a few words in the Jesus tradition and early narratives that explicitly speak of Jesus' family: his mother, brothers (Mark 3:20–21, 31–35, par. Acts 1:14), and sometimes even sisters (Mark 6:1–6). His mother is mentioned alone in several instances (Luke 11:27–29; *Gos. Thom* 79:1–2; John 2:1–12; 19:25–27); in several instances her name is also given. His father does not appear in the narratives about Jesus' adult life, but he is found as a memory (Matt. 13:55; Luke 4:22).

These passages do not tell us what a household was at the time of Jesus. That was taken for granted as common knowledge. The closest we come in the gospels to a description of households is this word ascribed to Jesus:

> Jesus said, "Truly, I say to you, there is no one who has left house [*oikian*] or brothers or sisters or mother or father or children or lands [*agrous*], for my sake and for the gospel, who will not receive a hundredfold now in this time, houses and brothers and sisters and mothers and children and lands, with persecutions, and in the age to come eternal life. (Mark 10:29–30)

It is uncertain whether this saying to the disciples can be traced back to the historical Jesus, but more important, this statement may help us understand the cultural and social location of his environment. Often this statement is referred to as an exhortation to leave family. But we should not immediately think of the modern nuclear family. The references to family members are framed by two words that situate them in a broader context. These words are *oikia* and *agroi*. *Oikia* here retains its meaning as "house," that is, the physical place in which the household lives, the center for work on the land, *agroi*—that which gives the members of the household their livelihood.[20]

Within this frame we meet the people who live in the house and work the land, described in their relation to the person who is leaving, and with their sex: brothers and sisters, mother and father, and children (we notice that "wife" is not mentioned). Thus, we are introduced to a three-generational household: the parent generation, the next generation consisting of at least some adult siblings, some of whom have children of their own. They all live in the same house and form a group who make their living from working the land.

This brief list then serves as an entry into a better understanding of house and household in Galilee. For the author of this gospel passage, household is presented as a social structure that was well known and taken for granted, one that did not need any explanation. It is remarkable that the statement speaks of leaving house first, before the household members are mentioned.[21] The house is a subject that comes before the people who inhabit it. A house is not just where the family lives, it is a place that is identified with the history and tradition of the household. Generations come and go, but the house remains.[22]

In a house it is the household as a social and working group that matters, more than the couple. Is this the reason that "wife" is strangely missing from the list of those who are left behind? Is it possible that the original saying did not refer exclusively to male disciples, but also included women disciples? If so, other versions that include "wife" may be later versions based on a desire to promote discipleship as a male prerogative.[23] The married couple is also absent from Jesus' interest elsewhere, in parables about life in the household. The emphasis on household members, not the married couple, may indicate that it is primarily the members as a working group, in interdependence on work to secure a living, that is in focus. There is one couple actually mentioned in the passage, that is, "father and mother." Maybe it is the patriarchal couple that matters, so that they, their children, and their grandchildren are members of the house, but not the wives of their sons. Must we surmise that some members of the household are invisible in this list? Thus, we find relations between the members of the household, emotional relations and relations in the sharing of work and pooling of resources. But there is also a relationship between the household members and the house, as source of identity and history. The location, that is, the house, is itself part of the social relations.

The mention of the household group not only serves as a list of those who are left behind when (presumably) a son is leaving, it also serves to identify the son in terms of the group to which he belongs. This function of the household group comes to the fore when the inhabitants in Nazareth raise their objections against Jesus (Mark 6:3 par.) at his visit in his home village. This saying may be part of the redactional activity of the evangelists, and may not be historically verifiable. But it reflects a cultural understanding of social identity: "Is not this the carpenter, the son of Mary and the brother of James and Joses and Judas and Simon, and are not his sisters here with us?" (Mark 6:3). In 13:55 Matthew has rephrased this sentence and included Jesus' father: "Is not this the carpenter's son? Is not his mother called Mary?"[24] In this list the larger family group is brought in to identify Jesus. He is described not only through relations to his mother (and father), but also to brothers and sisters. Most likely, they were his "real" brothers and sisters,[25] but that is hardly the point here. Rather, the point is to establish Jesus as part of a household group in Nazareth.

The response from Jesus to the negative reaction from the villagers in Nazareth follows in an apothegm in Mark 6:4[26] about the reception of a prophet: "A prophet is not without honor except in his own home town (*en tē patridi autou*) and among his own kin [*en tois sygeneusin*] and in his own house [*oikia*]." Here the household of the prophet is put within a larger context, of kin group and village. It is uncertain what is the most original version of the saying. Luke 4:24, John 4:44, the *Gospel of Thomas* 31, and pOxy.1 have only *patris*; Matthew 13:57 has *patris* and *oikia*, so maybe Mark's list is part of his redaction of the apothegm.[27] However, the triad of household, kin group, and home village (-town or -land) is part of a traditional pattern. A similar list is found in the description of Abraham's home place in LXX Gen. 12:1: "Leave your land [*gē*] and your kin group [*sygeneia*] and your father's house [*oikos tou patros sou*]."[28] Thus, the household is integrated into a structure that consists of the larger kin group, and the village community to which it belongs. It is also implied in the apothegm of Jesus that household, kin group, and village are all of one mind, and they belong to a close, maybe a closed, group.

These three texts, one ascribed to critics of Jesus, the others to Jesus or the early Jesus tradition, give a similar picture of how identity is placed in household, kinship, and village. These were three circles around the person that described him or her. They gave a location to individual identity, and at the same time represented a set of social relations. All texts describe this as a *given* location. Thus, the words of Jesus or from his tradition serve to identify house, village, and kinship as the primary locations for a person. The similarity of the descriptions indicates that they are typical. The interactions take place not just socially, but spatially, in specific areas: house, courtyard, and village. This was also the location of Jesus when he grew up; he was part of a household, a village, and a kinship group. He was also part of the social relations that were localized in these places. We surmise that there were power and hierarchies implied in these relations. For instance, there was the authority of the father and the power of the village leaders to accept somebody as an insider or to exclude him (or her) from the community. There were expectations about what sort of behavior was acceptable in the household, ideas about the honor of the family, and ideal roles for individual members.

JESUS IN "IDEAL DOMESTIC SPACE": THE CULTURAL CONSTRUCTION OF FAMILIES IN THE INFANCY NARRATIVES

The passage from Mark 10:29–30 listed the members of a household consisting of mother and father, brothers and sisters. Until the death of Joseph, this was how the household of Jesus existed. At the time of his visit to Nazareth (Mark 6:1–6) only his mother, brothers, and sisters are mentioned. What were the roles and functions of the members of this household, and what were the relations between them? This is again a question where it is difficult to get historically specific answers. The infancy narratives in Matt. 1–2 and Luke 1–2 confirm the identity of Jesus' parents as Joseph and Mary, but they are probably more relevant as sources to early traditions and ideology about "ideal parents" than as direct evidence for the historical Jesus.

With their description of the household and family in which Jesus grew up, the authors of the gospels created an idealized domestic space. They told a specific story, but the gender roles they portrayed as an ideal applied to others as well. Moreover, the authors placed Joseph and Mary within a network of places: Bethlehem, Jerusalem, and Nazareth, and their relations to these places are also revealing. The infancy narratives of Matthew and Luke tell a story of spatial practices. We hear of a miraculous birth, dangerous travels, and in Luke also offerings in the temple. But the texts also present "representations of space," that is, ideological underpinnings of these practices and the places in which they happen. The descriptions of Mary and Joseph in Matthew and Luke make their behavior appear natural and proper.

First, consider the background for these narratives in Luke and Matthew. It is not only scholars from the last two centuries who have shown little interest in Jesus' family background, this was also the case for the first evangelists. Birth and childhood stories were common features of ancient biographies, but only Luke and Matthew include these features in their story of Jesus. Mark and John (and the *Gospel of Thomas*) do not have them. They likely did know something about Jesus' origin and family. There is evidence for that (Mark 3:20–21, 31–35; 6:1–6; John 7:40–44; 19:8–11; *Gos. Thom.* 79). We may guess that they consciously distanced Jesus from this background. This may have been because Mark and John were most concerned with telling the story of Jesus as a mystery, and of identifying him directly with God, as his son, through baptism or even from the beginning of the world (Mark 1:1, 11; John 1:14). In any event, they showed less interest in the circumstances around his birth and early childhood.

It may be that this reticence on the part of the first literary gospels spurred the popular imagination and a desire to know more about Jesus' childhood. The result was a number of infancy gospels that told the history of Jesus' parents and stories from the childhood of Jesus.[29] These narratives are not so much historical sources as they are character portraits of Joseph and Mary and Jesus, and laudatory narratives of the miracles of Jesus as infant.

Since Matthew and Luke give infancy narratives as part of their theological program,[30] we shall expect that the portraits of Joseph, Mary, and Jesus will be in line with that program. Their narratives can be read from different perspectives, for instance, with an interest in the divine role and intervention in the birth of Jesus or as a continuation of biblical history writing and an example of "prooftexting." The description of the main figures, especially Mary, has also been studied as an expression of ecclesiology, as a picture of ideal believers. For the purpose of this study, I suggest that the portraits of Joseph and Mary be read within the context of gender roles and household patterns in Mediterranean societies in antiquity.

Luke's narrative in chapters 1 and 2 puts Mary, not Joseph, in the foreground. After all, it is she who is elected to a special task, and who gives birth to Jesus. Thus, it looks like a feminine story. However, the picture of Mary in Luke is drawn from a male perspective. It is a male gaze that organizes her place in the narrative and sees her as an ideal of obedience and piety. She is not a person to claim her rights; she is a woman who is obedient. Thus, she is not like many of the women in the First (Old) Testament descriptions, strong-willed and independent. Rather, she fulfills the ideals that the male world sets for her: she listens to the message from God (via the angel) with awe and respect. She shows her willingness to obey and to serve: she is the "servant" (*doulē*) of the Lord (1:38, cf. 1:48; 2:29; Acts 2:18). And after Jesus is born she listens to the messages about him from angels or Simeon in the temple, and she keeps the words in her heart (2:19, 33, 51). But this is not just a social role ascribed to women in society; it is picked up by Luke and given a place in his theology. These descriptions identify her as an ideal disciple (cf. 11:27–28).[31]

In Luke's infancy narratives women have an important role, with Mary, Elizabeth, and Anna as central figures. Particularly in the case of Mary, they have more prominent roles than the parallel male figures: Joseph, Zechariah, and Simeon. However, in line with Luke's general tendency his pictures of the women are ambiguous. Women have a central role in the narrative, but at the same time they are kept "in their place" in a way that emphasizes traditional gender roles.[32] Joseph has only a supporting role, although it is he who, as a descendant of David, initiates the journey to Bethlehem, and it is through him that Jesus belongs to Davidic ancestry. He is portrayed as pious and law-abiding, he brings Jesus to the temple, and later, in the narrative of Jesus at twelve years old, he performs his obligations to undertake the pilgrimage to Jerusalem (2:41–51).

The places in the infancy narrative are important. Bethlehem plays a role as the ancestral home of the house of David, and Jerusalem is the center of worship, temple cult, and pilgrimage. Mary and Joseph perform the expected rites in the temple (Luke 2:22–24), that is, they behave in ways that correspond to the holy place. Nazareth, on the other hand, is not a holy place in itself. It was rather insignificant, but it is characterized by its inhabitants, who perform pilgrimages and give the required offerings. Thus, the household of Joseph is characterized as pious and obedient, and indirectly Nazareth also partakes in this quality.

Matthew's story, different from Luke's, is explicitly androcentric.[33] For Matthew, gender is also a spatial metaphor. Male and female occupy different places in the narrative and its social hierarchies and social relations system. It is the male protagonist, Joseph, who is the main figure. The plot in the narrative is formed around Joseph's dilemma (1:18–19). Mary has been promised in marriage to him, but before he has sexual contact with her it turns out that she is expecting a child. Therefore, this cannot be his child. The central topic is Joseph's fear of the shame of an illegitimate child, fear of losing his masculinity because another man has entered into his sphere of ownership and control. This dilemma would be completely understandable to any male (and also female) reader in the first century.

Matthew's picture of Joseph is that of a masculine ideal. Joseph was just (*dikaios*, 1:19). This was the highest ideal for a Jewish male, personified in the figure of Abraham, the ancestor (Rom. 4). The content of what it meant to be just might change over the time and in various milieus, but the ideal played a permanent role in the image of a Jewish man. To be just expressed an ideal of behavior toward household, family, and neighbors, toward the poor and to strangers, but characteristically, it was bound to the relationship to God. God was just, and therefore also those who believed in him must be just. That Joseph was just was explained by his behavior toward Mary when he wanted to divorce her (1:19). Matthew builds the plot of his story on the social pattern of an honor/shame culture that was above all associated with male sexuality and masculinity.[34] Adultery by a woman, which would soon become visible for all in the village to see, was an attack against the honor of her husband. He was in his full right to demand a divorce, and that was expected to redress the injury he had suffered. In

Matthew's story, Joseph is portrayed as just because he wanted to divorce "quietly," so as not to bring public shame over her. It is not easy to imagine how this could happen "quietly" in a small village, but Matthew's point appears to be to describe Joseph's concern for Mary as an expression of his justice.

It is strange that Matthew tells the story of the birth of Jesus in a way that puts Mary, and thereby also Joseph, in an unfavorable light by even broaching the suspicion against her. In later Jewish and other anti-Christian polemics, this suspicion is turned into an accusation that Jesus was born out of wedlock.[35] It is possible that Matthew knew such accusations, since he explicitly brings up the problem that Mary was expecting a child before she moved into the house of Joseph.[36] Matthew situates the story about Joseph's discovery in the period between the two important phases of the establishing of marriage. According to later rabbinic sources, the first stage was betrothal with a formal exchange of promises. That took place when the woman (or rather, the girl) was twelve or thirteen years old, and transferred the authority over her from the father to her future husband. However, she continued to live at home for another year, and during this period it was required that she should not have sex with her future husband. After a year her husband brought her to his home in a formal ceremony.

The dilemma that Joseph faced was solved by a vision of an angel who convinced him that the child was not conceived by another man, but by the Holy Spirit (1:20–21). Therefore Joseph could without fear proceed with stage two of the marriage and bring Mary to his house. Matthew emphasizes that after Joseph did this, he did not have sexual intercourse with her until Mary had borne a child (1:24–25). In this way Matthew tells the story so that the honor of Joseph is preserved, Mary's reputation is defended, and the early birth of Jesus is explained through a divine intervention. Thus, Joseph's honor is of decisive importance, also, in the way in which the marriage is socially (if not sexually) fulfilled when he brings Mary into his house. In this way he legitimizes the birth of Jesus, and as the last part of that he gives the child a name (1:25) and thereby recognizes Jesus as his own son.[37]

This first narrative in the gospel establishes Joseph as the main protagonist in the infancy story of Matthew. And his role is continued. After the birth of Jesus and the threat of Herod to kill Jesus, the plot continues with a series of new visions and messages from angels to Joseph. He is told to go to Egypt (2:13–18), and after the death of Herod to return to Israel (2:19–21), and, finally, to go to Galilee and Nazareth (2:22–23). These places become part of the identity of Jesus, an identity that is established by means of the quotations from Scripture attached to each of them. Matthew's use of the Bible is often characterized as proof-texting. I do not find that an adequate description of what these scriptural quotations actually do to these places. It is better to say that they provide history for the landscape; they bring to life a memory that can be activated and applied to this particular place.[38] Landscapes and places are never empty of meaning, and that meaning often comes from their history. But it is obvious that the author had difficulties in finding memories and establishing a history for Nazereth, since

the only notion he put forward was a forced reference to "Nazarene" (2:23).[39]
There simply was very little with which Matthew could work, since there were
no references to the town of Nazareth in Scripture. But it was nevertheless important to Matthew to establish a link between Jesus and Nazareth, and the most
likely reason is that it was known to him that Jesus came from Nazareth.

In the infancy narratives, especially in Matthew, Joseph is established as an
important figure for Jesus. Joseph makes Jesus legitimate vis-à-vis the village community, where Jesus would become known as "the son of Joseph." For the theological interpretation of who Jesus was, Joseph's role was decisive, since it was
through him that Jesus' Davidic descent was established. But after the infancy
story Joseph disappears completely. In the main text of the gospels he exists only
as a memory. In the skeptical reaction to Jesus from the villagers in Nazareth,
Matthew brings up the tradition that Joseph was known as a village carpenter:
"Is not this the carpenter's son?" (Matt. 13:55).

The historical evidence about the relationship between Jesus and his parents
is slender, but the infancy narratives as well as other gospel passages can say something about cultural expectations. Jesus' obedience to his parents is part of such
expectations. But we must be aware that in ancient Mediterranean societies we
cannot speak in a general way of relations between "parents and children."
Because of the central importance of gender, parental relations were not expressed
or imagined in a general way, but always specified as "father and son/daughter"
and "mother and son/daughter."[40]

Luke provides the most interesting picture of the relation between mother and
son in his description of Mary and Jesus. Through studies of many different
Mediterranean societies, anthropologists have found that a close and very special
relationship between mother and son is characteristic for these societies, and of
great importance for family relations.[41] The upbringing of children was the task
of the mother; this resulted in an emotional closeness and in some sort of sym-
biotic relation between mother and son. We may compare the intensity of the
relations between mother and son to that of the relationship between a husband
and wife in the modern world.[42] It was expected that the mother would identify
with her sons through suffering; it was a cultural expectation that mothers should
suffer because of their sons. In Luke, Mary is portrayed as the suffering mother
from the very beginning, from Simeon's prophecy that "a sword will pierce
through your own soul" (Luke 2:35). Mary carries on the conversation with Jesus
when he is found in the temple after he stayed behind in Jerusalem during the
Passover pilgrimage (2:48–50). In these episodes the reader sees the basic elements in a mother-son relationship. In the gospels there are some traces of this
special mother and son relationship in Jesus' later life as well. When Mary reap-
pears after the infancy narratives, she comes in a new role. Joseph has disappeared,
and she appears to be the head of the household (Mark 3:21, 31–35). In John's
Gospel there is no such clear break with Jesus' family as in the synoptic gospels.
Even if Jesus distances himself from his mother early in the narrative (John

2:1–12), Jesus' handing her over to the care of John in the crucifixion scene (19:25–27) presupposes the traditional mother-son relationship.[43]

There is no material in the infancy narratives or later in the gospels on the relation between Joseph and Jesus.[44] What is striking, however, is that so many of the narratives and parables of Jesus focus on the father-son relationship. Thus, it is through this other material that we can perhaps trace some aspects of Jesus' relation to father figures—not in an individual, psychological sense, but in terms of a culturally shared meaning.[45] The main link between Jesus and Joseph seems to be that the genealogy of Jesus goes through Joseph. It is via Joseph, and not via Mary, that the descent from David is established (Matt. 1:1–17; Luke 3:23–38). Genealogy links persons to a continuity of kinship and legitimizes their position by associating them with their ancestors; in some instances the ancestors are women (Matt. 1:3, 5, 6). This descent from David is an example of how the old tribal system surfaces, which identified households with a specific tribe, and thereby to a perceived unity of Israel. In that way each household was part of the whole. The ideology and theology of Israel centered around two institutions, the household and the monarchy, standing for the whole.[46] This was reflected in the way the understanding of God was formed by these two institutions, kingdom and household. And the people also understood itself in relation to God through metaphors from household roles, like wife, son, daughter, slave, and so on.

After the demise of the Davidic monarchy, the Jerusalem temple with its priesthood was established, with some of the same role as the monarchy. Politically, economically, and not least ideologically, it would define the identity of Israel. In the infancy narratives we see how the household interacts with the temple and the (vassal) monarchy. In Matthew, the household of Joseph—and all households in Bethlehem with infant sons—are confronted with the power of King Herod, the ruler who is threatened by a possible Messianic contender (2:1–18). This is portrayed as an utterly negative relationship. Luke, on the other hand, portrays a positive relationship between the household of Joseph and Mary and the other central institution, the temple. They fulfill all the religious obligations of the household: circumcision, purification offerings, and pilgrimages (Luke 2:21, 22–38, 41–51). Thus, in Matthew we get a picture of households living in a space that is dominated by the vassal king, and where one has to find a way to secure a place of one's own. Luke portrays a holy place, the temple, that also dominates the space in which the households live, but in a positive way. Coming to the temple is one way to commit the household place to "the law of the Lord," so that when a family returns home, that place shares in the sanctity of the temple (Luke 2:39).

We started by saying that the infancy narratives have little historic value for specific events in Jesus' life. The value that they have is more paradigmatic, in terms of the picture they give of ideals and patterns of behavior. In particular, since family and household relations within different areas of the Greco-Roman and Jewish world showed so many similarities,[47] we get a picture of ideals that influenced the cultural context of Jesus. The infancy narratives in Matthew and Luke may be read as normative attempts to describe Jesus as part of an ideal household. Joseph and Mary are portrayed as members of larger kinship groups and of a village community, and uphold clearly defined roles for husband and wife. These narratives integrate Jesus into a culture with strong ideas about household and gender roles. We may say that their authors are not just accepting ideas, but also shaping and creating an ideal domestic place and arguing for a specific identity of place.[48]

GALILEAN HOUSES AND THE SHAPE
OF DOMESTIC SPACE

The infancy narratives describe the household of Joseph in idealized space, in a culturally and ideologically created world. But this is not the only information that we have about household and family in first-century Galilee. Archaeology and history of architecture provide information about the setting for these households, the very places where they lived their lives, their houses and villages. It is not so, however, that this is "objective" or "neutral" information. Archaeological finds are also in need of interpretation, and archaeologists are becoming increasingly aware of the problems of interpretation.[49] The meaning of a place is not given once and for all; it is socially and culturally determined, and therefore open to changes and alterations. Archaeologists are concerned not only with the form and structure of buildings, but also with their function and with the social significance of domestic shape.[50]

What is the interaction between social relations and specific locations? We are first interested to find out how house and village were socially and culturally shaped in Palestine at the time of Jesus. But we are also interested in whether Jesus also shaped the space of house and village through his activities.

We do not have any information about the house in Nazareth in which Jesus grew up. There is very little left of domestic structures from early Roman times in Nazareth, except some cisterns, storage bins, and caves. What there might have been is covered under the church buildings that were built over the ancient village. Recent projections suggest that Nazareth was a small village with maybe only four hundred people, basically an agricultural village with some traces of terracing, as well as of grinding stones, storage silos, and winepresses.[51] We have no evidence exclusively about Jesus' house, but there is much evidence generally about houses and household activities in Galilee that is relevant for the time of Jesus. A number of types of houses from the early Roman period have been found. The locations include the city of Sepphoris, and villages like Yodefat, Meiron, and Kirbeth Cana, as well as Gamla in nearby Golan.

Much information about houses in Palestine, in particular Galilee,[52] is available in recent excavation reports, but now also in special publications on houses in Hellenistic, Roman, and Byzantine times.[53] From the earliest period in Palestine, there were two main types of houses, the "simple house," typical of rural areas, and "the courtyard house" found in more clusterlike or urban types of settlements.[54] It is a sign of socioeconomic changes in the Roman and Byzantine periods that we find three other building styles: the villa (*domus*), the large farmhouse, and the house with shop (*taberna*). All of them probably existed in the first century C.E., so they are relevant for the period of Jesus and the Jesus movement. These different forms of houses reflect differences in economic resources as well as in social status, and we can surmise that households of varying sizes and composition inhabited them.

The "simple house" was typically a square building, divided into two or more rooms. It was situated at a courtyard. Even if this type of house could vary much in size, most were quite small. These probably were houses for single families that did not have many members. Several such houses have been found in villages in Galilee.[55] The other traditional house most often found in towns and villages is the "courtyard house," with an inner courtyard. It had one entrance into the courtyard, and around the courtyard were several dwellings, divided into more rooms. This type of house could be the home of a large family with more generations living together, with married sons and their wife and children in separate dwellings, as for instance, the family mentioned in Mark 10:29–30. Such a house could also be shared by several families, either with family ties or without. The courtyard served as a common place for various types of work, especially the preparation of food.

The period of Hellenism and Roman rule saw great changes in the patterns of landholding in Palestine, with larger areas of land collected into the hands of an elite. That is reflected also in the houses for the elite who owned these estates, which have a definite Roman style.[56] They are built in the style that we know from Roman villas (e.g., from Pompeii), with a number of rooms around an atrium. These rooms could be nicely decorated with mosaics and murals. In particular, the dining room, the triclinium, was often decorated with mosaics. A couple of these large houses are found in Sepphoris.[57] The best example of the villa is the so-called Dionysiac house, named after its mosaics. It reflects the wealth, culture, and lifestyle of the elite. Such elite households were quite large and also included more distant relatives, people in dependent positions, as well as servants and slaves.

A fourth type of house was the large farmhouse, different from the villa in that it was "a working farm." Several examples of this house from the Herodian era are found in various parts of Palestine, although not yet in Galilee. Typical of this house was a large area enclosed by a wall, which for the most part was used for different types of farm work, for example, threshing or wine and olive presses, as well as for storage for the various forms of produce from the farm. These farms included large areas of land or large orchards or vineyards.

The last type of house is designated "house with a shop (*taberna*)." The first examples found in Palestine are from the Hellenistic period, but most of them are from Roman and Byzantine time.[58] This type of house was very common in cities and towns in the Roman Empire. One can, for instance, see many examples of them in *insulae* in Ostia and Pompeii.[59] Often part of a larger house along a street, for example, an *insula*, they had one room toward the street, which was the workshop or the shop, and one room in the back that served as living quarters. This type of house reflects a specialization of production into various forms of craftsmanship. In Galilee such workshops are found also in other types of house, like the simple house or the courtyard house.[60] These finds suggest that a household often supplemented farming with various types of crafts.

This overview has served to indicate what types of place we can imagine for households in Galilee. There are, however, some houses that are not retrievable, the dwellings for the very poor. They were so poorly built that remains did not survive for very long, and very rarely are the areas where the poor lived even excavated.

Do these different houses give any indications of the socioeconomic situation of the inhabitants? On the basis of various house types and literary evidence, Santiago Guijarro has attempted to divide the population in Galilee into four different family types: large, multiple, nucleated, and scattered.[61] The very top, the elite that made up only a small fraction of the population, maybe 1 percent, included Antipas, his family, top administrators, and others; they lived in the villas in large, extended households and controlled much of the income of the land, both through taxes and from their own estates. The inhabitants of the courtyard houses included lower-level administrators (e.g., tax collectors), retainers of the elite, and also landowners with small estates, and fishermen. Within the courtyard house, there could be two or more related families, who could support one another in time of need. Guijarro suggests that this group made up about 10 percent. The large majority of the population lived in a "simple house," a one-household dwelling. Most households were small. They had few resources in time of need, and they were peasants, craftsmen, or day laborers. And finally there was a large group of homeless—beggars, people who had lost their land and had no work. Guijarro calls their family type "scattered," because it would not be possible for them to keep a family together.

Used with imagination, the finds from archaeological excavations can teach us something about the activities and social relations of the household. A typical example of a courtyard house in Capernaum is described in the following way: "Inside the courtyard of Capernaum, parts of *tabun* ovens survive, fishhooks are strewn about, and agricultural implements are scattered about, such as grinding stones, presses and loom weights, illustrating how the families' work and lives centered around the courtyard."[62] Similar finds are made in Yodefat[63] and at Meiron.[64] From this picture we may draw various conclusions. First of all, we are far from the modern "home," separated from the workplace. The house then was both dwelling and workplace, and the family was a working group. This makes the distinction between "private" and "public" meaningless. This modern distinction has played a large role in descriptions of ancient societies, frequently combined with a division between the roles of men and women. In such descriptions, women were associated with the inner house as the private sector, and men with work outside the house, active in the public sector.

A strict division between men's and women's spaces does not appear to be a plausible interpretation of the finds from houses in Galilee and Palestine from Roman times. The different types of installations found, from winepresses and grinding stones to spindles, indicate that men and women worked together within the house and courtyard. Women were active participants in the work of the household, and apparently not enclosed in a "private" area of the house. The Greek house in antiquity had a division between "private" and "public."[65] But the Palestinian house may have functioned more like the Roman house, without such clear distinctions.[66] In Roman society the home of the elite was at the center of public life. Instead of a dichotomy between public and private, there was a spectrum from the complete public to the complete private. Access to various parts of the house was dependent on the status of the visitor—the higher the status, the more house was accessible. Within the Galilean house we may see this spectrum of access from the courtyard to the house itself. The courtyard served as a workplace. From the implements that were found in Capernaum and other places, it is obvious that it was a space for both men and women and for children. Thus, the courtyard did not divide genders, but integrated them.

The courtyard was also a meeting place for all who lived in the dwellings around it, and for neighbors and relatives. This function was all the more important since many villages did not have any public buildings or meeting places.[67] Thus we may presume that meetings of kin and neighbors took place in the courtyard. This was particularly so for the households that shared a common courtyard. These might be families that belonged to the same kin group, for instance, married brothers with their wives and children.[68] But even if they were not directly relatives, their dwellings "shared walls, courtyard workspaces, water cisterns, and common rooftop areas."[69] This is an example of how a society shaped domestic space through its architecture, the way in which houses were built and space could be shared. But this common space was also shaped by means of common activities. These activities might include sharing of work, lending and borrowing, and common meals. A word by Jesus echoes what it might be like to live in such close quarters: "What you have whispered in private rooms shall be proclaimed upon the housetops" (Luke 12:3; *Gos. Thom.* 33.1).[70]

That was at the public end of the spectrum. But the house could also be closed off from the outside. The wall around the courtyard had only one entrance, which could be closed with a door, sometimes with a very elaborate closing mechanism.[71] Thus, the courtyard was protected against view from the outside, as well as against unwanted intruders. The walls around the house were physical expressions of boundaries. But there are also other examples of boundary markers that expressed the identity of the household vis-à-vis outsiders. It is possible to understand how the inhabitants of a house defined themselves vis-à-vis others by studying the material culture.

Four archaeological indicators in particular reflect a space that is shaped to signal Jewish identity.[72] The first is stone vessels; another is the presence of stepped pools, *miqva'ot;* third, ossuaries for secondary burials; and the fourth, absence of pork in the finds of bones. Stone vessels are the most common find. They were used to contain liquid, and to be used for washing hands. The stone did not attract or spread ritual impurity, and the presence of stone vessels in many buildings therefore indicates a concern to keep the building and its inhabitants pure. The same was true of the stepped ritual pools, the *miqva'ot*. They are found in most excavated cities and villages in Galilee, for instance, in Sepphoris, Yodefat, and Meiron. Many of them are dated to the first century C.E. Large ones are found near olive presses, and may reflect a commercial interest, to produce kosher olive oil for sale, often for export to Jews in the Diaspora. But in most instances the ritual pools are in private houses, and their meaning must be associated with a conscious attempt to shape domestic space and to define it as Jewish space in terms of purity. However, they are also found mostly in houses that reflect a high socioeconomic status.

These first two indicators are fairly specific. The other indicators are a bit more tenuous, in that they are not so well documented, but the two often work together. The absence of pork in studies of bone profiles of zoarchaeological data correlates well with evidence from literary texts that Jews avoided pork. It is difficult to be more precise about the specific ideas that the inhabitants of these houses had about their practice. Archaeology cannot tell us accurately about that. But the finds indicate a material layout and a use of the buildings and utensils that demonstrate that the inhabitants of these sites shaped their environment and their social practice in a way that can be characterized as "Jewish" in contrast to "Gentile."

The way in which burials take place may indicate significant changes in structures and relations between members of households. There seems to have been a transition away from the large, communal family tombs that were typical of an earlier period of Israelite history. By the late first century B.C.E., burials were in small family tomb complexes, with *loculi* for individual bodies or ossuaries in which the bones were placed in a second burial that took place one year after the first burial. Burial practices in Galilee were similar to those in Judea.[73] This change in burial practices suggests that the extended family as an economic, social, and ideological unit had split up into smaller, household-based family units.[74] The role of the extended family, as well as of the family patriarch, may also have diminished. The extended family could therefore no longer be relied on to help in periods of crisis and need.

But with the social and economic changes in the late Hasmonaean and Herodian period, the smaller household unit and the role of the father were also threatened. There was a centralization of property and power in the hands of the elite, and thus especially the landholders of small estates and also tenants found themselves in difficulties. In periods of crisis, people who are already at the margins of society are hardest hit, and young men without property were especially vulnerable.[75] This may have led some to leave the household and the authority of their father. Some may have joined the Essenes. Individual burials in Qumran, also of young men, indicate that they have left their household and their place in the family tombs. The foundations of new cities by Herod and his sons, other large building projects, and new industries—for instance, in fish processing—opened up new opportunities, particularly for those who could not find occupation and sustenance in their own household. This was a situation that weakened the authority of the male head of the household, and that increased the opportunities and choices for younger males.

HOUSE AND HOUSEHOLD IN THE JESUS TRADITION

Did Jesus as a son in a household experience and react to these tensions? As already indicated, we do not know much about the particular household and place that Jesus came from. It seems fairly certain that he came from Nazareth; there is evidence that he was called "Jesus of Nazareth."[76] Likewise it is at least very possible that his father was a carpenter (*tektōn*),[77] that his mother's name was Mary, and that he had brothers and sisters. But more important here than these specific historical pieces of information is the question how house and household appear in Jesus' words, what place they have in his mental universe.

I shall focus on two large groups of material from the early Jesus tradition, namely, the parables and Q, and I shall point to two recent approaches to that material that will prove helpful for our purpose. The first is a study by Bernhard B. Scott of the parables of Jesus from the perspective of the *place* that they inhabit.[78] This is a perspective that reflects the cultural setting of the parables in a Mediterranean context and provides a means to structure parables into coherent groups. The first set of parables is grouped under the heading "Family, village, city and beyond." This is because "in the ancient Mediterranean world everyone had a social map that defined the individual's place in the world. It told people who they were, who they were related to, how to react and how to behave. At the center of the map was the family, esp. the father, then came the village, finally came the city, and beyond, to the ends of the world."[79]

The individual received his or her identity from being placed in this map, with family (household) as its center. It was from a shared understanding of what life was like that the audiences of Jesus would listen to his parables. Thus, images or stories from household and village in parables were more than just topics, they actually reflected a location from which to experience life, and served as a place to identify with the protagonists of the parable. There is a shared perspective and experience of identity between the audience that listened to the parables, the figures of the parables themselves, and the "voice" of the parable, the implied author.[80] We may, with some caution, say that there is at the very least a connection between the implied author of the parables and Jesus.

We may imagine a location for the parables within the houses and social patterns that the excavations have made it possible to identify. It was the elite, the small group of rich, who lived in the villas. If we have seen the Dionysiac villa in Sepphoris, it is easy to imagine that house as the scene envisaged by the words "those who are gorgeously appareled and live in luxury are in kings' courts" (Luke 7:25). Likewise, the entrance to a villa seems a likely scene for the parable about Lazarus outside the gates of the house of the rich man (Luke 16:19–21). Maybe a large working farm was the envisaged dwelling place for the rich man who contemplated what to do with his large crops, and who planned to pull down his barns and build larger ones (Luke 12:16–22). The householder (*oikodespotēs*) who went out to hire workers for his vineyard, and who clearly needed many workers, must have had a large vineyard, and is another plausible occupant of a large farmhouse (Matt. 20:1–16). Maybe also the father with two sons in Luke 15:11–32, who was asked to divide his inheritance, had a large farmhouse; it is clear from the story that he had many servants and hired workers. These stories may be told from the perspective of "below," with neither the implied author nor the audience sharing the social location of the characters in the story, but the large farms nevertheless provide plausible settings for the stories.

House and household as a shared locus of identity appear to play a similar role in another large group of early material from the Jesus tradition, in Q, as Peter Richardson has pointed out.[81] Richardson sees a correlation between the main themes of the Q document and a social setting in towns and villages in Galilee and Golan. Excavations in Jodefat, Gamla, and Kirbeth Cana show that these communities were centered around houses and courtyards, with only few traces of public buildings. We find the same pattern in the Q material, and again, not just as an individual topic, but as part of the compositional macrostructure of Q. There is a movement from Jesus' relationship with John in the wilderness by Jordan in the first part of Q (3:7–7:35) to a "familial setting" among towns and cities in Galilee in the next section (Q 9:57–10:22). This emphasis on household continues in the following unit, with contrasts between the poverty of the followers of Jesus and the Pharisees' concern for purity (Q 10:23–13:35). Finally, the last part of Q (12:2–22:30) continues to focus on household activities in a rural and agricultural setting, for instance, on masters and servants and divisions within the family. We may conclude that "Q's core imagery is house and householder as models for community behavior." And many of the issues that are raised in these texts are related to life in the household: "Poverty, debts and supply of daily bread are endemic issues within some households (Q 11:2–13), while other wealthier households have servants and laborers . . . (Q 12:35–6; 19:12–25). Some followers leave the domestic responsibilities . . . (Q 9:57–62) . . . , perhaps sundering familial relationships to acquire new ones (Q 12:49–59; 10:21–2)."[82] Thus, Q does not present an idyllic picture of households in Galilee, but the household structure is the given pattern of life as it is described by Q.

The picture that emerges is at the compositional level of Q. But many of the passages in question are ascribed to early layers of Q, and thus belong to the earliest Jesus tradition.[83] Moreover, this is not a question of whether individual sayings or parables go back to Jesus. It is a matter of a perspective on family and village as an expression of identity, or of house and household as a core image. That is, house and household are part of the parables and sayings at the level of that which was taken for granted, the culturally given. If there is any link between Jesus as a historical person and the early tradition of material under his name, there can be little doubt that this perspective on house and household belongs to the link. That the material comes from various sources and genres supports this conclusion. In addition to parables and early sayings, we have seen that narratives about Jesus like Mark 3:31–35 and the infancy narratives in Matthew and Luke place him within house and household.

The question is not whether Jesus was part of a household for most of his life, but what that meant to him, and how that influenced his public activity and proclamations. There can be no doubt that the social world of the household was at the center of Jesus' parables; it was the perspective from which he viewed the world. Likewise, house and household were core images in the sayings traditions that go back to Jesus. This should not surprise us. Archaeological excavations have shown that in village societies with few traces of specifically public buildings or places, houses and courtyards were at the center of community life. But we have also noticed how descriptions of domestic space were shaped by ideological patterns and historical traditions.

I think it has become clear that Jesus was not a modern individualist. When the gospel material is read with the various lenses of place, this material comes alive in a new way. It is part of a cultural context with a strong focus on the household as the primary location for its members, and this praxis was supported by cultural ideals. Moreover, studies of houses in Galilee at the time provide specific examples of the spaces where the household of men, women, and children actually lived their lives. Viewed against this context, it becomes obvious that, as a person growing up in Galilee in his time, Jesus was utterly grounded in house and household. He was not just an idea, nor was he a modern individualist. If he was a true human being of his time, his identity was based on his being placed in a particular household group and locality. He lived in a society that was strongly communal and placed in a locality. This was the world that he was part of and that he interacted with.

But to see Jesus as part of a world focused on house and household is not a conclusion, it is simply the beginning of a study of Jesus within his place. It is when we recognize the importance of this "groundedness" in place that we can start to appreciate what it meant to break away from this place. If house and household was the primary location of identity for Jesus, what happened when he left his household of origin?

Chapter 3

Leaving Place

Farewell to Household

At some point, probably in his late twenties, Jesus left his household in Nazareth, became a disciple of John the Baptist, and eventually started as a preacher on his own. This break from his household was an important event in the life of Jesus, although in most presentations of the historical Jesus it is not identified as significant.[1] Is this because his first socialization is not regarded as important for the man he became, so that a "break away" experience does not mean much? But if house and household were places for primary socialization and locations for social identity, to break with these places or to leave them was of great importance and ought also to receive serious attention in a study of the historical Jesus.

An example from a traditional society in the Middle East today may serve as an illustration of my point. On one of my visits to St. Catherine's Monastery in Sinai I made my usual hike up to Mount Moses. On the top I encountered two young men working in the coffee shop (!) there. They belonged to the Bedouin tribe that worked as the servant community for the monastery. They were obviously intelligent young men; they were studying a book in Hebrew on the birds of Sinai when I came along. They could also speak English very well. So, striking up a conversation with them, I asked what seemed the obvious question about future plans and education for young men with bookish interests: "Will you go

to Cairo to study?" They were startled at this naive question and started explaining the structure of the Bedouin tribe to me. The tribe was made up of several
large family groups, each with its own head. There was also a group of family
heads that made up the leadership of the tribe, and these men came together to
make important decisions. Leaving the tribe for prolonged periods was a question that must be decided by this council; the request had to be submitted to this
group of heads of all families. Therefore, a plan to go to Cairo to study was not
up to an individual to decide, not even together with his father. "And besides,"
said one of the young men, "if I went to Cairo, who would I be? I would be
nobody." Without his family and tribe, alone among large groups of people
whom he did not know, and for whom he would be unknown, he would lose his
identity. It was his family and the collective group of the tribe that provided him
support, a place to be and to belong, so that he knew who he was. Away from
that group, he would be simply "no-body."

This conversation brought home to me the importance of a communal society, where the individual was located in a group and its specific location. The
young men whom I talked to were in a direct way placed in their household, clan,
and geographic area in Sinai. "Identity" did not exist as a separate entity apart
from this. It was not something that was located in the individual, and which the
individual might bring with him- or herself. Nor did these young men have positive associations with the rite-of-passage act par excellence for young Western-
ers, leaving home to find a new place. In many modern countries this is almost
taken for granted as a cultural act that is part of the way in which a modern individual constructs himself or herself. That "leaving home" is taken for granted may
be one reason modern Jesus scholars have paid so little attention to Jesus' break
with his family, or to his call to followers to leave their households.

In the previous chapter I emphasized that Jesus was part of a household, both
in terms of a physical location (house) and of the social relations that took place
there. Also part of the household as place was its ideological representation, for
instance its ideal roles for members and household as a microcosm of a people
and of the world. All these factors are implied when we say that the identity of
Jesus was located in the place called household. In this chapter I will look at texts
that seem to imply that Jesus dislocated identity from the household, both for
himself and for those who followed him. This terminology is technical, borrowed
from the quotation from Lee Edelman in chapter 1,[2] and I shall therefore alter-
nate between that and terms from everyday language. We may also say that Jesus
became a "displaced person," and that he made those who followed him displaced
persons as well.[3]

In the gospel narratives, the transitions in Jesus' vocation are described as
movements in place. Jesus' baptism by John is described as following a journey
from Nazareth in Galilee to the wilderness on the other side of the Jordan (Mark
1:9–11; Matt. 3:13–17). Moreover, after baptism, Jesus goes out into the wilderness, which is the scene for the temptation story. And the beginning of Jesus' independent ministry, after the arrest of John, is marked by his transition from Judea

back to Galilee. However, this is followed by another transition, which to varying degrees becomes visible in the gospels, from Nazareth to the lake region and Capernaum. Matthew tells us explicitly that Jesus returned to Galilee and that he left Nazareth (to which he must have returned) and settled in Capernaum "by the sea," where he began to proclaim the kingdom (4:13–16). Luke on the other hand has Jesus start his proclamation in Nazareth (4:16–30), and it is after the initial rejection in his home village that he turns to Capernaum (4:31–32). Mark says only that Jesus returned to Galilee and began to proclaim the kingdom (1:14–15), but after the calling of the first disciples along the shores of the Sea of Galilee, his gospel locates Jesus in Capernaum for his first synagogue scene (1:21).

Thus, common to the synoptic gospels is a picture of Jesus that combines changes in his life with transitions in place. The gospels present Jesus' leaving of village and household in Nazareth not just as a practical move. His leaving was also linked to changes in his life—accepting the baptism of John, being tempted in the wilderness, and starting his own mission. Some of these changes in place implied a conflict with household and household relations. From this picture in the narrative sections of the synoptic gospels, we shall turn to the importance of leaving house and household in the earliest traditions of Jesus' words.

The texts discussed here have as a common thread that to follow Jesus meant to leave one's household, and that this led to conflicts with or within households. These texts come from the early Jesus tradition, from Mark, Q, and the *Gospel of Thomas,* and mostly present three (or at least two) independent witnesses to a saying or story. The combination of these sources with a common perspective strongly indicates that we are dealing here with a tradition that takes us as close to the historical Jesus as we can possibly get. I divide the texts into three groups here, in terms of their relationship toward household as a primary place of identity and toward new locations. The first group of texts have Jesus as their subject, and appear to represent the absolute negation of place (Mark 6:4; *Gos. Thom.* 86; Q 9:58). They take an identity rooted in house and village for granted, but dislocate it. They negate this place. Other texts address followers or would-be followers of Jesus and call them to leave their household or predict crises in their families.[4] But there is a significant difference between these texts, so for our purpose they will be divided in two groups. The second group is made up of texts that speak of leaving the household without knowing where to go (Q 9:59–60; Q 14:26; *Gos. Thom.* 55, 101; Q 12:51–53; *Gos. Thom.* 16; Mark 1:16–20). The third group is made up of texts that create an alternative place (Mark 3:31–35; 10:29–30). Those who leave the known and taken-for-granted household structure to follow Jesus establish an alternative place as a fictive kinship household.[5]

In the analysis of these passages, I will first identify the location of the place that is negated, the social relations that take place there, and the meanings attributed to location and relations, that is, the underlying ideological representation. In terms of social psychology we may speak of the household as the primary location of identity, in which *socialization* of the child takes place. Consequently, to break with the household means to dislocate this identity, and to move to another location that is different socially, spatially, or metaphorically (one or more of the three), and to be *resocialized* into that location.[6] The puzzling aspect with many of the sayings of Jesus is that they speak about breaking with the household and moving away from it, but do not mention any socialization into a new location.

JESUS IN NO-PLACE

In his book *Getting Back into Place*, Edward S. Casey actually starts with the opposite of place, with a discussion of what it means to have no place to be. Changes of place and separations are facts of life from the very earliest phase of life; they are part of being human. Therefore, we experience different kinds of difficulties related to space. One of the most serious is that of being *unplaced*, caused by constant movement: "Not only may the former place be lost but a new place in which to settle may not be found. With increased mobility and range comes increased risk, above all the risk of having no proper or lasting place, no place to be or remain."[7] Casey says that the very idea or image of a no-place-at-all causes the deepest anxiety. This panic can be caused by major destructions, like war, but also by more casual events, like being lost or being without lodging for a night: "In such situations we find ourselves entering into a special form of panic: place-panic. For we confront the imminent possibility of there being no place to be or to go. We feel not so much displaced as *without place*. . . . No wonder, either, that fleeing in the face of our own panic, we resort to elaborate stratagems to avoid the void that looms before us."[8] This fear of the void seems almost to be a constitutive part of human existence. Most philosophers from the most ancient to the modern have struggled to eliminate the idea of the void that threatens the reassurance of being. Therefore, in the works of many philosophers *being* and *place* are connected. And, on a practical level, people rely on territoriality to maintain stability and security—for instance, in the form of a home place—in contrast to the insecurity of being placeless.

In some of Jesus' sayings we see this fear of being without place, of losing one's place, come to the fore. Just because house and household were so important as locations of identity and security, the possible loss of location or of being excluded from one's place was threatening. The most prominent example is the saying in Q 9:58 and *Gos. Thom.* 86.

> Q 9:57–58: And someone said to him, "I will follow you wherever you go." And Jesus said to him: "Foxes have holes, and birds of the sky have nests, but the son of man does not have anywhere he can lay his head."
> *Gos. Thom.* 86: Jesus said, "the foxes have their holes and the birds have their nests, but the son of man has no place to lay down and rest."[9]

This saying in Q is the first of two sayings that have to do with the contrast between Jesus' lifestyle and a life placed in household and family relations (Q 9:57–60). This saying presents "the son of man" as a wanderer who "does not have anywhere he can lay his head"; *Gos. Thom.* 86 adds: "and rest."[10] This is a picture of a man without house and shelter; we might say a vagabond or a homeless person.[11] But why is it not enough to say that the Son of Man has nowhere to lay his head? Why contrast that with the statement about foxes and birds? What exactly does this contrast do? Comparisons between human beings and animals were not uncommon in the ancient world, but the point of the comparisons could vary. A well-known example is found in Q 12:24: "Consider the ravens: They neither sow nor reap nor gather into barns, and yet God feeds them. Are you not better than the birds?" This comparison builds on the idea of a hierarchy among creatures, with humans as the highest. However, the point is not a reversal of this hierarchy, but an argument *a minori ad majus:* If God provides for the birds, he will also take care of what human beings need. There is also another assumption at play here, maybe in tension with the first one. Animals could be an ideal for humans ("consider the ravens"), since animal behavior was regarded to be closer to nature.[12]

But the comparison between the foxes and birds on the one hand and "the son of man" on the other in Q 9:58 seems to be based on a different assumption. It seems to evolve not around a point about nature, but about civilization and what it was that characterized civilized, that is, human, life. The images used of the foxes and the birds and the terminology used of their dwellings indicate that they have permanent dwellings, something that was the sign of human society, a mark of civilization. In light of that, the dislocation of "the son of man" takes on an ominous meaning. This person is not only dislocated from a more to a less privileged position in society. He is simply dislocated from civilized society, with its characteristics of permanent human dwellings; he is made less than the foxes and the birds. One commentator says that "the contrast of foxes and birds having a place in the world and 'the son of man'—however that idiom may be understood—having none, points to a dislocation and an inherent injustice in the present fabric of things."[13] Thus, it has to do with identity being *placed,* and a dislocation. This is more than an unfortunate situation for one person among many others. It has to do with being dislocated from one's place; and without place one's identity as a civilized human being is also lost. The contrast is one of order versus disorder.[14]

There is a similar argument in one of the speeches of Gracchus in Plutarch's life of Tiberius Gracchus. Here he laments the wretched conditions of the poor commoners, who suffer under the luxurious life of the unjust rich. In order to drive his point home, Gracchus contrasts the situation of the poor, not with the rich, but with animals: "The wild beasts that roam over Italy have everyone a cave or lair to lurk in; but the men who fight and die for Italy enjoy the common air and light, indeed, but nothing else; houseless and homeless they wander about with their wives and children" (*Vit. Grac.* 9.828c). Here the poor are denied the very premise of human living, settled life in houses. And the contrast to animal life makes their plight even more cruel: the animals are settled, but the poor are deprived of the very sign of human, social life—they have no place.

Likewise, in the sayings about "the son of man" in Q 9:58, he is contrasted with foxes and birds. It is they now who share in the place world. The world is turned upside down. The contrast between human life and animal life has been reversed. The human is in "no place." Thus, the saying points to a more fundamental problem than that this person lives like a tramp and a vagabond. It speaks about a person who has been deprived of all that which comes with having a place, a person outside of human community and the identity that goes with it.[15] But who is this "son of man"? It is likely that this saying refers to Jesus. An argument against taking "son of man" here only in a generic meaning, as a human being, is that the saying in all likelihood is not a proverbial saying, something of a general character. No parallel statements have been found, either in Greek or in Jewish literature, that would make it plausible that this referred to a proverb that one could expect to be known to the hearers or readers.[16] If the saying goes back to Jesus, it means that he has used it about himself or, at the very least, included himself in this "son of man." This does not, of course, imply that it was used in a christological sense, or in the meaning of a future, an eschatological, figure. A suggestion by Mahlon H. Smith is worth considering. In searching for possible parallels or allusions for this statement, he points to the Targum of Psalm 8, which speaks of "the son of man,"[17] who is made a little less than God, and who has all creatures put under his feet, including "the birds in the sky." The irony of the statement would then be that the one who has no place to lay his head is identified as "the son of man," a figure whom God has made the head of creation! If this suggestion points in the right direction, it is a cryptic statement that reverses popular expectations and values. In that regard it would be similar to many other words of Jesus, which have just that effect (e.g., Luke 6:20; Mark 10:15). However, even if the suggestion is attractive, the link to the Targum is weak. The most obvious impression is that of the unsettling picture of Jesus in non-place, contrasted with the picture of animals that have what humans in an ordered society should have. This is the portrait of a person as transgressor of the boundaries of human society.[18]

There is also another saying that places Jesus outside of human society; one version of it is found in Mark 6:4: "A prophet is not without honor, except in his own hometown, and among his own kin, and in his own house."[19] The saying about "a prophet without honor" has become so familiar, included in a common stock of images that are taken for granted, that it does not any longer surprise us. This life without honor appears as if it should be a part of the role of a prophet. This attitude is no doubt a result of the fact that the role of the prophet has fallen out of use; there are no longer prophets around. Therefore, we may hold a very reverential view of prophets, as august men (why are they always thought of as men?), who spoke a message lifted above ordinary human lives. Then we are certainly on a wrong track for understanding the meaning of this saying. It shatters the image of a prophet as a distant person; this is a prophet entangled in household and kin, integrated into a hometown or village.

We have discussed the scene about the rejection of Jesus in Nazareth (the Markan passage 6:1–4) above, and seen how it described the household and village network. Now we will focus on the conflict that the saying about the prophet makes visible. The original form of the saying has been much discussed. Its setting in the Nazareth rejection story may be secondary, as it is found in a different setting in John 4:44 and as an independent logion in *Gos. Thom.* 31. However, all interpretations of the saying presuppose a context of conflict,[20] and there is good fit between the saying in Mark 6:4 (par) and the present context.[21]

What type of place is it that becomes visible in this saying, and what are the specific social relations involved? The place is identified both in terms of location and social relations, as *patris*, that is, "hometown"; *sygeneis,* the kinship group; and *oikia,* the house(hold). This is a description of a village society and the components that made it up, the kinship groups and the households. The particular activity of this community in relation to the homecoming prophet is awarding or withholding honor (*timē*). This is a revealing description of a "little community."[22] The main values were measured in honor and shame, and were part of the interaction within the community.[23] "Honor" is the value of somebody in the eyes of others. It is a value rating that is always part of a competition within the community, where the individual is subject to the evaluation of the others. Honor and shame are intimately connected with place: they are the status of somebody in his or her place. It is possible to be honorable in a humble position, and one can incur shame by going beyond one's place, not respecting one's position within the community.

This appears to be the problem that is reflected in the saying that his own community does not award the prophet honor. So, what could be the reason? Arland D. Jacobson suggests that it is because prophets speak of things that the community would prefer to leave unspoken.[24] But that would apply to the words of the prophet in general, not only in his own village. And therefore it would not seem to explain why just his hometown would reject him. The context in Mark 6:1–4 points to another possibility, which I find more plausible: the prophet is met with disapproval because he puts on airs. He pretends to be something more than he is entitled to from his place in the village. In a way it is familiarity that gives the reason for rejection, but it is just because the familiarity of the community is challenged.

One important aspect of familiarity in a small community is to "know one's place."[25] Social and geographical place is structured; it has, for instance, "a sense of social location, of genealogy, kinship, authority, superordination and subordination."[26] And it is this element of "knowing one's place" that comes to the fore in the reaction from the villagers. The criticism in Mark 6:3 is an attempt to shame him back into his proper place. Maybe to speak of him as "son of Mary" is part of that shaming, to call him "the bastard son of Mary."[27] But also, apart from that, somebody whose brothers and sisters lived as ordinary young members of the village should not behave as if he were a prophet! There is a distinctively male gaze in these comments, with the possible slur on Mary, and with the way Jesus' brothers are all named while the sisters are lumped together in a group, without names. There is a contrast between this Jesus, whose place in the village they know, and his teaching, which raised the question: "Where did this man get all this?" (Mark 6:2; *pothen* indicates "source," but also means "where," spatially).[28] And there is no question that this remark casts doubt about the source of his powers: Was it a source that was unfamiliar, that came from the outside, and was even demonic? (Cf. Mark 3:22–27; 11:27–33.) In this way this criticism was a challenge to Jesus, to get back into his proper place or to realize that he had gone beyond the limit of his proper place.

To this challenge the aphorism in Mark 6:4 can be read as a riposte:[29] Jesus refused to be shamed into his (old) place within the village, to be bound by the honor-shame paradigm of the community. The saying "A prophet is not without honor, except in his own hometown . . ." upped the stakes. He claimed honor outside of his community, so that the shame fell on the community that refused him the honor that was rightly his. The social interaction in this challenge-riposte exchange serves to define the location where it takes place and the meaning of this location. The critics of Jesus spoke out of the conviction illustrated by the quote from J. Z. Smith that place has "a sense of social location, of genealogy, kinship, authority, superordination and subordination."[30] In terms of this meaning of place, Jesus, by presenting himself as a prophet, had rejected the order and structure of the place. He was not acceptable within this place. He had placed himself outside this social location. His only option to come back into it was for him to accept his "place" in this social location as determined by genealogy, kinship, authority, subordination, and the rest. But Jesus breaks out of the mold and will not be limited by the place defined by his lineage and household. He opts to stay outside of it: by refusing to give him honor, the village has also removed him from their place. It is they, not he, who have moved him beyond their limits.

The Markan version of the saying compares the hometown of the prophet, where he is not honored, with other places where he apparently is honored. Thus, the hometown as a negative place is contrasted with other places that are given a positive image. There is here an ideological difference between places,[31] which is similar to the woes of Jesus over Galilean towns that would not believe the miracles that he worked (Q 10:13–15; Matt. 11:20–24), or over Jerusalem, which rejected the prophets sent to her (Q 13:34–35).

The sayings from Q 9:58 and Mark 6:4 present Jesus as a person outside of human community and dislocated from places that give identity. The first saying points to absolute estrangement, the other, using the language of the prophet, is not desperate, but defiant. The ties to homeplace are loosened, the honor and recognition that one expects there is found elsewhere. We find here a self-confidence in Jesus' identification as prophet, but we do not hear of other places that give recognition.

CALLED INTO NOT-YET PLACES

The second group of texts address would-be followers of Jesus and ask them to leave their home place, likewise without pointing to an alternative place. An underlying presupposition of these texts is also the importance of the household as a place of origin. It is summed up well by this quotation from Francis Bacon: "Place is the beginning of existence, just like a father."[32] Bacon's statement draws a parallel between "place" and "father," in that they both stand at the beginning of existence. We may also see it as a statement about the importance of the father for the first place, the home place. In the previous chapter we spoke about the social or mental map of ancient peoples in the Mediterranean that defined the place of the individual in the world. At its center was the family or the household, especially the father.[33] The result was a map that organized the world starting with what was in center and moving toward the periphery. But this mental map also organized the world in terms of hierarchy, so that to be in the center also meant to have authority and power.

It is this aspect of place that becomes visible in all its force in Q 9:59–60:

> But another said to him: "Master, permit me first to go and bury my father."
> But he said to him: "Follow me, and leave the dead to bury their own dead."

The place of the would-be-disciple is the household, where he as a son stands in a position of obligation to his father, who is now dead. The meaning of this location is one of social obligation, subordination, filial piety, responsibility toward ancestors, a matter of honor and shame and of social standing in the village community. Thus, it is difficult to imagine a place where the social relations are imbued with such a thick web of meaning. It is this web of meaning that is challenged, even put down, when the household and its place in the kin group and ancestry is described as "leave the dead to bury their own dead." Who are the "dead" who will bury "their own dead"? Are they "the metaphorically dead," or even, the bones of the dead ancestors in the ossuary?[34] It is difficult to give an accurate interpretation of this gnomic saying, and that is not the point of such sayings anyway. But at the very least we can say that the saying was applied to the household context that the son was asked to leave—the household was characterized as "dead," in contrast to the call to "follow me." The house as the all-important place, as the location of identity, is challenged. The house that took on an ultimately important meaning at the moment of transition from father to son is reinterpreted. It is no longer a place of life; it is identified as a place of the dead. Moreover, life is not found in another location. The call is to move and to follow Jesus, without any clear indication of place.

This dialogue in Q 9:59–60 is set in the context of a challenge to leave the household behind for a wandering life. Thus, it is a close follow-up of the previous saying about "the son of man," who is without house and place.[35] It is the call to leave one's primary location of identity and obligations, one's social place, for a life following Jesus into no-place that is the main topic of this passage. It seems to be a text that rips apart the social fabric of households and local communities.[36] These are call stories or discipleship quests that show would-be disciples in the tension between living in the place that they know and venturing out into unknown places. This Q logion portrays Jesus as calling people out from a fixed place into a location that is not yet defined. It is described as "following Jesus," and Luke adds the task: to proclaim the kingdom of God (Luke 9:60).[37] The transitions in the lives of the disciples, in order to follow Jesus, are described as *movements,* not as entering into a fixed place.

But Luke and Matthew make the understanding of this location more specific through their redactional activity in framing this saying. In Luke, this brief dialogue (together with 9:57b–58 and 61–62) is set in the context where Jesus sets his face to go to Jerusalem (9:51). The small collection of sayings is introduced by a typical Lukan phrase, "As they were going along the road" (9:57a). To "be on the road/way" is the typically Lukan way to describe Christian life. Christians are identified as those who follow "the Way" (Acts 9:2). The specifics of the journeys of Jesus and the disciples as they are described in the gospel narratives are not always clear, as has often been noticed by commentators. But more important than the precise path followed is "the *course and direction of the journey itself,* its tenor and import."[38] Therefore, Luke significantly prefaces his travel journey of Jesus (9:51–19:27) in a way that locates Jesus in relation to the goal for his journey: "When the days drew near for him to be received up, he set his face to go to Jerusalem" (Luke 9:51). This sentence provides the direction that is implied in the call stories in the Gospel of Luke. The call from house into no-place, or into journeying with Jesus, has an implicit direction that is understood by the reader: Jerusalem is the place of Jesus' suffering and death, but also the place from whence the journey continued to "all nations" (Luke 24:47). Matthew likewise understood this saying as an example of the disciples' life. The dialogues in 8:19–22 are inserted in Matthew's rewriting of the Markan story of the crossing of the sea that made it into a discipleship story (8:18–27). The expression "to follow Jesus"—taken from the dialogues (8:19, 22)—is also added to the introduction of the story of the crossing: "When he got into the boat, his disciples *followed* him" (8:23, my italics). Thus, through this redactional process, to "follow" Jesus (an enigmatic saying in 8:22) is given the specific meaning of discipleship and becomes a main theme in Matthew's Gospel.[39]

Q 9:59–60 is an example of an unsuccessful call story.[40] It is a story that shows the power of the quote from Bacon: "Place is the beginning of existence, just like a father." Life for the man who received the call from Jesus was rooted in obligations that derived their strength from the combined power of place and father, bound together in the location of the house and household. Therefore, I am puzzled by readings of this text that make Jesus' attitude to Jewish law the most important aspect, to the degree that "this logion has become a kind of shibboleth for the assessment of Jesus' whole relationship with Judaism."[41] Then one has made the question of household obligations into primarily a "religious" issue about the attitude to Jewish law. This seems to me a reading that compartmentalizes religion in a way that it was not compartmentalized in the first century C.E. Responsibilities for burials and the issue of impurity are discussed in Jewish legal texts, of course, since these were texts dealing with all aspects of life. But to make Jesus' call here primarily into a question of his relation to Jewish law seems misguided. To focus on religion is to shift away from the way in which Jesus presented a challenge to the household structure. The specific religious issue seems more pertinent to theological discussions about law and gospel and Christian-Jewish dialogues today than to the meaning of Jesus' call.

In Q 9:59–60, the dialogue between Jesus and "another [man]" is without context. But such dialogues must very early have been made into narratives. We find them in the stories that tell how Jesus called his first disciples, and shall look at Mark's version in 1:16–20.[42] That Mark has preserved the radical sayings about leaving household is a good indication that they in fact were part of the earliest Jesus tradition. He did this although they did not fit completely with the rest of the history as he narrates it. The call stories of the two couples of brothers—Simon and Andrew, James and John—are stereotypical stories of how Jesus called disciples. They are examples, so to speak, of how the radical challenges of Luke 9:57–60 were turned into narratives about successful calls. Moreover, whereas the previous sayings took place in undefined locations, this narrative is localized: it takes place along the shore of the Sea of Galilee. That provides the specific setting of the narrative and introduces the Sea of Galilee as one of the primary locations for Jesus in Mark.[43]

Mark 1:16–20 consists of two call narratives with identical structures: (1) Jesus meets two brothers at work in fishing boats (1:16, 19); (2) Jesus calls them (1:17, 20a); whereupon (3) they leave their nets (or their father) in the boat (1:18a, 20b); and (4) follow Jesus (1:18b, 20c). The stories have the same pattern, and in both instances the brothers belong to a working group of fishermen. In the second story this is described as a household group, led by their father, but including also "hired laborers." It is explicitly said that John and James leave their father in the boat with the hired hands; thus, this notice in a glimpse lets readers see their place in the socioeconomic system of fishermen at the Sea of Galilee.[44] When the brothers left that place, the effect was both that the livelihood of their household was threatened, and that their father was dishonored and suffered a loss of authority. Moreover, they were called out of a very specific location into an uncertain task ("fishers of men") and into a movement ("follow me") rather than into a new place.

This double story gives names and faces to the radical call to follow Jesus, and provides the main disciples as examples of those who left everything and followed Jesus, in contrast to the unsuccessful call stories (Mark 10:17–22). The idealized picture given by Peter in 10:28 likewise portrays the disciples as those who have "left everything." But this does not seem to be the full story in Mark.[45] In addition to this picture there appears to be a different story hidden underneath, of disciples who keep their ties with their households, who remain in their houses. When Peter and Andrew had left their nets, that is, their work and thereby their place in the economic and social structure of the household, they followed Jesus to the synagogue in Capernaum, where he performed his first exorcism (Mark 1:21–28). Afterward they brought Jesus to their house and a household that included Peter's mother-in-law, whom Jesus healed (1:29–31). Many think that the "house" in Capernaum that serves as the base for Jesus in Mark's Gospel (e.g.,

3:20, 31–35), refers to Peter's house.[46] Maybe this is a conscious ambiguity in Mark's narrative. If so, it seems to be repeated in the story of the calling of Levi, the tax collector, who "rose and followed him" (Mark 2:14). The following scene depicts Jesus at table with "tax collectors and sinners" in "his house" (2:15). It is possible that this refers to Levi's house,[47] and that to "follow" Jesus did not mean that he left his house and household. That disciples kept contact with household members is also indicated by the presentation of one of the women at the crucifixion of Jesus: "Mary the mother of James the younger and of Joses" (Mark 15:40). Thus, Mark has preserved the radical call to leave everything, but it is modified by the stories he tells.

The narrative rendering of the calls to follow Jesus have made it almost seem natural to break up from a household to become a follower of Jesus. Not so in the sayings tradition; here we sense the agony over the break and the extremely strong bonds to house and household. In some instances the call to become a follower did not mean to leave the household physically; instead there seems to be a distancing from the group that created unbearable tensions within the household. The strange thing about these sayings is that they leave the person who is called in limbo, called to leave and to follow Jesus, but without a new place to go, either socially or in terms of location.

This tension is clearly felt in some sayings that indicate that one must "hate father and mother," if one is to become "worthy of Jesus."[48] The sayings in Q 14:26–27 and 17:33 (Matt. 10:37–39; *Gos. Thom.* 55, 101) may point us in the direction of an understanding of this dilemma. Leaving is almost impossible and at the same time something that is required. Q 14:26–27 starts with the exhortation to hate father and mother, son and daughter, and then continues with a parallel statement about "taking up one's cross":

> [The one who] does not hate father and mother can not be my disciple; and [the one who] does not hate son and daughter cannot be my disciple. The one who does not take one's cross and follow after me cannot be my disciple.

The saying in Q 17:33 speaks about finding and losing one's life: "[The one who] finds one's life will lose it, and [the one who] loses one's life [for my sake] will find it."

To a modern mind there is here a puzzling combination of denouncing the household group and of denouncing oneself, in terms of "one's cross" and "one's life." Especially many young people have felt that they needed to leave their families in order to find themselves as autonomous individuals. But to a Mediterranean mind in the first century, "household" and "self" were not two separate entities, but two aspects of the same condition.[49] The self was located in the group; in these sayings the household is described not in its economic and hierarchical sense, but more explicitly in its affective and emotional function. This comes from the collectivist culture that is built primarily on the group, and therefore individuals are defined by means of their family and their place of residence. "The self is always an aspect or a representative of the in-group, which consists of related, gendered persons who come from and live in a certain place."[50] My conversation with the two young Bedouins at the top of Mount Moses showed how this might be true in a collectivist society today also. Moreover, "loving" is an expression of this position in a group, not an individual choice: "Collectivism is associated with *homogeneity of affect;* if ingroup members are sad, one is sad; if joyful, one is joyful."[51]

Therefore, to "hate" is more than an affective emotion, it carries with it an act of distancing, of separation.[52] And the cross that one must take up is not a general suffering "for the sake of Jesus" (as in Mark), but implies the loss of community and alienation from family.[53] Thus, it is the social location of the addressee, his or her primary place of identity, support, and loyalty, that is challenged by the demand to "hate," in order to be "worthy of" Jesus. We see a displacement, a dislocation of an identity that is moved away from the primary group. Granted that we speak of people for whom a modern, individualistic identity was not an alternative, what is the new place for identity? There is a relationship to Jesus, in that the goal is to become "worthy of me." Therefore, there is a movement from the household as the primary social location and identity to a place in the esteem of Jesus. However, no new set of social relations becomes visible here. There is no reintegration into a new location or a new social system.

The previous passages have spoken about followers of Jesus who have left their household and severed themselves from the other members of the household, and thereby caused conflict. The conflict has been viewed from the perspective of those who left. Another saying that is preserved in Q 12:51–53 and *Gos. Thom.* 16 looks at the household in which the conflict exists from within:[54]

> [Do you] think that I have come to hurl peace on earth? I did not come to hurl peace, but a sword! For I have come to divide son against father, [and] daughter against her mother, [and] daughter-in-law against her mother-in-law. (Q 12:51, 53)[55]

Here household is viewed as social relations between family members, based on the authority of the older generation. Moreover, the relations are typically described as specific to each gender. It is interesting that the daughter-in-law is here made socially visible in her own right and in her relationship with her mother-in-law, not just as the wife of one of the sons in the family (Luke 14:26; 18:29). In the system of patrilinial households, it was the bride who left her father's house and moved into the house of her husband's father. The conflict is one between the generations, and within each gender. The split occurs between father and son, mother and daughter, and mother-in-law and daughter-in-law. It is the social fabric of the household that is affected; it is not described as simply the younger generation confronting the older. The result is the destruction of the household.[56] The house as a structured place, as a microcosm of authority and order, of support and solidarity, is destroyed.

The harshness of the saying lies in the fact that it is Jesus who is the cause for division. The saying about division is introduced by a word of Jesus that he has not come to give peace, but a sword.[57] We get the impression that the destruction of the household is an intended one; it was caused by Jesus (Q 12:51). The breakdown of household structures is not viewed as an unfortunate effect, but as something that Jesus intended[58] and that belongs in the context of conflicts in households caused by followers of Jesus. This context is supported by Matthew's redaction; he combines this saying (10:34–36) with the saying about followers of Jesus who must "hate" members of their household (10:37–39). The breakdown of household relations illustrates what that hate might result in for those who followed Jesus. The list, starting with son, daughter, and so on, suggests that the conflict was caused by members of the young generation of the household.

In the Q tradition, the conflict in the household is, so to speak, left hanging. In the statement in Q 12:51–53 there is no way out. *Gospel of Thomas* 16, however, has a longer ending, with "and they will stand solitary [*monachos*]." In the *Gospel of Thomas* that is a term for those who have broken away from family life and have adopted the radical lifestyle of the "solitary" (49; 75). Mark, Matthew, and Luke make "following after" or "the way" into spatial metaphors for the situation of the disciples of Jesus after their dislocation from the household. The *Gospel of Thomas* does not use this metaphor,[59] but instead to "stand alone/solitary." This is one of a series of terms for the true disciple in the *Gospel of Thomas,* together with "elect" (49), children of the light (50), and others. The term "solitary" may also imply a lifestyle of sexual asceticism, but this is not certain.[60] Thus, the *Gospel of Thomas* indicates by his redaction of the saying that the conflict within the household caused by those who followed Jesus could not last. A household could not bear such division over time; the result was that one chose, with the *Gospel of Thomas*'s expression, to stay "solitary." But there is no suggestion of an alternative community for the solitary ones. This metaphor partly indicates the differentiation and distancing from the household, but it may also be a way of expressing an identity "with Jesus" (30, 108).[61]

ENTERING A NEW HOUSEHOLD

We started out with sayings that envisaged the "dislocation of identity" from its place, and that created a "zone of possibilities," but only as possibilities, not with a specified new place or location for the subject. But there are a couple of sayings where the dislocation is combined with a new location, where leaving one's household means entering into a new and different household. The picture of Jesus sitting in a house, surrounded by listeners, declaring them to be his family while his own family stands on the outside, is well known from the story in Mark 3:31–35 (Matt. 12:46–50; Luke 8:19–21). Moreover, it is a good example of how real and metaphorical locations and space were used to bring across a meaning. But this seems to be the case not only of the Markan story, but also of the sayings tradition behind it, which is witnessed in *Gos. Thom.* 99 as well as in the Gospel of the Ebionites (Epiphanius *Haer.* 30.14.5).

The *Gospel of Thomas* has this version: 99:1 "The disciples said to him, 'Your brothers and your mother are standing outside.' 2. He said to them, 'Those here who do what my Father wants are my brothers and my mother. 3. It is they who will enter the kingdom of my Father.'" The contrast between inside and outside, combined with the contrast between the family of origin (mothers and brothers) and a new type of "family," were probably part of the original saying. This is an example of how *place* is used to create difference. Although there is no reference to a specific "where" of the outside, or the very use of a word for "outside" conjures up a contrast between "outside" and "inside," and between insiders and outsiders. Household and family are the quintessential insiders, and particularly a mother in relation to her son (cf. Luke 11:27–28).[62] Therefore, to place mother and brothers on the outside spatially creates a shock effect in the story; it actually means that they are outsiders to Jesus. There is a new group of insiders who make up the mother and brothers of Jesus. And they are constituted not by birth, but by doing "the will of my Father." This is fictive kinship, but, importantly, it is not a group that is added on to the family, an extension of familylike relations. The contrast to the outsiders shows that the idea is one of substitution. There is here a reversal of the "natural order." Fictive kinship is the only kinship.

Mark has turned this saying with its brief introduction into a narrative that more extensively uses the *house* to describe the location of the controversy, as well as to emphasize the metaphorical contrast between inside and outside. First, he introduces a house as the place for Jesus, surrounded by a big crowd, when he first mentions that his family ("his own") come to find him (Mark 3:20–21). And second, he actively employs the image of the house with an outside wall and a courtyard, in his redaction of the story.[63] To the saying in 3:32, that "Your mother and your brothers are outside," he adds a narrative repetition of the information that they were standing outside, explaining that they sent a message to him, presumably since they could not get in because of the crowd (3:31). The story is built around the contrast between the inside, where Jesus and a group of followers are sitting in the house or in the courtyard, and the outside, where his original insiders, his mother and brothers, are. This contrast replicates very well the contrast in Jesus' saying about who his mother and brothers are: (not those of his family, but) those who do the will of God. That his mother and brothers are outsiders is emphasized by their role in 3:21. Because they believed the accusations that Jesus was "beside himself," that is, that he had an unclean spirit, they came to bring him home. The accusation in 3:21 is similar to that directed at him by the Jerusalem scribes in the Beelzebul pericope in 3:22–30. Thus, in Mark's Gospel Jesus' family is portrayed in the same way here as in 6:1–6, participating in the rejection of him by his hometown.[64] It is Jesus who has left the household, who has opted out of the given structures of authority and loyalty, but instead of being defensive, he attacks. He confronts his household of origin: those who do the will of God are his household. This is similar to the rhetoric of Q 9:58 and Mark 6:4; it is the old household that is the problem.

Thus, the picture of Jesus in Mark 3:31–35 is not just that he finds a new kin group, but that he establishes a new household. Jesus is placed in a house, and this house becomes a center for Jesus in his wanderings.[65] Moreover, "house" becomes an important architectural metaphor in Mark for the new community in conflict with other "houses," the synagogues and the temple.[66] In this passage Mark establishes the family and the house as metaphors of social relations and place for the followers of Jesus. But so far little is said of the function of the group.[67] This becomes much clearer, however, in a dialogue between Jesus and Peter in Mark 10:28–30.[68]

Following the story of the rich young man, who did not want to leave everything he had (Mark 10:17–27), the dialogue in Mark 10:28–30 between Jesus and Peter spells out the hope for those who have left everything:

> Peter began to say to him, "Lo, we have left everything[69] and followed you." Jesus said, "Truly, I say to you, there is no one who has left house or brothers or sisters or mother or father or children or lands, for my sake and for the gospel, who will not receive a hundredfold now in this time, houses and brothers and sisters and mothers and children and lands, with persecutions, and in the age to come eternal life."

We have earlier seen how Mark 10:29 painted a picture of the house, household, and fields, that is, the physical location for the social group and their relations, as well as the source of living for the household. The point is here not just the household as family relations or authority structure; houses and lands point to property and sources of sustenance in an agricultural society. This list also suggests that it is based on pre-Mark traditional material, since it does not square with the story of Peter and other disciples leaving not fields, but fishing nets. Besides, Mark gives the impression that they did not really leave their families either.[70] So, the saying seems to presuppose disciples who lived in farming villages, and who left their families and their source of sustenance to follow Jesus.

However, in Mark 10:28–30 they do not leave just for "the way." They are promised a full return—of house, social household group (except father), and even fields. But there is a qualifying note, "with persecutions." It may be that this mention of persecution is the best key to the picture of the situation that is presupposed. It goes well with sayings in the Q tradition, where to "follow Jesus" was a source of conflict, which broke out into the open when it resulted in leaving the household. It meant to withdraw from obligations to the family; it brought shame on them; and rejection and social ostracism were natural results.[71]

The mention of persecution qualifies the hundredfold compensation, which is the crux of this passage. Why should one leave one's household ("everything") only to receive the same back? Does not Mark speak more in terms of a wise investment than of renunciation?[72] But the mention of persecution suggests that there is a difference between what one has left and that which one is promised in return. The parallel to "hundredfold" in Mark 4:10–20, the explanation of the parable of the sower, bears this out.[73] In times of tribulation and persecution it becomes visible who they are who follow the word and bear good fruit, up to a hundredfold, and who so much cling to their riches that they fall away. The hundredfold are signs of the kingdom (4:20; 10:23, 25), that which cannot be planned—it is a mystery (4:11), the reversal of first and last (10:31). Thus, as the story of the rich young man in Mark 10:17–27 shows, leaving households means renunciation. But Mark's picture of compensation shows a truism: a criticism of existing structures is often, paradoxically, presented in similar structures. And apparently the only alternative that Mark could imagine to the household that one left was a new household.

In 10:30 Mark draws a picture of groups of followers sharing houses and working fields, that is, establishing new household groups. These groups were envisaged as fictive kinship groups, just as in Mark 3:34–35.[74] This is a strange picture, indeed, in that it envisions communities rooted in the villages, as alternatives to the households the followers had left. This looks more like an idea of an Essene-like community, although it is unclear whether the idea is that these are new families of procreation, with their own children. "Wives" are not mentioned, so that might indicate that both men and women were followers. Moreover, the new structures may be indicated by the strange mention of "mothers" in plural, and the absence of a mention of a father in the new community.

It is difficult to judge what relationship this picture has to a social context behind the saying. It is only Mark who has the promise of new household, house, and lands "in this time." Matthew 19:29 has placed the fulfillment of the promise in the future, and redrafted it as unspecified "hundredfold." Luke 18:30 has a vague promise that they will receive "manifold" in "his time," and the promise of eternal life gets more prominence. So it seems that Matthew and Luke did not want to portray the community of followers as fictive, alternative households made up of those who had left their own households.[75]

What is a plausible historical and social context for this marginal position, a result of leaving the family or being forced out from a conflict situation? Jerome H. Neyrey has suggested that the social situation is reflected in the macarisms (blessings) in Q 6:20–22.[76] He argues that the situation of poverty, hunger, sorrow, and persecution that these macarisms project is a result of being ostracized from one's household and family, and thus being left without resources and a place in the community. The sayings in Q 12:51–53 and 14:26, about conflicts in the family and hatred toward household members because one is a disciple of Jesus, provide a plausible reason for such a reaction from the family. This must have meant disregard for filial obligations of obedience and respect, and this offers a plausible scenario for the ostracism described in the macarism on those who were persecuted (Q 6:22). Neyrey's argument runs on the level of the Q community, but if, as it is commonly held, these macarisms go back to Jesus, the social context that he proposes is even more plausible.

Neyrey makes the fourth macarism[77] his starting point in his search for a context: "Blessed are you when men hate you, and when they exclude you and revile you, and cast out your name as evil, on account of the Son of man" (Luke 6:22).[78] The terminology used for "hate, exclude, revile, cast out" is not the terminology used for formal or informal excommunication from the synagogue.[79] Rather, "hate" and "exclude (separate)" are related to groups and group loyalty, and imply separation or banning from a social group. The other two terms, "revile" and "cast out," are terms of shaming; they imply acts of dishonoring and attacking the public honor of somebody. Thus, we are within the area of reproach and punishment within the village community as part of an honor and shame society, just as we saw in Mark's picture of how the prophet Jesus was shamed (Mark 6:1–6). A person who was reproached in this way would lose his reputation and standing in the community, and would be excluded from formal and informal business and contacts. Moreover, this punishment was not just inflicted by the village; in that case, the household and larger family would have given support and protection. The cultural context for the saying must be one in which the household also is a source of this attack. The result, Neyrey suggests, is the situation that is described in the first three macarisms: those who are excluded from their household are reduced to poverty, even begging, and hunger, because they have lost their place of work and source of sustenance and support. And this also leads to grief and sorrow at the loss of family. Thus, a plausible case can be made that all of the four macarisms deal with situations experienced by followers of Jesus. They suffer "on account of the Son of man" and they are promised a reversal of fortune in the kingdom (Q 6:20) or in heaven (Q 6:23).

Such a reading of the macarisms makes it possible to see the conflict behind them in a new light. Instead of a general suffering of the poor, and an expulsion from the synagogue, they speak to a social conflict on village and household level. And we can see the point of view for those on the other side, who remain in the households and villages. The latter are trying to deal with disobedient sons and daughters, household members who have shown disregard for filial obligations and responsibilities toward the household. "Following Jesus" was hardly an excuse for this sort of behavior, which, when carried to the extreme, met with social ostracism.

But this type of behavior from sons (and daughters?) in the household cannot have been totally unknown. The parable of the prodigal son, Luke 15:11–32, may possibly be read as a story that reflects this kind of experience with unruly sons.[80] The son in this story left of his own accord, and with his acts of claiming his part of the land, and leaving, put the future of the household at risk. When he had spent all of his property, that is, become poor (15:14a), a great famine came, and he began to be in want (15:14b). He was forced into a dishonorable location, feeding pigs (15:15–16), where he "came to himself" and lamented that he had left his father's house (15:17). Thus he was poor, hungry, and full of sorrow when he wanted to return. That is, not only had he spent his father's possessions, but in a shameful way, so that the return should be greeted with punishment and humiliation, rather than with feasting (instead of hunger), joy (instead of sorrow), robes of honor (instead of shame and poverty).[81]

Of course, there are many differences between the parable and the macarisms, not least that the situation of wants and shame in the parable was brought about by disobedience to the father. Neyrey, however, has suggested a reading of the cultural context of the macarisms that suggests a similarity in the social consequences of leaving household and village. It was an act that was regarded as shameful, and particularly toward the father as the head of the household. Read in this way, the picture of the father in that parable becomes another example of reversal, of contrast to culturally expected relations.

The macarisms are easily read as expressions of a unique Christian experience. And, within a Christian context, leaving household to follow Jesus is understood as a honorable cause. But it may not have been understood in that way in first-century Palestine. I suggest that the social and economic changes of the period provide a more plausible context to understand the conflict that was a result of followers of Jesus leaving their households. In the previous chapter we saw that these changes threatened the households as viable socioeconomic units, and led to a concomitant weakening of household ties and of the authority of the father. Social and economic pressures led to social uprooting, especially among the young, who were in a marginal situation already.[82] Young men were therefore susceptible to joining groups like "freedom fighters," as well as to being attracted by John the Baptist or the Essene community. It is quite likely that the Jesus movement would appear as playing to these tendencies. From several of the sayings of Jesus, as well as from the list of disciples, it appears that many young men followed him. In that perspective, both the prodigal son and the sons (as the most likely addressees of the macarisms) might from the outside have been regarded as sharing in a pattern of behavior that destabilized households even further.

THE PLACE OF THE INTERPRETER

It is difficult to imagine exactly how the words about leaving households and hating household members were heard. It is even more difficult to envisage what effects they might have had on social behavior, and how "outsiders" in Galilee reacted to that behavior. But we must try to establish a context within which to understand and explain these words. I have suggested that social uprooting and the following pressures on households and families in Herodian Palestine was part of the context for the conflicts caused by Jesus. And I suggest that this scenario helps us to understand the words of dislocation from household in the early Jesus tradition within their historical context in first-century Galilee.

For discussion of some of these problems, I will use as an example a short article by John W. Pryor, "Jesus and Family—a Test Case,"[83] which summarizes positions held by many other scholars.[84] It is especially useful since it sees that the main challenge of interpretation is to explain how Jesus' critical words about family and household might have been understood in a Jewish milieu. Pryor says: "To the Eastern mind, such a comment of Jesus can mean only one of three things: (i) he has callously turned his back on his cultural and family obligations and should be thought of as a reprobate; (ii) he is mentally unstable; (iii) he is consumed by a passion which in his eyes relativizes all other obligations."[85] After giving these three alternatives, Pryor defends the third alternative, with little mention of the second,[86] and absolutely none of the first! In defense of the third alternative, Pryor argues that such a *relativization* of all other obligations on the basis of a special allegiance to God was well known in Jewish tradition.[87] However, even if this were the case, Pryor would have to prove that it was likely that this was how Jesus and his followers were perceived, and how they perceived themselves. But this is not the line of argument that Pryor follows. Instead he attempts to show that Jesus did not intend to attack the family. In a discussion of Mark 3:31–35, the "new family," Pryor claims that "Jesus' words do not need to be seen as an attack upon the family *per se*. . . . What he is doing is to *bear witness* to a community of women, children and men which *transcends* that most precious of units in Jewish culture, a community which, *if needs be*, takes precedence over the family."[88]

In a discussion of Q 12:51–53, about conflict in the household, Pryor argues that Jesus did not laud the disintegration of the patriarchal family. In line with Jewish tradition he must have looked on it as a tragedy, and the readers must have understood it in the same way, unless "Jesus spoke these words without clearly indicating that he considered such an eventuality 'a good thing.'"[89] Pryor overlooks that, regardless of whether Jesus considered the divisions in the household to be "a good thing" or not, in Q 12:51 he clearly says that he will intervene to cause them to happen. Finally, on the question of what it means that Jesus does not mention "fathers" in the new household, Pryor argues against Schüssler Fiorenza: "The fact that Jesus fails to mention fathers in the 'kingdom family,' far from denigrating the father role elevates it, for the heavenly father becomes the pattern of all human fatherhood."[90]

In every instance Pryor chooses a reading that, in order to show how seriously Jesus takes the family, does not take the words of Jesus seriously. What is the meaning of that little qualification of family that Pryor makes, family "*per se*"? If Jesus' rejection of his mother and brothers is not an attack on family per se, but only on his mother and brothers, does that mean that it is less serious? And is it plausible to say that Jesus shares the Jewish sorrow over the disruptions of households, when he actually says that he has come to cause it? And finally, can the disappearance of fathers from the picture of the new fictive family really mean that fathers are now taken up into heaven and partake in God's absolute fatherhood?

With his interpretation Pryor will argue that Jesus falls into the last of the three possible options into which the Eastern mind[91] might put the words of Jesus on the true family, that of a person "consumed by a passion which in his eyes relativizes all other obligations." Pryor here argues not from Jesus' intention, but from the assumption that the community had such a category that they could put Jesus into, so that his disruptive words would be understood only as "relativizing" and not as threatening family life "per se." But there is nothing in the textual evidence

he provides that indicates that the Jewish community would put Jesus and his followers in such a category.[92] Instead, the texts speak of conflicts and hate! Pryor
does not discuss the two other options he imagined that the "Eastern mind" could
use to interpret Jesus' words. One of them, that Jesus was mentally unstable, he
lumps together with the third option, discussed above. And the first option he
only mentions, but does not even comment on. This is the verdict that "he has
callously turned his back on his cultural and family obligations and should be
thought of as a reprobate." To me, this appears to be the most plausible interpretation of the "outside" reactions, and in line with the interpretation of the Beatitudes in Q 6:20–22 and the parable of the prodigal son, Luke 15:11–32, offered
above. Also, the reactions from Jesus' household and the village community as
they are constructed by Mark in 3:21–22, 6:1–4, point in the same direction, as
well as Q 9:59 and the reactions one can project to that challenge.

One may suspect that it is the family as a modern institution that is the ideological starting point for Pryor, not the possible reactions of Jesus' Jewish milieu of
his time. The family was a central Jewish institution, but in Pryor's discussion "family" becomes an almost metaphysical concept. Is this the "family per se," which
cannot be shattered? Is the starting point that the idea of family as a universal institution has a value, which one cannot imagine that any in their right mind will want
to shatter? It seems to me that in many discussions of Jesus' relation to households
in his time, the underlying issue is the preservation of families today.[93] And since
they are regarded as God-given institutions par excellence, and Christian churches
have become the champions of defense for families, it is beyond comprehension
that this might not always have been so. It is apparently not possible to imagine
that Jesus should have been critical of family life "per se." And since his critical attitude to his own household cannot be denied, it becomes imperative to invent a
"family per se" that will not be affected by this criticism. Can we understand this
reaction as a sort of "place panic" that Casey discussed (see "Jesus in No-Place,"
above)? That was a panic of being without place. Many of us feel deeply that
"home," in the sense of family, is "the beginning of place." And it is this very feeling of secure place that is threatened if we entertain the possibility that Jesus was
"anti-family." But maybe we should be willing to entertain that possibility. I think
that we would then be closer to understanding the reactions to Jesus in his own
time than if we conjure up a magical "family per se" that would remain secure in
place regardless of what Jesus said or did to his own family.

But Pryor and others who share his position are not alone in combining the
discussion of Jesus' relations to family and present-day controversies over family.
Pryor argues against scholars like J. D. Crossan and E. Schüssler Fiorenza, who
hold that Jesus "sought to overthrow the patriarchal family."[94] We may compare
this accusation with Crossan's phrase in commenting on Q 12:51–53: "Jesus will
tear the hierarchical and patriarchal family in two along the axis of domination
and subordination."[95] This clearly is the language of modern social and political
analysis, which identifies this type of family as old-fashioned. Crossan views it
primarily as hierarchy and domination, that is, from the perspective of power,

not in terms of support, solidarity, and loyalty. The language he uses has borrowed much particularly from feminist analysis of the inequality of women within families from the 1960s onward. The position of the author is one of moral superiority. It ought to be obvious to any reader in his or her right mind that such families ought to be torn apart. Let me add that my point here is not to be critical of this feminist position and its impact, but simply to identify the location of this language. It is in and by itself a modernizing language, and it is not strange that readers might surmise that the purpose of the historical argument is to fight a modern battle.

I have found it useful to enter into this discussion of the social and mental location that we as readers and interpreters occupy when we try to make meaning out of words in the Jesus tradition. But let us now actually return to the attempt to make meaning out of the words from the earliest Jesus traditions about leaving household.

JESUS AND THE CHALLENGE OF DISLOCATION

We started this chapter by asking what meaning it had that Jesus left his household and his village, Nazareth, at the outset of his public activity. This was an important question because it was associated with the traditions of Jesus' conflicts with household and village. Moreover, in the tradition about Jesus' calling of his disciples, the disciples were also called to leave their households. Therefore, we studied passages about Jesus and his situation vis-a-vis family and households, together with passages that spoke about the situations of followers or would-be-followers. A remarkably similar picture resulted from material in three different traditions: Q, Mark, and the *Gospel of Thomas*. Although they also showed individual differences in the way they used this material to develop their own perspectives, this coherence in the main points makes it possible to be fairly confident that they originated with Jesus.

First, I think we may say that Jesus was a "displaced person." The prophet saying in Mark 6:4 puts Jesus within a context where the primary value for a man was his honor, in the eyes of his significant others. And in a Mediterranean setting in the first century, the household was the most significant group of others. To be refused honor from that group was to be put outside of that location, to be marginalized and displaced. But the saying about no honor in the home place also suggests a critical stance toward the home place: Jesus seems confident that a prophet deserves honor. It is the home place that stands to lose. The other saying, about having nowhere to put his head, was not just an indication of a vagabond existence. It meant to be in no-place, without any location that could give social identity. Thus, as a saying coming from Jesus, it could also be heard as an expression of transgression, deliberately placing Jesus at the outside, in no-place, to challenge the places that were taken for granted, which had authority. Therefore, we should not read these passages as if Jesus were passively accepting the verdict, but rather as dislocating himself from the places that gave or withheld honor and identity, the household and the village community. Thereby Jesus questioned the value of their activity as well as their power to grant or withhold honor.

The enigmatic character of these sayings was repeated in sayings to followers or would-be followers. The household was in a hyperbolic sense said to be "dead," as a justification for leaving behind even the most vital filial obligations. And disciples were asked to "hate," in other words, to distance themselves from, their family relations in the household. It appears that Jesus intended the resulting conflict within the household. Finally, an alternative family of origin and social relations was suggested in some texts. However, the implications of this suggestion were not spelled out. The idea of a new place for the hearers or the readers was very vague.

Let us try to reflect on the importance of these observations. The perspective of these sayings is noticeably different from that of the parables and other sayings of Jesus. In the previous chapter we pointed out how central the image of the household was to Jesus. But it is also remarkable that at the center of that household was the householder, the master or father. Or we might rather say that it is unremarkable, because that was the normal way of mapping the world, starting with the household and the father as its head. In the sayings about leaving or being outside of the household, the perspective is different; the sayings mostly address a son, sometimes possibly a daughter. Jesus does not speak as the head of a household and he does not address other heads of households. Sometimes Jesus addresses a married son, so that leaving means also to leave married life. But most of the time couples do not receive attention. Jesus takes a much broader view of the household. It is a location, a set of social relations, of obligations and loyalties, above all to the father and mother of the family. Thus, what comes in view is household as place in its totality of relations, location, and meaning, that is, as the primary source of identity.

That is the reason why leaving the household is so unsettling, since it means to be displaced from one's place of identity. And the trouble with these sayings is that they do not immediately open up a new place into which a disciple might settle. Jesus invites or calls people to "follow me," to "become my disciple," but this does not in itself provide a new place. It seems more a call to follow him into his lack of place. Followers are called into this "no-place" existence, with the household as its primary opposite. Nonburial of father and "hate" toward family expresses the severing of ties to the household and a call for spatial distancing. But this distancing may also happen without a distancing in place: it may be expressed by the conflicts within the household. This saying might indicate a tension that is unresolved. The solution to this tension is suggested in a saying about a new family of fictive kinship, made up of those who do "what my father wants." They are identified as "insiders" in contrast to Jesus' natural family, who are characterized as "outsiders." It is not stated, however, that those who make up the "new family" have left their own household. They may have distanced themselves but still remained physically in their household.

The primary theme in this group of sayings is one of dislocation. The given position in all instances is the house, the household, and household relations. In all instances this is understood as highly significant, for identity, social structure, integration in community, and so on. To leave this location therefore causes disruption of social relations and meaning. But there is very little in terms of an alternative to the household as a center for life and identity. The addressees are asked to follow Jesus into "the road" or "way," "to stand alone." Very little in these sayings points toward a new fellowship, a community that can serve as an alternative. There is no new house or household visible, only conflicts in the old, which is to be left. It is a strangely undefined place that one is called into, maybe a "zone of possibilities" that are not yet put forward.

We can understand how seriously this experience of dislocation must have been felt from how quickly it was attempted to find a solution—a new, defined place. This, I think, explains the redaction of these Jesus sayings by the *Gospel of Thomas* and in particular the way in which Mark turns them into narratives. We find various strategies. Q appears to presuppose a radical dislocation, and to stand by that position, without clear descriptions of a new integration. The *Gospel of Thomas* has the saying of those who do the will of Jesus' father as "my brothers and my mother," in contrast to Jesus' real mother and brothers who stand "outside." But insofar as Thomas imagines a new place, household and family do not seem to be his primary images. Instead of an alternative family, his alternative is "to stand alone," to be solitary (*Gos. Thom.* 16, 30, 49, 75). This does not necessarily imply a total lack of sociability or community; it is possible to share this status, and the *Gospel of Thomas* speaks of those who stand alone in plural. But identity is expressed more in terms of origin than in terms of social community. The *Gospel of Thomas* 50 speaks of those who come from the light and, in a parallel statement, of being sons of "the living father." Ultimately, it is a question of sharing the identity of Jesus. And that one can do by "standing alone."

For Mark, on the other hand, "standing alone" is not a solution. He seems fully integrated in a worldview where household and family are at the center of the world, and where that holds true also of the alternative world of Jesus. He has some of the radical sayings of Jesus, about the prophet and the new family (6:4; 3:34–35), but he puts them into a narrative context that explains them, while it also appears to "domesticate" them. Most significantly, Mark provides a social and spatial location for the new, fictive kinship group. Jesus has a house (2:15; 3:20, 31–35), and that becomes a center for him and the group of disciples, and, metaphorically, for the Markan community.[96] This integration into a house is significant for Mark's adaptation of the radical call to leave work, household, and father in other narrative contexts as well (1:16–20; 10:29–30). For one thing, we may surmise from the narrative that the disciples did not totally leave their old household and family members. Moreover, instead of the total loss of household, house, and living that they (presumably) left, they are promised the same in return. The text (Mark 10:29–30) seems to aim at social integration into a movement that is located in the same type of place, with house and fields to cultivate.

The vision takes the form of the structure that it negates, something that is not unusual in protest movements. However, this new place is qualified. There are major differences from the old. There is no father figure in the new household, and that appears to be not by default, but by design. And life in this household includes persecution, probably in the form of social exclusion from their old household and village.

Thus, Mark's narrative in one way seems immanently plausible. It describes Jesus as staying in houses, and the disciples as not really leaving their households, but only venturing out with Jesus on his small trips in the vicinity of Capernaum. But when compared to the *Gospel of Thomas* and Q, and when we study the reinterpretations that Mark has made, it becomes clear that it is part of a conscious construction of a picture on the basis of a few sayings. The method is the same as we can see in several instances in Mark when a word from the saying tradition with multiple witnesses becomes the basis for a narrative.[97] Consequently, I venture to say that the picture that Mark gives of Jesus located in a house that serves as the location of his new household is a Markan construction.[98] This does not mean that it could not be historically plausible, but arguments for historicity need to meet the criticism rendered above. Moreover, it could also be argued that Mark's picture reflects his own time, a gradual movement toward integration of families and households into the group of followers of Jesus.

The earliest tradition, which takes us closest to Jesus, is represented by sayings from Q, *Gospel of Thomas* and Mark before they were reinterpreted within Mark's narrative structure. These sayings are critical of the household and see or predict the conflicts that were the result of following Jesus. To use the terminology of Edelman, they present a dislocation of identity, and that creates "a zone of possibilities." But it remains basically an opening, and does not offer a new embodiment, location, or resocialization. Therefore, these sayings represent a location that is outside of the house and household, a liminal position.

We have studied the rhetoric of the Jesus sayings and have attempted to draw a picture from that. But what was the function of this rhetoric? What was the possible historical situation that this rhetoric created? If we look at the rhetorical situation implied in these sayings, it points to an "in-between position," having left one's original household, but not yet integrated into a new position. Victor Turner's works on "*rites de passage*" provides a model to postulate a social process behind the rhetoric.[99] The model, originally used for youths in transition to adult status, has been usefully applied in many other contexts, among them to the study of early Christian groups.[100] This model postulates three stages: The first stage is separation from one's original place, status, and position. The result, in the second stage, is the state of liminality, a position that is ambiguous, "in betwixt and between." Finally, in the third stage the passage is completed and the person is reincorporated into society with a new position. When the model is applied to the formation of early Christian groups, this third stage is represented by the formation of a new group or position, into which integration takes place. Looking at the material we have studied, we may say that Jesus' sayings in Q and the *Gospel of Thomas* present a picture of the second stage, the liminal phase. Mark, however, has integrated the words of Jesus in a context that represents the third stage, integration into a (re)established household structure.

Supposing that the sayings in Q and the *Gospel of Thomas* are closer to the position of Jesus, we may suggest the following picture: The sayings of Jesus were primarily addressed to young men, calling them to leave their position in the household. Most of these young men do not seem to have been in a marginal position in society (e.g., poor or "sinners," sick, etc.), but well integrated into their place in the house and village structure. Therefore, by leaving to follow Jesus they experienced the effects of separation: they became displaced; they were stripped of that which defined their position and status. They entered into a liminal stage, outside the known and accepted structure of their household and village society. We noticed that the sayings of Jesus appeared to be at least mostly directed at men. If women are not directly excluded, they are at best only implicitly addressed in the exhortation to "leave" and to "follow." But other sources clearly imply that there were women in the Jesus movement.

This picture raises at least two questions that we shall follow up in the next chapters: What were the consequences for men of entering into a liminal position, not just as a brief transition in a rite of passage, but for a longer period? Since they were men in a male-dominated society, I am particularly interested in what it meant to their male position. And second, since we know so little of how women entered the Jesus movement, how can we imagine the relations between the men who had entered a liminal stage and the women in the group?

Chapter 4

Leaving Male Space

Eunuchs in the Jesus Movement

Young men who left their households and followed Jesus became displaced persons. By putting themselves "out of place" they represented a provocation to the very order of the community. One of the most provoking ways that men might be put out of place was by being—or standing accused of being—a eunuch. It is probably such an accusation that caused the eunuch saying in Matt. 19:12, one of the strangest words attributed to Jesus: "For there are eunuchs who have been so from birth, and there are eunuchs who have been made eunuchs by men, and there are eunuchs who have made themselves eunuchs for the sake of the kingdom of heaven. He who is able to receive this, let him receive it." Although there are strong arguments for regarding this as a saying of Jesus, it is little used in descriptions of the historical Jesus. This may be because the image of *eunuch* threatens common presuppositions about Jesus as a male figure.

In this chapter we shall use the eunuch saying for entry into a discussion of what it meant to Jesus and his followers to leave their place as males in a household.[1] Within a house and household, everybody had "their place," both in terms of material practice, what kind of work they did, and in terms of social and ideological place. Men had their specific place as fathers, sons, brothers, and husbands. Their position was privileged compared to that of mothers, daughters, sisters, and wives. To leave this male place in the household meant to abdicate from an important part of their identity as men.[2] Outside of this location their identity was threatened and open to question. It is this questioning of masculine identity that will provide the starting point for our investigation.

With this focus on Jesus and his male followers, I may open myself up for the criticism that once again a male scholar overlooks the question of women in the Jesus movement. This is a criticism that has been raised by many feminist scholars, most effectively in many studies by Elisabeth Schüssler Fiorenza.[3] I am not suggesting that there were no women among the followers of Jesus. And I see the importance of studying earliest Christianity from a feminist perspective, to rectify a traditional picture that has focused exclusively on men. But when, as in this chapter, I focus on how male identity was challenged by Jesus, it is actually a perspective that is inspired by feminist criticism. Feminist interpretation has questioned the traditional image of women that was once taken for granted, and has produced a new picture showing women in a diversity of roles and places. In this study I want to challenge the traditional image of men that has also been taken for granted. Just as it too long was taken for granted that the first followers of Jesus were mostly men, their masculinity was likewise taken for granted. It is this image of masculinity that I want to question. As a result, I hope to show that if men left their masculine places, there was an opening also for new relations with women and children in the Jesus movement.

Withdrawal from one's (male) place is part of a larger discussion of *asceticism*.[4] Often asceticism is spoken of in terms of what specific practices or things are given up, but a more fruitful approach places these specific practices within the larger context of the purpose of asceticism.[5] One such suggestive attempt at a definition says that "Asceticism may be defined as performances within a dominant social environment intended to inaugurate a *new* subjectivity, *different* social relations, and an *alternative* symbolic universe."[6] The emphasis on "new," "different," and "alternative" places asceticism at odds with "the dominant social environment." According to this definition, asceticism is a set of performances that will create something other than that which exists within the dominant culture. That is, asceticism is a critical activity. It is an attempt from a nondominant, even marginal position, to create something that transcends or even transgresses the existing order.[7] In the sayings of Jesus it is the patriarchal household that is the "dominant social environment." We may therefore characterize it as "male space." By that I mean not only the practical and social structure of the house and the household activities, place in practical terms, but also the ideological and mental structures and the place of men, women, and children within that space. Therefore, I will look at the asceticism of Jesus, his call to leave male space, as a challenge to the standards of masculinity in antiquity.

In antiquity asceticism was viewed in terms of self-control and -mastery, and it was regarded as a masculine characteristic. Eunuchs, on the other hand, were regarded as "half-men." These views on masculinity and asceticism were shared by early Christian writers, some of whom, all men, commented on Matt. 19:12. They strongly defended the ascetic renunciation of sexuality as a male virtue, and therefore distanced Jesus from any association with castrated eunuchs. Against this background, I will return to the saying in its historical context and examine the saying in the context of a break with the masculine, patriarchal patterns of society at the time.

But first we shall see how modern interpreters of the passage in Matt. 19 have defended the masculinity of Jesus against the accusation that he was a eunuch. It appears that they find it threatening to imagine that the masculinity of Jesus may be questioned. It may be permissible to view Jesus as an ascetic, but not to question his masculinity. Here I think that we are dealing with strong cultural patterns and presuppositions among (mostly) male scholars.

UNSETTLING A MALE SPACE:
MODERN INTERPRETATIONS OF MATT. 19:12

The history of interpretation shows that Matt 19:12 has caused problems to interpreters throughout the centuries.[8] Even today, modern interpreters are in a quandary how to explain it. I am interested to find out why this saying has been so problematic as it obviously has been, and I suggest that it has to do with the interpreters' presuppositions about masculinity, both that of Jesus and his followers and that of their interpreters. The eunuch is a highly problematic and ambiguous figure who, because he is a male figure, threatens the very idea of masculinity. To imagine Jesus or his disciples as eunuchs, as men who were physically unfit for marriage, unable to perform sexually, is perhaps an unsettling picture. But this strange and uncomfortable picture of the eunuch is a useful place to start. By so effectively denying masculine sexuality, it suddenly makes us think about the sexuality and masculinity of Jesus. To start "off center," with the image of the emasculated man, may help us to see more clearly what male images we hold of Jesus, what presuppositions about masculinity we bring with us when we try to construct our picture of "Jesus the man."[9] In texts from antiquity we find that the figure of the eunuch often was the "other" that triggered reflection on male identity.[10] In this effect the eunuch shared similarities with women as the "other" over against which masculinity was defined. We will start with modern interpreters and then move back to early Christian expositions of this saying.

Most often the eunuch saying in Matt. 19:12 has been regarded as a conclusion to the conflict dialogue between Jesus and the Pharisees about divorce. In Matt. 19:3–11 Jesus sharpens the command against divorce, and especially against remarriage after divorce. The following verse has often been interpreted in light of this discussion, as an exhortation to a divorced husband to live in chastity or celibacy. The most common understanding of "eunuchs for the sake of the kingdom of heaven" has therefore been that it meant "chaste" or "celibate," and that it had nothing to do with castration.

However, many commentators have realized that Matt. 19:12 does not fit well together with 19:3–9, and have suggested that it was Matthew's redaction that

combined the two sayings.[11] Thus, it is very likely that Matt. 19:12 was originally an independent saying, and there are good reasons to think that in some
form it goes back to Jesus.[12] Although it is attested only in Matt. 19:12 in the
New Testament, the suggestion that it is an ancient saying is supported by a version of the saying in Justin I *Apol.* 15:4 that most likely is independent of
Matthew.[13] If the addressee for the saying is no longer a divorced husband who
is encouraged to live a celibate life, we may have to consider other possibilities
for the implications of the word "eunuch."

If it was an independent saying, it probably goes back to a polemical exchange
with Jesus' opponents.[14] The opponents may have used the word "eunuch" to
denigrate or slander Jesus and his disciples, in effect to remove them from their
position as "real" men. In response, Jesus picked up the word, and accepted it:
yes, in a certain sense they were eunuchs, unable to live a married life. The saying lists three different types of eunuchs. The first two were commonly known
in antiquity, also from Jewish sources (*Jebamot* 8.4): one by nature, that is, from
birth, the other through human intervention, by castration. To these two Jesus
added a third, referring to his disciples. They were eunuchs of a very special type,
not by nature, not "man-made" by forced castration, but "for the sake of the kingdom of heaven." In the first two instances the term "eunuch" was commonly used
not of someone who was celibate or who abstained from marriage, but of someone who was physically (made) *unfit* for marriage and incapable of performing
sexually. The central question is therefore whether the last group was parallel to
the others in this respect, or whether "eunuch" was here used in another, figurative meaning.

Many scholars have accepted this proposal of a polemical exchange as the context of the saying, but when it comes to further interpretation, they still do not
seem to grasp the challenge that the use of this word eunuch posed.[15] In his otherwise very perceptive discussion of the asceticism of Jesus, Dale C. Allison provides an illuminating example. He twice mentions that this saying in Matt. 19:12
may be pejorative or due to slander,[16] but finds that it could still be a word by
Jesus since it corresponds to his habit of taking up slander and using it for his
own purpose. But this seems to be forgotten when Allison offers his own interpretation of the saying. He says that

> [Jesus'] urgent eschatological mission was sufficiently important and con-
> suming as to disallow family entanglements. This is, after all, and as argued
> above, the plain meaning of Mt 19:12. The eunuchs that Jesus defended
> were those who, as heralds of the coming kingdom, had as little time for
> marriage as for business. To leave all for the sake of the grand cause was to
> leave behind the world and its attendant affairs once and for all. If the dis-
> cipline of the Spartans was to prepare for war, and if the exercises of the
> Greek athlete were to prepare him for the athletic contest, the asceticism of
> the pre-Easter Jesus movement was similarly a strategy to meet a specific
> goal. The missionary endeavor to restore Israel in the face of judgment
> demanded complete dedication. In other words, the proclamation of the
> coming kingdom required sacrificing a normal course of life.[17]

It is noteworthy that Allison here so easily enters into a language of asceticism that is full of stereotypical masculine categories. Within one sentence it has acquired "discipline," "prepare for war," "exercise," "athlete," and "contest." The Spartan warrior and the Greek athlete are the ideal figures, the "grand cause" of exploration or conquest is the metaphor. In this interpretation, the insight that "eunuch" was a word of slander has gotten lost. There is no trace left of the specific meaning of being a eunuch in the saying in Matt. 19:12. Allison continues an interpretation of the saying as an exercise in the manly business of self-mastery over the body and mastery over the world, and the result is a disciplined virility. But the image of a eunuch in fact represented the very opposite of the masculine discipline of the Spartans or of the Greek athlete. His was a body that had been emasculated, and therefore did not conform to the ideal standards of the male body that Allison invokes. Thus, in the context of various images of "eunuch," the associations that the word evoked could hardly have been that of warrior or athlete.

I use this quotation not so much to single out Allison's interpretation in particular for criticism, but to illustrate how it belongs to a tradition of male interpretation that has had great trouble in interpreting this verse. This is not so much due to individual shortcomings but because of a cultural pattern that views the world from a masculine perspective. For male authors, asceticism is so obviously a masculine place, a war field or a sport arena, and this perception filters the information that can get through.[18] Therefore we may ask: What position did the eunuchs represent within the field of male asceticism that made them so unsettling? Let us first look at how masculinity and asceticism were combined and how asceticism was regarded as a male ideal.

ASCETICISM AS MALE SPACE

The masculine ideals of the warrior and athlete invoked by Allison have a long tradition and actually go all the way back to antiquity.[19] This idea implied not only mastery over others, but also mastery over self, self-control. The dominant meaning could change over time and in various situations. On an individual basis, there were different aspects to the mastery or control that a male could exercise. One was the mastery over others in the household, performed by the male head of the house, reflected for instance in the household codes in early Christian letters.[20] Another was the mastery over self in terms of control of one's body. In the ancient world there were two areas that were of primary concern regarding self-control: sexuality and food.

This masculine ideal was shared by many cultures within the Greco-Roman world; there were many similarities between ancient Greek, Roman, and Jewish ideals.[21] Therefore, we shall use passages from the Jewish authors Philo and Josephus about ascetic movements as examples of this ideal of male self-mastery. These passages are particularly useful since they have often been adduced as parallels to leaving home in the Jesus movement. But the explicitly masculine character of this ideal of renunciation has not been discussed, and as a result it has been taken for granted that Jesus' asceticism built on the same ideals.[22]

Continence or renunciation of sexuality was based on the ideal of self-mastery or self-control. In Jewish sources, as well as in Greek and Roman ones, this ideal was gendered as male.[23] In contrast, a lack of self-mastery was gendered as female. Self-mastery was part of a set of masculine virtues, like courage, whereas weaknesses like softness and servility were associated with women. Among Jewish writers in the first century C.E., Philo emphasizes that through ascetic regimens men can transcend their corporeal and feminine aspects, and he portrays his male heroes as possessing the self-mastery that was required. Women, on the other hand, lacked this self-control, and are identified with negative and unmanly characteristics.[24]

Philo's description of the Therapeutae in *De Vita Contemplativa* is a good example of this masculine self-control. His picture of the Therapeutae is most likely not a historical description, maybe not even meant to be,[25] but it tells much about the gendered value system that Philo shared with many of his elite contemporaries. The Therapeutae followed an ascetic lifestyle in a male community, with the goal to do philosophical contemplation. There were also women in the community, but they are described as having renounced their femaleness by becoming "virgins." They had sacrificed that which made them women, bodily pleasures and desire for children, and behaved like men in their yearning for wisdom (Philo *Contempl.* 68–69). Thus, masculine and feminine do not correspond directly to (biological) man and woman; there is a possibility also for women to "become male," but then they must leave behind "the ways of women."

This criticism, or rather disdain, of women becomes even more outspoken in Philo's description of the Essenes (*Hypoth.* 11:1–18). He sets up a contrast between marriage, which due to the character of the wife is described in negative terms, and communal life (*koinōnia*), which is characterized by the ideal of self-control (*enkrateia*). Philo's view reflects the position of popular Greek moral philosophers. He portrays a wife as selfish, jealous, casting shame, foreign to communal life. In contrast, communal life is identified by male characteristics—it is not jealous, it has a sovereign mind, and it is not slave, but free.

Josephus's picture of the Essenes, as a male community, follows the same lines (*B.J.* 2.119–61; *Ant.* 18.18–22). Their special virtue, he says, is control of their passions. He says that they do not oppose marriage on principle, but then goes on to a very hard criticism of women: "They wish to protect themselves against women's wantonness, being persuaded that none of the sex keeps her plighted troth to one man" (*B.J.* 2.120–21). Philo and Josephus are male voices, addressing other men. Their heroes are all men, or women who have become like men. The dangers are represented as women. In these pictures of the Therapeutae and the Essenes, the ultimate male mastery over self was represented as ascetic community life, free from everything that was identified with women. In Josephus and Philo the ascetic body is determined as male; asceticism is a male space.

Women have to become male in order to enter that space. This shows, though, flexibility—that it was possible for some women to "become male."

This was a discourse in which the masculine ideal (be it in men or women) was contrasted with the feminine counterimage. The language of asceticism could be inscribed in the culturally formed language of male-female contrasts, with binary opposites. Philo and Josephus were thoroughly familiar with the Greco-Roman cultural ideals, and they displayed in their writings a typical combination of masculine self-control and sexual abstinence. Asceticism and masculinity as ideals were combined, so one might say that asceticism was entering more deeply into a male space, not leaving it. This was the reason that the combination of asceticism and an emasculated man, a eunuch, who had left male space, was so controversial.

EUNUCHS IN BORDERLAND

It was this ambiguity, that the eunuch represented renunciation but also had renounced masculinity, that made it so difficult to find a defined place for the eunuchs. In attempts to characterize them, we find that eunuchs did not have their own "essence," but only a position in relation to others. They could be described in relation to men as "half-men" (*semiviri*), and in slander they would be compared to women as "soft" and "feminine."[26] Although they were men, they were prime examples that "man" was not a category that all who were born male automatically belonged to but was something that had to be earned and defended. To be a man was an honorable position, but it could always be put into question, and a man must always be prepared to fight for it. In antiquity, as well as in many modern cultures, this male honor was associated above all with a sexual role as the one who initiated and dominated a sexual and social relationship.[27] In all these areas the eunuch was at a disadvantage and could not compete.

Eunuchs are known from antiquity in the East as well as in the Greco-Roman world.[28] The best-known examples from the Middle Ages were the court eunuchs in Byzantium,[29] and at Muslim courts. In modern times, the imperial court in China and shrines in Mecca and Medina had well-known groups of eunuchs.[30] The following description refers primarily to eunuchs and attitudes toward eunuchs in antiquity.

First, to be a eunuch due to involuntary castration was an indication of an inferior or disadvantaged social position. After loss in war, members of the losing army or tribe might suffer castration as an act of ultimate shame and emasculation. Prisoners of war might also be castrated and sold off as slaves. Thus slave trade was the most common source for castrated slaves in the Western parts of the Roman Empire. Consequently, slaves were (mostly) at the bottom of society, and at the will of their master, to fulfill both his needs for work and his sexual desires. Some young men were castrated with the specific purpose of being sold as slaves for sex.

Their social situation as castrated males made eunuchs useful in several specific areas. In the Persian and other Eastern empires, eunuchs were important and powerful officials for the king. This was also true in the late Roman and Byzantine empires. Likewise, eunuchs could hold important positions in private households, for instance, as guardians of women or teachers for sons. Their social position resulting from their sexual status might give some explanation for this. Since they were cut off from having a family of their own, they were outside the power of family structures, and therefore could more easily serve as confidants for rulers or masters and mediate between them and the outside world. Eunuchs were part of a complex social structure, in which their ambiguous social and sexual status made them useful. An Arabic collection of verses, anecdotes, and proverbs from the fourteenth century, on the ideal home, places eunuchs in a significant and highly charged part of a wealthy house: in the vestibule (*dihliz*), the hallway between the door and the actual dwelling.[31] The vestibule served as the corridor between the public and the private. The eunuchs were guardians of the vestibule, and decided who was allowed to enter further into the house and who was denied entry. The eunuchs acted as representatives of the master of the household in the area that protected the inner, sacred space of the house. But their in-between position, socially and sexually, made the eunuchs vulnerable and exposed to criticism and slander.[32]

The various groups of eunuchs were either eunuchs by birth, or castrated, mostly against their will. They correspond therefore to the first two categories listed in the saying in Matt. 19:12: "eunuchs who have been so from birth," and "eunuchs who have been made eunuchs by men." But there was one more group, those who had chosen to become eunuchs—in the words of Matt. 19:12, those "who have made themselves eunuchs" for a higher purpose. This group was, in antiquity, mostly associated with cults that originated in Asia Minor, especially the fertility cults of Cybele (and Attis) from Phrygia[33] and of Dea Syria from Syria.[34] This institution of self-castrated men was called galli.[35] They had special functions at festivals, in particular at processions, but they were not priests. There was likely a link between the main myth of the Cybele and Attis cult, in which Attis castrates himself (or is castrated by Cybele), and the act of self-castration by male devotees during the main spring festival. Castration may therefore originally have been associated with a fertility rite, and its ascetic connection may be a later development.[36]

These galli do not seem to have had a fixed organization, but were wandering groups, with song and music. They carried with them a picture of the goddess, gave oracles, and begged. For local participants in the cults of Dea Syria and Cybele, visits by these groups of galli must have served as contact with the goddess. Groups of galli were more common in the Orient than in Rome and the Western parts of the Roman Empire. But the galli of the Cybele cult, originating in Phrygia, must have contributed to the spreading of the cult also in Greece, Rome, and the Western part of the Mediterranean.[37] One reason for the fascination the galli evoked was their chastity, which was especially important in relation to fertility rituals.

In contrast to popular opinion, the literary elite was more skeptical. We have most of our knowledge of the cults, the festivals, and also the institution of the galli from detailed descriptions in Lucian of Samosata, Apuleius, and other satiric writers.[38] Lucian and Apuleius turn a very critical eye towards the galli. Their narratives are satirical and critical, and thus their information about the cults is one-sided. Lucian (*Syr. d.* 20ff.) tells the myth of Combabus, which is related to the practice of castration. He says that after they were castrated, the men became "as women" (*thēlynontai*), no longer dressing as men, but wearing women's clothes and doing women's work. Apuleius (*Metam.* 7.24–31) tells how a band of galli traveled through villages and lured people to give them gifts, how they performed acts of flagellation and self-mutilation almost as theater. He describes them as *semiviri* and *effeminati* (7.28), and tells how they, although they posed as chaste priests, were caught in the act of seducing a young man.

Such descriptions provide a stock list of accusations against the galli.[39] In addition to accusations of greediness, which puts their begging in a bad light, the main attack was directed at the effect of castration on their masculine role. There is a whole series of invectives that shows how difficult it was to define somebody who had gone beyond the secure male boundaries. They are neither men nor women, they are "half-men" or effeminate. The accusations of sexual misconduct revolve around a lack of masculinity as well as a lack of chastity. When the Cybele-Attis cult was officially established in Rome, excessive elements and the institution of galli were curtailed, for instance, by laws against castration. But the galli remained an ambiguous sign of the Oriental cults, partly admired, partly despised.[40]

Eunuchs occupied an ambiguous place in various respects: They did not fit into the common ways of making boundaries and drawing borders. They could not be placed securely either as male or as female. Likewise, the galli threatened the distinction between sacred and profane. And, maybe most provoking, the eunuchs could not be placed within the area of chastity. They also appeared to belong in the location of desire. Thus, the challenge of eunuchs was that they could not be securely placed, they were in a position of "betwixt and between," in a permanent liminal position.

THE MASCULINE ASCETIC
IN EARLY CHRISTIAN WRITERS

Early Christian writers, who belonged to the educated class of men, shared masculine ideals and the critical attitude to eunuchs common among the Roman elite.[41] With regard to the galli of the Cybele and other cults, these Christian writers showed their abhorrence toward the excesses of Oriental cults.[42] These cults were part of the religious and cultural context when Christian writers discussed what place eunuchs might have within Christian asceticism. But eunuchs not only represented the pagan "other," religious competitors from whom the Christians could distance themselves. Extreme asceticism in the form of castration was also practiced among Christians themselves.[43] It must have been a problem in many communities, since the Council of Nicaea in 325, in its first canon, condemned self-castration and decided that self-castrated eunuchs could not serve as priests.[44]

The interpretation of the eunuch saying in Matt. 19:12 is part of a controversy among early Christians over how radical sexual asceticism should be. There are relatively few direct references to Matt. 19:12 in gospel commentaries and homilies of the early church.[45] One reason may have been the fear that it could support radical asceticism. In the second century, Justin tells about persons who took the saying about making themselves eunuchs for the sake of the kingdom in a literal sense (1 *Apol.* 29). The eunuch saying from Matt. 19:12 is mentioned in a context that deals with *sōphrosyne*, moderation or self-control. This makes it likely that Justin understands Jesus' eunuch saying in the sense of chastity,[46] that is, in a figurative sense, and not about castration.

This hypothesis is supported by the following story about a young man who wanted to become a eunuch (1 *Apol.* 29). Set in Alexandria, this story gives interesting insight into the situation after the decrees against castration by several Roman emperors, starting with Domitian.[47] A young man in the Christian community contacted doctors to have them make him a eunuch. But they said that they were forbidden to do that, unless he received permission from the prefect, Felix. The prefect, however, refused to give his permission. Justin tells how the young man then decided nevertheless to remain celibate, supported by his own conscience and that of his fellow believers. Here the contours of an interpretation of the eunuch saying become visible. If castration was not possible, it was still possible to remain single, and that decision could be supported by one's conscience. Thus, one's decision to remain single and true to one's conscience was more important than physical castration.[48] With this story, Justin has laid out much of the pattern that later interpretations of Matt. 19:12 would follow in their arguments for a figurative understanding of the eunuch.

Early Christian writers were concerned to interpret Matt. 19:12 in such a way that it supported a commitment to chastity, but prevented this commitment from going too far. So how do they argue that "[making] themselves eunuchs for the . . . kingdom" shall be read not literally, but figuratively?[49] There are some instances in which the writer shows horror over the "murder" involved in castration. But in most cases the arguments seem to be driven by a logic where two possible causes for an act are positioned as binary opposites. Clemens of Alexandria (*Paed.* 3.4.26) says that a true eunuch is one who is not married, not because he does not have the (generative) power (*mē dynamenos*), but because he does not want to (*mē bouloumenos*). Clemens thus sets up a contrast between somebody who is a eunuch, either by nature or by castration, and a man who makes a deliberate decision not to marry. And it is obviously the latter who is the morally superior.

This figurative understanding of "eunuchs for the kingdom" is found also in Origen. In his commentary on Matt. 19:12, Origen (*Comm. Matt.* 15.1) is concerned with consistency in interpretation. Therefore he protests against what he sees as an inconsistent interpretation, which takes the two first classes of eunuchs in a literal sense, and the last one in a figurative sense. On the basis of 2 Cor. 3:6 (letter versus spirit), Origen holds that either one must understand all three of them in a literal way, or all of them in a figurative way. He argues for a figurative interpretation of all three groups of eunuchs.[50] Origen, notwithstanding the reports that he had castrated himself as a youth,[51] associates himself with those who were opposed to a form of extreme asceticism that practiced castration. Origen recognizes that those who were castrated may have undergone this operation out of fear of God, but he considered it to be a misguided fear, and too much love for renunciation. And his main argument against taking the third group (eunuchs for the sake of the kingdom) in a literal sense is that eunuchs would attract slander, even shame, both from outsiders and from people within the Christian church. Christian eunuchs were probably part of his social environment, but they were not highly regarded by the mainline groups that Origen now represented, and were exposed to slander and shame. One wonders how it could be possible for Origen to write this if he actually had castrated himself. But if he in fact had done it,[52] it might explain why he was relatively mild in his criticism of castration and why he was concerned with the shame and slander that eunuchs experienced. He distanced himself from the eunuchs, but nevertheless showed a certain sympathy. Eunuchs were not made into something totally "other."

Origen's figurative interpretation of the third group, those who were eunuchs "because of the kingdom," is filled with masculine metaphors (*Comm. Matt.* 15.4). His starting point is that castration is performed by the word of God, which is "sharper than any two-edged sword" (Heb. 4:12). The ideal eunuch is a man who takes this word, which the apostle also calls "the sword of the Spirit" (Eph. 6:17), so that he may cut out the passions of his soul, without touching the body. Since passions are gendered female,[53] by cutting out the passions the masculine sword (word) of God turns the ascetic man into "a real man," since his physical body is not touched. Thus, the eunuchs are "dephysicalized,"[54] and as a result the ascetic male can preserve and heighten his masculinity. Origen's figurative interpretation was clothed in war and warrior categories, those most masculine of male images.

For Jerome also it was important to make a moral distinction between eunuchs who had been castrated and true Christian ascetics. In his commentary on Matt. 19:12 he argues that the first two groups of eunuchs (by birth and made by men) are inferior to the last group, those who are eunuchs because of Christ. His argument is similar to that of Clemens of Alexandria, that the first two groups are eunuchs from necessity and not from (free) will.[55] This binary opposite between necessity or lack of power on the one hand, and will on the other, is a contrast between the negative and the positive with regard to moral value. Commonly, also, the contrast between feminine and masculine is associated with such binary opposites. In this set of comparisons, the eunuchs come down on the feminine and morally negative side. Whether the terminology used is "nature," "necessity," or "lack of power," all these terms refer to the physical fact of being a eunuch.

They made him unfit for the physical aspects of marriage, sexual intercourse, and procreation, but did not require an act of will or a moral decision. Thus, being a eunuch in the physical sense was devalued; it came down on the "left" and feminine side of the comparison, and therefore it was also lower in the hierarchy of values.[56]

Jerome makes this absolutely clear when he goes on to contrast the two groups, the involuntary and the voluntary eunuchs. To leave no doubt, he identifies the voluntary eunuchs as truly masculine, saying that "although they could have been men, they made themselves eunuchs for Christ."[57] In the allegoric interpretation of "eunuchs by men," Jerome follows Origen, and attributes such castrations to the influence of philosophers, the cult of idols, or to heresy. In the description of what the cults do to their adherents, he employs stock accusations against the gallis of the Cybele or other Oriental cults: "They are softened into feminines [emolliuntur in feminas]." Only those who have (figuratively) castrated themselves for Christ will obtain the kingdom of heaven. Jerome exhorts his readers in an exposition of Matt. 19:12d: "He who is able to receive this, let him receive it." It is necessary that he consider his powers (vires). And it is as if the voice of the Lord exhorted and encouraged his soldiers to receive the reward for their chastity: "He who can fight, fight! Conquer and triumph!"

This whole discourse on the ideal spiritual eunuch versus the two other types in the flesh is expressed as a contest over masculinity. It is obvious that the very question of entering into a position of nonprocreation brought the fear of losing male power and virility. So therefore it was imperative for Jerome to say that "to castrate oneself [spiritually] for Christ" was nothing of the sort. Those who did it might have been (real) men, and in a way they continued to be just that, because to be a virgin required strength. It was like being a soldier, to go into battle, to win a prize. Spiritual eunuchs had nothing in common with the (real) eunuchs of Oriental cults, who were written off as feminine, or with more radical Christian ascetics, who were written off as just "simulating chastity." Jerome wanted to show the superiority of the spiritual eunuchs over the bodily ones. His real fear seems to be the loss of virility and masculine status that being a eunuch represented. This is why he argues so vehemently that voluntary chastity is a truly masculine endeavor that wins the prize, the kingdom of heaven. And he uses the most masculine of all images: these men are soldiers of the Lord, with the Lord himself as commander in chief. Thus, the military metaphor is appropriated for these men who had actually rejected the world with its military power.[58]

When we look at this early history of the interpretation of Matt. 19:12, "real" eunuchs have all but disappeared from Jesus' saying about those who are eunuchs for the sake of the kingdom of heaven. They have been subsumed under the category of continence or celibacy. And the reason for a spiritual interpretation of this third group of eunuchs is not just the extreme demand that castration represented. It has also to do with the figure of the eunuch and the representations of that figure. The eunuch was an intensely problematic and ambiguous figure. The problem was that the eunuch represented both the goal, asceticism, and something extremely problematic—a lack of virility and of masculinity. And for these male writers (in antiquity and today) masculinity was more difficult to give up than married life or sexuality. The challenge was how to combine asceticism with masculinity, to turn the body into an ascetic male by spiritual means, without touching the body with the knife. In this male space the eunuchs did not fit. Implied in the figure of the eunuch was the shame of losing masculinity.

The traditional interpretation of Matt. 19:12 attempted and succeeded in domesticating the eunuch saying, and brought it back home into a male space. It made the spiritualized eunuch into a male ideal and stripped the saying of its "queer" qualities. Characteristics of the eunuch that seemed to contradict the male ideals were removed and attributed to the "others," one's opponents—the heretics or those who belonged to other cults. In this way that which was offensive about the saying, that it identified Jesus and his followers with eunuchs, was interpreted away. Consequently, the renunciation practiced by Jesus and his followers was interpreted in light of an utterly masculine asceticism, far removed from real eunuchs. That appears to be a successful strategy, which still works today.

JESUS IN QUEER SPACE?

There is one early Christian writer who stands out from this hypermasculine reading of Matt. 19:12, and that is Tertullian (d. ca. 220 C.E.). Tertullian did not attempt to distance Jesus and his saying from "real," castrated eunuchs as did other early Christian writers. Therefore I will use him as an introduction to an attempt at an alternative reading of the eunuch saying.

Tertullian's writings give witness to the popularity of the Phrygian cult of Cybele in the western part of the Roman Empire, and he makes several references to the act of physical castration among galli in the cult of Attis.[59] Tertullian is somewhat of an exception among early Christian writers since he seems to be open to the possibility that the term "eunuch" implied a physical castration.[60] He has references to Matt. 19:12 in several of his works, and it is obvious that for him, too, "eunuchs" for the kingdom may refer to asceticism without castration.[61] However, he partly takes this position for granted, without discussion, and partly seems to leave open the possibility of castration. His main interest is to push for an ascetic position.

Tertullian stands out also because of the terminology that he uses. He rarely employs the Latin transliteration *eunuchus* of the Greek term, but prefers the Latin *spado*. This was a common Latin word for eunuch, whether by nature or by castration, and it could also be used of any impotent male. Tertullian uses *spado* for the first category of eunuchs (by nature) in Matt. 19:12, but it is more remarkable that he also uses it for the last category, eunuchs for the kingdom of heaven.[62] This must have given his writings on the topic a shock effect, particularly when he identifies Jesus as *spado:* "For the Lord Himself opened the Kingdom of Heaven to eunuchs and He Himself lived as a eunuch [or he himself being a eunuch, *ut et ipse spadone*]. The Apostle also, following His example, made himself a eunuch [*ipse castratus*] and indicated that continence is what he himself prefers" (*Mon.* 3.1).[63] Not only does Tertullian use the coarse word *spado* about Jesus, he even speaks of Paul as "castrated," a shockingly strong term if what Tertullian meant was a continent lifestyle.

In *Mon.* 7:3–4 Tertullian again referred to Matt. 19:12c and those who made themselves eunuchs for the kingdom of heaven. The context is a discussion of the levirate marriage, the demand that a man marry the wife of his dead brother, if the brother had died without offspring (Deut. 25:5–6). One of the reasons Tertullian gave for this custom was that "eunuchs and the unfruitful [*spadones et steriles*] were despised."[64] But now the command to perform levirate marriage was no longer valid, Tertullian argued. One of the reasons he gave was the eschatological argument, "the time is short." Another argument was that procreation was no longer viewed as necessary. That resulted in a different evaluation of the eunuchs: "Now no longer are eunuchs despised; rather they have merited grace and are invited to enter into the kingdom of heaven."[65] When he refers to how the eunuchs were despised, he may refer not only to the statements in the Torah, but also to the social and religious position of eunuchs in his own time. Tertullian argued that eunuchs were not to be despised and related how their position was reversed by Jesus. Tertullian talked about how the Lord, that is, Jesus, has *opened* the kingdom of heaven for them, and how they are *invited* into the kingdom of heaven. That is, what had previously been closed to eunuchs, because of the negative judgment upon them, is now open for them: the eunuchs are "coming out of shame."

Tertullian seems to be the only early Christian author to have spoken expressly of Jesus as "eunuch" (*spado,* see also *Mon.* 5.6). Especially in *De Monogamia* it seems clear that Tertullian takes *spado* to mean a "virgin," but by using the word *spado* he employed a term that was in common use to refer to castrated men. It may have been an attempt by Tertullian to rehabilitate the word, but in that he was not successful.[66] The word may have brought associations that were too close to self-castration. Tertullian's association with the Montanists and their radical asceticism probably did not help either.[67] Tertullian's view on marriage and second marriage became more aggressively ascetic as he moved closer to Montanism. His use of Matt. 19:12 in *De Monogamia* (from his Montanist period) provides insight into this aggressive asceticism. There he positions himself against both the orthodox and the heretics of the Marcionite type.

The way Tertullian uses *spado* about Jesus shows that he was aware that it was a controversial term. He employs Jesus, and Paul in an even more controversial way, to defend a radical ascetic position. Moreover, he retains a terminology that must have created associations with the galli, the eunuch devotees of Cybele and Dea Syria. So Tertullian's rhetoric has some of the same qualities as that of Jesus in the original saying. It retains the controversial point of reference, but transforms the meaning. His discussion of this saying shows Tertullian at his most brilliantly irritating, and he had few followers in his use of *spado* to characterize Jesus.

Tertullian's interpretation, focusing on the ambiguous and the (previously) shameful position of the eunuchs is, I believe we shall see, a better guide to understanding the contemporary implications of the Jesus saying in Matt. 19:12 than that of later writers who spiritualized the term eunuch. The traditional masculine reading of the eunuch saying has stripped it of its controversial content, so that we should try to return to the controversy of its original context. Therefore, we shall first look at what could have caused the use of the term eunuch as slander against Jesus and his group.

One possibility is that slander was primarily caused by a comparison with the eunuchs who were mentioned in Jewish Scripture.[68] However, the Jewish material does not necessarily explain the use of the term *eunouchos*. Jewish authors did not use this term, either to describe celibacy positively (as Philo or Josephus did), or to reject it (as the rabbis did).[69] And the Torah did not use the technical term *saris* (eunuch) when it denied "[him] whose testicles are crushed or whose male member is cut off" access to the temple (Deut. 23:1).[70] It is the man whose body no longer possesses masculine characteristics who is excluded. But this picture of the eunuch as a single individual does not provide a sufficient model for Jesus and his group of followers. Most other references to what in the LXX is translated as "eunuchs" are to the royal court eunuchs.[71] They were court officials, often in high positions, and they do not provide an immediate parallel to this type of wandering group.

Another possibility is closer at hand: that the slander against Jesus and his group was caused by a comparison with eunuchs who belonged to Hellenist cults. In that case there would be more elements that were similar than just being castrated eunuchs. The social situation of belonging to a group of eunuchs, and the activities associated with the group, may have seemed similar. It is quite likely that bands of castrated galli, belonging to the Cybele or Dea Syria cults, were known in Palestine in the first century. The Dea Syria cult had its center in the north of Syria, in Hierapolis, near the Euphrates, but it had many cult centers farther south.[72] Archaeological finds point toward cults in Damascus, the Bekaa valley, Beirut, and Ptolemaïs-Acco. In Hermon an altar has been found with an inscription of a servant of Dea Syria who was sent out to collect money, which would point to one of the functions of the galli as beggars for the goddess. As for the Cybele cult, in addition to Syria, there are also finds that indicate veneration —if not necessarily cult places—of Cybele in Sidon, Neapolis (Nablus), and Ascalon.[73] And as the galli were not bound to temples, but were wandering groups, they may have wandered between the various cult places of the goddesses.

Thus I find it possible and plausible that Jews in Palestine could have known about these wandering groups of galli, who were worshipers of Cybele and Dea Syria. It might have been the impact of groups of galli, disturbing in their out-of-maleness state, known to be exotic in behavior and clothing, filled with religious fervor, walking around begging, that inspired the slander against Jesus and his followers.[74] Was not "eunuchs" fitting slander for these men who had left behind all the standard practices of a male place, whether they were castrated or not?[75]

It was probably a slander of this kind that Jesus took up and turned around and used positively when he said, "There are eunuchs who have made themselves eunuchs for the sake of the kingdom of heaven." But what might the meaning of the term "eunuch" have been in this context? We ought to be skeptical when a saying that has been so notoriously difficult to interpret suddenly is declared to have a "plain," "natural," or "obvious" meaning.[76] What is considered "plain" and "obvious" is always that "eunuch" and "to make oneself eunuch" do not have a literal meaning, but *must* be understood figuratively as celibate, as somebody who has rejected marriage. It is strange that although many commentators will interpret the saying of Jesus independently of its present context in Matt. 19, their interpretation ends up with the same result as when read in this context: to make oneself eunuch is to choose an ascetic rejection of marriage.

We find a typical example in an otherwise careful and insightful interpretation by Ulrich Luz.[77] Luz claims that in pre-Christian times "eunuchs" were not the same as "unmarried" (Ehelose); this was a meaning that has come up because of Matt. 19:12, and was first recorded in Athenagoras in the second century C.E.[78] But a few pages later when he comes to his own interpretation of the Jesus saying in its pre-Matthean state, Luz argues that the "obvious" meaning of "made themselves eunuchs for the sake of the kingdom of heaven" is to understand it allegorically ("*natürlich übertragen zu verstehen*") as "to make a decision for an unmarried state or for sexual asceticism." And this is followed up by another assertion that Luz also finds "obvious": if the saying is a reply by Jesus to slander from opponents, "quite naturally" ("*natürlich*") one cannot draw any inferences about the duration of this unmarried state for this third group, while the first two groups of "physical" eunuchs were permanently unfit for marriage.

But an interpretation of the third group of eunuchs as "unmarried" or "sexually ascetic" is far from obvious. The meaning of the saying of Jesus might not even have been clear for Matthew himself or his readers. The hermeneutical comments that surround the saying and serve as a redactional link to its context (Matt. 19:11, 12d) suggest that it was considered a riddle or a secret.[79]

In an attempt to find a solution to the riddle, it has been discussed whether there are any formal criteria that could determine whether the last group of "eunuchs for the sake of the kingdom" is to be understood figuratively or literally. This suggestion takes up the point that Origen had already made, that the meaning of "eunuch" in the three parts of the saying ought to be the same, either literal or figurative. Matthew often uses a list, or formula, with three elements, just as with the three groups of eunuchs in 19:12. A study of such formulas suggests that Matthew parallels elements on the same level of content or meaning. If this is the case also in 19:12, the three groups should either all be taken literally or all allegorically.[80] That the two first groups should be taken allegorically seems forced, since they refer to well-known groups that are historically verifiable, and very few interpreters have suggested that.[81] But a literary comparison with other formulas in Matthew that occur in sets of threes cannot on the other hand decide for a literal meaning of the last group of "eunuchs for the kingdom."

Thus, Origen's modern disciples have rejected his solution that all groups of eunuchs should be understood in a figurative way. They have not dared, however, to opt for the other consistent solution, that all groups are "real," that is, castrated eunuchs.

Maybe the issue cannot be solved by recourse to a consistent logic of interpretation. But this discussion shows that it is not "obvious" or "natural" that "eunuch" in the third group must be taken to mean unmarried or chaste and not castrated, and some interpreters have wisely left the question open.[82] Some have made the same observation we did regarding the terminology of Tertullian. The choice of words was such that it was offensive.[83] "Eunuch" was a shocking term in the context of the Jesus saying, and making it into "chaste" or "unmarried" cannot solve the problem. The phrase "eunuchs who made themselves eunuchs" is also puzzling, as the verb *eunouchizein* is a hapax legomenon in the New Testament. The parallel in the second group, "the eunuchs that have been made eunuchs by men," makes the meaning "to castrate" most plausible, so that it refers to the physical act itself.[84] But maybe it also has a broader meaning, "to make oneself eunuch," that is, not only physically, but also in terms of social and cultural roles.[85] This would imply that the person enters into the role, identity, and/or lifestyle of a eunuch. This would follow directly from castration, but it is also possible to imagine that Jesus was using hyperbolic language. In other words, he said that some had chosen to become "social eunuchs." This can remain only a hypothesis, but it would point to a specific context for the eunuch saying: it is really about "leaving a male place."

Eunuch is a term used of a man, but of a man who lacks many of the characteristics of a "real man." Therefore eunuchs were unfit for marriage. This affected a broad spectrum of the role of a man. Jesus' saying should be read in the context of masculinity as it was constructed through role models, demands, and expectations for men in Jewish society. One aspect was, of course, sexuality. Another was power, and a third was place, to be integrated as husband and father in a household. All these aspects of male identification were challenged by the figure of the eunuch.

With the figure of the eunuch Jesus held on to a metaphor that violated masculine identity. It was a metaphor that moved those men that experienced castration, either literally or figuratively (e.g., by slander), out from a secure male place into an uncertain zone of ambiguity and suspicion. It would be tempting to say that Jesus by the phrase "because of the kingdom" made an allusion to the king's eunuchs, that is, the court eunuchs,[86] and transferred that title to the kingdom of heaven. But the association with the kingdom would not take away the ambiguity of the phrase.[87] Most shocking to Jesus' Jewish environment was probably the way in which he associated the shameful identity and life of eunuchs with the kingdom of heaven, even saying that it was "for the sake of" the kingdom, that the kingdom actually motivated it.[88] By picking up the slander, Jesus both rejected it and confirmed it. It must have worked as a defiant defense for a strange group of single men who associated with women and even with children.

Consequently, the combination of eunuchs and kingdom is not a positive ideal, as it is when "eunuch" is read as "celibate," alongside Matt. 19:1–9. Rather, it is a controversial saying by Jesus, and to be placed together with other statements about the excluded groups that are to be included in the kingdom. The saying in Matt. 19:12 is similar to sayings of Jesus where he picks up on or responds to criticism and slander; for instance, when he associates sinners and tax collectors with the kingdom (Matt. 21:31; Luke 15:1–2).[89]

This leaves Matt. 19:12, I think, with a message that is not fully explored. I think it is highly significant that the saying, just because it was and continues to be so countercultural, probably goes back to Jesus in some form. Because he does not simply refute the term "eunuch," but takes it up and plays around with it, so to speak, Jesus creates an ambiguity over the male identity of himself and his followers. If the origin of the saying was slander from Jesus' opponents, its point was to dislocate Jesus and his followers from their identity as "real" men, to move them out of that space and into an "outside" position. And Jesus does not question this position; he takes up and identifies with the word "eunuch," and now puts it into the new context of the approaching kingdom.

The eunuch saying of Jesus questioned the masculine identity that was taken for granted for Jewish men in the first century. And the difficulties of interpretation show that it also challenges modern presuppositions about masculinity and the male identity of Jesus. Jesus has been seen through the lenses of modern masculinity, which have provided the categories within which to understand him. Since the masculinity of Jesus has been taken for granted, it has been impossible even to contemplate that Jesus might be a eunuch in a physical sense, that is, castrated. The intellectual energy of both ancient and modern interpreters has been spent on rejecting that possibility in order to defend the masculinity of Jesus. As a result, the possibility that Jesus embraced the term "eunuch" as a designation for himself and his followers, and the meaning this term entailed (with or without castration), has not been explored.

Eunuchs were men who were permanently out of place, in a liminal position where there was no possibility of integration into the order of masculinity. The institution of eunuchs is not well known in the modern Western world, and that may be one of the reasons that it is difficult to find suitable models of interpretation and understanding. I suggest that the modern term that can best provide a lens for viewing the material and a category for interpretation is that of "queer." This is in contrast to suggestions that Jesus could be understood by means of categories like feminine or gay. These would be categories that once more attempted to view Jesus in terms of a fixed identity, as feminine in contrast to masculine, or gay in contrast to heterosexual. "Queer," on the other hand, does not indicate another category. Rather, it signals a protest against fixed categories.[90] As a protest or opposition to fixed categories of identity, it points out that all categories are historically and socially constructed, and that human experiences are forced into these categories. The use of the term "eunuch" in antiquity illustrates this point. It defied categorization. It did not fit into the categories of either male or female.

In modern terminology, it is sometimes spoken of as "third gender."[91] The term queer is often used in questions of gender and identity, but it can be used in much broader terms than sexuality. It concerns power, social roles, place in hierarchies, in short, all aspects of identity. I suggest, therefore, that "queer" is the most useful term to apply when we try to make sense of Jesus' eunuch saying from a modern perspective.

The closest parallel to the function of this saying I can imagine is the way in which oppressed or marginal groups take up pejorative names used by the dominant culture and adopt them and use them about themselves, as a way to turn the labeling and oppression around. Marginalized groups thereby turn the terms into something else. Terminology that has been used to keep groups and individuals in "their place" suddenly becomes something else, more dangerous and undefined. Blacks and gays are two communities where this has been used as a counterstrategy against the abuse of power in labeling. Maybe those who identify themselves as "queer" in protest against fixed male or female identities provide the closest parallel to Jesus' use of "eunuch" today.

We started by stating that the eunuch saying has been little used in historical studies of Jesus. The reason may be that it was regarded as so strange, almost weird, that it could not easily be integrated into a plausible picture of Jesus. I suggest, however, that the saying about those who made themselves eunuchs for the sake of the kingdom fits very well with other sayings of Jesus about *who* belongs in the kingdom. This is what we shall explore in the next chapter.

Chapter 5

Entering Queer Space

The saying of Jesus about himself and his male followers as "eunuchs for the sake of the kingdom of heaven" was an expression of new place for those who had left the male space of the household. The eunuch represented a different type of place in terms of the common indicators of how space was organized, with distinctions between male and female, pure and impure, sacred and profane. Measured with these categories for space, the eunuch was ambiguous, and represented a *queer space* that blurred and twisted categories. In this chapter we shall explore the links between the eunuch saying of Jesus and other, related sayings about *who* are placed in the kingdom in Jesus' sayings: barren women, children, and people who live like angels, that is, asexually.[1] Taken together, the sayings of Jesus about entering the kingdom create a picture of a symbolic world that breaks with traditional role models and establishes new identities. One aspect of asceticism was to establish a new identity for the persons involved.

But for a new identity to take form, it needed to be established with new social relations and to be supported ideologically by an alternative symbolic universe. Since there is little direct information about social relations in the gospel material, I will postpone a discussion of possible hypotheses about the social composition of the Jesus movement. There is more material about an alternative symbolic universe—that is, sayings about the kingdom—so we shall start there. Next, using models from social anthropology, I shall explore possible links between this symbolic world and the social world of the Jesus movement, where women and men were united in a new community.

The third part of the chapter will focus on a different but related expression of asceticism: renunciation of food in fasting. Fasting too has commonly been interpreted in light of the masculine ideas of self-control and protecting boundaries. Jesus' nonfasting has been taken to mean that he was not an ascetic. But his feasting may have had a function similar to that of his eunuch saying: to break boundaries and therefore to pose an alternative to the dominant social environment, that is, what we have described as the purpose of asceticism.

CHILDREN, BARREN WOMEN, AND ANGELS IN THE KINGDOM

To compare Jesus' sayings about eunuchs with those about barren women and children may not be so strange as it sounds. There are parallels in other ancient religions. These religions also describe a similarity between the eunuch, the child, and the virgin, particularly in relation to fertility cults.[2] It seems a paradox that the unfertile served a goddess of fertility, but the cult required ritual purity, and eunuchs, virgins, and children represented the chastity that was needed.

Matthew's Gospel explicitly combines the eunuch saying (19:12) with a saying about children (19:13–15). In the story we hear about the lack of esteem that children suffered; the disciples tried to prevent the mothers from bringing their children to Jesus. The logion itself says: "Let the children come to me, and do not hinder them; for to such belongs the kingdom of heaven" (Matt. 19:14). The same logion is found also in Mark 10:14 and Luke 18:16.[3] In an act of reversal, the kingdom is ascribed not to adults but to children. In Matthew this logion stands by itself. In Mark and Luke it is followed by another logion that employs the children as good examples for the disciples to follow, that is, the logion receives a moralistic interpretation (Mark 10:15; Luke 18:17).

Gospel of Thomas 22:1–3 has a different version of the saying: "Jesus saw infants being suckled. He said to his disciples: 'These infants being suckled are like those who enter the kingdom.' They said to him: 'Shall we, then, as children, enter the kingdom?'" *Thomas* combines the logion about the children and the kingdom with a saying to the disciples that is not moralistic, but speaks about the identity of those who will enter the kingdom. The list is characterized by the typical *Thomas* idea of making "two into one"; for instance, "when you make the male and the female one and the same, so that the male not be male, nor the female female" (22:5). Here the idea seems to be that celibate asceticism negates sexual and other differentiations. And the child serves as a metaphor for those entering the kingdom, because it is considered "asexual or presexual or nonsexual."[4] The well-known reversal saying about the first and the last is in *Gos. Thom.*

4 also directly related to infants: "The man old in days will not hesitate to ask a small child seven days old about the place of life, and he will live."[5] Q has a similar reversal saying in Jesus' thanks to his heavenly Father that he had hidden wisdom from the sages and the learned, but revealed it to babes (*nēpiois*, Q 10:21–22). In most instances where we find the reversal motif, infants are examples of God's reversal of status. Thus, the kingdom is characterized by a reversal; in the kingdom spatial hierarchies are turned upside down. But in the combination of sayings in *Gos. Thom.* 22 and Matt. 19:11–15, the element of chastity or blurring of gender lines is also present, so that there seem to be similarities between children and adults who no longer have their sex-specific roles.[6]

There seem to be two main perspectives in the Jesus sayings on children. One starts from the inferiority of the children, so that lifting up children becomes a reversal of the social order, presenting the community with a new picture. The other one is more hidden; it focuses on the child as belonging to a stage before sexual diversification, even before sexuality at all, and therefore representing chastity.[7]

Sayings about barren women constitute another group of sayings that are attributed to Jesus and associated with the eunuch saying.[8] The primary text is the blessing of women who never bore children, which is found in slightly different versions in Luke 23:29 and *Gos. Thom.* 79:

> For behold the days are surely coming when they will say, "Blessed are the barren, and the wombs that never bore, and the breasts that never gave suck." (Luke 23:29)

> A woman from the crowd said to him, "Blessed are the womb which bore you and the breasts which nourished you." He said to [her], "Blessed are those who have heard the word of the Father and have truly kept it. For there will be days when you will say, 'Blessed are the womb which has not conceived and the breasts which have not given milk.'" (*Gos. Thom.* 79)

The sayings in Luke and the *Gospel of Thomas* are most likely independent of each other. There are also several sayings of woes to childbearing or pregnant women that form counterparts to these blessings[9] and indirectly support their authenticity. Thus, it is probable that the blessings of barren women have their basis in Jesus' message.

The Lukan version adds, "Blessed are the barren," and emphasizes even more the motif of a reversal of status for women who do not have children. Throughout Jewish Scriptures the barren woman was pitied. Since childbirth and procreation were part of God's promise to Israel, her fate was described as a punishment, which only God could lift.[10] Her position was one of social shame, parallel to that of the eunuch. In a late Wisdom text, probably from Egypt during Roman rule, barren women and eunuchs are promised a reward and a reversal of their position by Yahweh (Wis. 3:13–14).[11] Several Jewish apocalyptic texts from around the first century C.E. also have blessings of barren or childless women, partly because of the eschatological trials and tribulations. Now, in Jesus' words, barren women, like the eunuch, are blessed, in contrast to the presupposition that child-birth and pregnancy were desirable for women. But we should not understand this as a reference to life as a virgin, an exhortation to follow an ascetic lifestyle. The sayings about the womb not conceiving and the breasts not giving milk do not speak of abstinence from intercourse, but rather about the function or non-function of the female body.[12] The body was unable to function in a "normal" way for a woman's body, just as the body of the eunuch was unable to produce offspring.

Similar blessings of barren women in Jewish apocalyptic texts suggest an eschatological horizon for these sayings of Jesus. But like the eunuch saying, they also had a function within the Jesus movement. The descriptive statement of the reversal of status for barren and childless women in an eschatological future could have a prescriptive function among the followers of Jesus. Such statements might signal a reversal of status already, here and now. There is an example in a related saying about chastity and an absence of marriage in heaven. The question of levirate marriage in heaven (Mark 12:18–27 par.) receives this response from Jesus: life in heaven, in imitation of angels, is a life without sexuality, that is, without marriage. In Mark 12:25 and Matt. 20:30 this is a future vision, but in Luke 20:34–36 we find a version of the saying where implications are drawn for the present. Jesus' words apply not only to heaven. It is "those who are accounted worthy to attain to that age and to the resurrection," who *now* "neither marry nor are given in marriage."[13] Thus, the word about a future in heaven that is asexual and without procreation was turned into an encouragement to renounce marriage already in the present.

This picture of heaven may suggest a return to the beginning of creation, the presexual being. It may be that this being was understood as a male being, so that leaving a sexual state for women meant "becoming male."[14] This is probably how we may understand *Gos. Thom.* 114, Jesus' response to Peter's critical words about Mary: "I myself shall lead her in order to make her male, so that she too may become a living spirit resembling you males. For every woman who will make herself male will enter the kingdom of heaven." This "becoming male" saying was probably added later to the collection of sayings in the *Gospel of Thomas.*[15] It shares the notion that we found in Philo and early male Christian writers: "Femaleness is the focus of passion, earthliness and mortality, and hence must be transcended or transformed if one is to return to the original state of primal perfection."[16] In the first century Paul might also fit into a similar pattern in his argument in Gal. 3:28 that "in Christ" the distinction between male and female is taken away. They are both "one," that is, male.[17]

With his sayings Jesus pointed to life in a kingdom that was far from the ideal patriarchal household. Those who belonged there, or who entered into the kingdom, were eunuchs, children, barren women, and couples who split up to become (sexless) angels. We do not know what practical consequences these sayings had on the listeners; it is possible that they were hyperbolic imaginations more than advice to make them change their lives. This picture of the kingdom strikes me as somewhat unexpected, because sexuality does not figure prominently in Jesus' teaching. As a result there are not very many sayings about sexual renunciation either. But the links between the various groups that have come together in these sayings and the image of the kingdom as a non- or asexual place are striking.

These texts are not social descriptions of life in the group of followers of Jesus. They are all sayings that refer to the kingdom, or to life in the resurrection, in the time that will soon come. Thus, they present what we might call a symbolic world, "spaces of representation," in the terminology of Harvey and Lefebvre. And with the composition of the groups that are included in the kingdom, the kingdom cannot be enlisted as a male place, reserved for those who have become male by leaving the female behind (*Gos. Thom.* 114). Jesus does not seem to speak the male ascetic language. In his sayings, the idea of renunciation seems to be combined with that of reversal of a male-dominated world. The male world in which "everybody knows his place" is turned upside down; the eunuch, the barren woman, and the child without status are all lifted up. It is the least valued, those of little status, "the others" who are lifted up, blessed, and accepted into the kingdom. They may represent purity and chastity, but not because they have become male. And it is not the ideal masculine athlete or warrior, but the eunuch who represents the new "man."

CONSTRUCTING A NO-MAN'S-LAND

The images of eunuchs and children, barren women, and angel-like beings represented the ideological space of the kingdom. But what did Jesus and his followers look like in social space? What type of embodiment did the group represent? What were the relations between Jesus' followers? A symbolic universe may represent an ideal image for a social group, but we cannot draw direct inferences from the ideal image regarding the group's social structures. Any attempt to describe social roles and relations in the Jesus movement must be hypothetical. When the information is scarce, as it is in this case, we must build on theories that may suggest plausible scenarios. Our starting point was that Jesus asked his followers to leave a male place. The question now is what type of space the community of followers represented?

It was not only sexual renunciation that would make the followers of Jesus look emasculated. For men, sexuality and procreation were bound up with the social role of being a husband, either as householder or as a son living in his father's household. In the previous chapter we looked at the specific role that sexuality played in the definition of masculinity; now we must look at the importance of men's place in the household. The writings of the New Testament provide many pictures of men within households in the Jewish and Greco-Roman world of the first century. The male role is identified with that of the householder as overseer, father, husband, supplier of resources, person responsible for his house

and its inhabitants, and so on. We have already pointed out how central the figure of the householder was in the Q tradition and in the parables. The New Testament letters, especially in their household codes, provide vivid illustrations
of the role of the housefather.[18] A comment on the role of Hermas in the early
second-century work *The Shepherd of Hermas* sums up the relationship between
this role and the understanding of masculinity: "It follows that manliness, as it
finds expression in the *Shepherd*, consists of effective leadership of one's household. That the 'real' man is an ideal *paterfamilias* is a truism in antiquity."[19] The
masculine role of the son, especially the eldest son, was closely linked to that of
the father. The son was going to succeed his father, to take his place (cf. Q 9:58).
This created bonds of loyalty, expectations of obedience, and identification where
the son acts on behalf of the father. In short, the son's place in the household was
his basis for honor and respect within the community.

For Jesus to present himself without a house, in a no-place, was therefore to
be deprived of a role either as a householder, which given his age would have been
his normal position, or as a son in a household. Thus, his masculinity was threatened. He did not behave as a "real man." He was "out of place." And when we
looked at Jesus' call sayings and sayings about leaving the house or about conflicts in the household, most of them were explicitly or implicitly addressed to
men. Thus, these passages are about leaving a place of social identity, a place that
defines and structures that identity, and a place in each case that is male—that of
a son, husband, or heir. But the house and household were more. They were the
workplace, the property, and the social basis for a place in the village. They
spanned the whole spectrum of social life and work. Therefore it was not a matter of "just" leaving the household behind and going on with one's life. To leave
and to follow Jesus' call was to forsake a definite masculine space and to enter
into another space, which, however, did not have a given identity in the same way
as the "counter" or "hyper" masculine space of banditry, which may have been
another alternative in first-century Galilee.[20]

The young male followers of Jesus had left their established, if inferior, position in the male world and were in a liminal situation. A recent study of poor
homeless men in contemporary San Francisco may be helpful for thinking about
what it might mean to a man's masculinity to be without a home.[21] This study
found that many of these men saw themselves as failures with regard to the dominant idea of masculinity, called "hegemonic masculinity." This "hegemonic masculinity" connected gender identity to relations of power that privileged one
group of men, most often affluent, white, heterosexual men, that is, the householders of our time. Other men, typically poor whites, blacks, and Latinos, and
homosexuals, many with HIV/AIDS, were trapped in a negative image of themselves compared to this hegemonic ideal. Their coping strategy in a hostile environment often was to develop a countermasculinity, for instance by displaying
aggressiveness. But there was also another, more positive reaction, to develop a
different type of masculinity. We may speak of this as a "versatile masculinity,"
not based on an "essence" of masculinity, but on a social process of accepting dif-

ference within their community. On the basis of such acceptance it was possible to change and to develop a different set of values: honesty, caring, interdependence, and respect.

This example suggests that in the case of Jesus and his followers we should also look for different ways of being masculine. Perhaps we should even look for some alternative forms of masculinity that encouraged acceptance of a new set of values, not associated with the previous, hegemonic ideal of masculinity. In Galilee in the first century it was possible to choose a countermasculinity of banditry and force. Young sons might leave households to join groups of social bandits.[22] But when Jesus, as a potential householder, left hegemonic masculinity, he did not choose such countermasculinity. In the passages we have read, we get the impression of a movement of young adult men who left their households, and consequently the patriarchal relations within which they were located, including their closest family group. They left their livelihood, their work, and their inheritance. Could this be a movement of younger sons, who would have less to lose than their elder brothers?[23]

In many cultures, younger brothers are more prone to leave home, just because the obligation toward parents and inheritance puts more pressure on the elder to stay home. It is not difficult to imagine groups of young men formed for a countercultural purpose, even banditry, but with very conventional masculine expressions of identity. But that does not seem to be the nature of this group of followers of Jesus. Jesus' group was decisively changed by the presence of women, some of them the mothers of disciples, who also followed Jesus.

It is difficult to get a full picture of what the Jesus group was like, I think partly because we are so used to a dominant model of interpretation based on the story of his male disciples. The call stories are interpreted within a conversion pattern of "before" and "after," of abrupt "leaving" and "following." And this following is continued with Jesus' commissioning his disciples to mission, selecting twelve of them, and, finally, promising them rewards in the future kingdom. This way of seeing the Jesus movement as based on changes in time seems to have a special relation to men: all the call stories are about men, and likewise the selection of the Twelve and the promises given to them. But there is more to male dominance in scholarship on early Christianity than a one-sided historical reconstruction on the basis of these call stories. Scholars themselves also have a tendency to imagine that these stories describe a universal paradigm in which the religious ideal is a calling and a total break with the past in order to follow Jesus. This paradigm shapes our image of discipleship, and other ways to follow Jesus are filtered out. The result is that women, who are not addressees of the call sayings or the commissions, are reduced to the narrative fringes of the group.

I suggest that we look at the narratives of Jesus and his movement not from a *temporal* perspective, but from a *spatial* perspective. The time perspective of the story line lends itself to the presentation of male disciples, and the "conversion," or "breakaway," patterns were culturally appropriate to describe male behavior. Moreover, the temporal perspective also lends itself to a modern construction of history-based progress and change that reinforces male domination. But if we change from a temporal perspective (from "before" and "after") to a spatial perspective, from a history determined by the call stories to the landscape of the narratives, women will become more visible. They are not so prominent in the main story line, but we realize that alongside the inside group of male disciples there was another group called "women." In fact, there was also an insider group among the women themselves; we find several texts that give the names of some of them and then add "many others" (Luke 8:2–3; Mark 15:40–41).[24]

This inner circle of women is present in places that were important for Jesus' activity: they followed him in Galilee, and went up to Jerusalem with him. Moreover, they, and not the male disciples, were present at the cross, at the burial place, and finally at the empty tomb. Thus, within the narrative, the places of their presence become more and more significant. Considering the difficulty the gospel authors had with accommodating the presence of women in their narratives, there can be no reasonable doubt that women were present in those places. And women are also portrayed as those who most clearly followed Jesus into ideal space, described in terms of "service" (*diakonia*).[25] But women are not "called" in the same manner as men are. There are no call stories for women, and therefore these women disappear within the dominant pattern of interpretation. It is primarily the apocryphal gospels and their depiction of women in prominent positions, especially Mary of Magdala, which make us aware of the potential for an alternative reading of the canonical gospels.[26]

One of the difficulties in gaining a clear picture of the men and women who follow Jesus is that men and women seem to be described in different ways in the gospels, with different relations to place. Men are on the move, while many women remain in their households while they "serve" (e.g., Mark 1:29–31; Luke 10:38–42). It is difficult to judge whether this reflects the situation among the followers or whether different patterns in describing men and women as followers of Jesus are culturally determined by the authors' milieu. In his studies of early Christian literature, Richard Valantasis has identified various types of ascetics, that is, various ways in which we can try to understand their main intent and their characteristics. The description of men as followers of Jesus seems to bear some resemblance to those Valantasis speaks of as the *pilgrim* type.[27] This is the ascetic subject "who travels from place to place to construct a subjectivity transformed by the experience of not having a stable home or by the encounter with holy places and people." If withdrawal is central to the ascetic experience, what does this type of ascetic withdraw from? Valantasis proposes that "the pilgrim withdraws from one society in which the pilgrim has been socialized and habituated in order to withdraw toward, or to progress toward, another society that holds the promise of transformation and encounter with newness." The call and the abrupt break with their house and household appear to be typical features of this type. This type of asceticism may be located in a place similar to the one we have found for Jesus and his followers, in an intermediary state: "The social vagrant's social ambivalence, mobility and itinerancy construct a fluid society, and the pilgrim's active living in that fluid society constitutes the asceticism, until arrival at the pilgrim site completes the transformation."[28]

There is a serious flaw to this hypothesis—Valantasis does not pay any attention to the question of gender, whether there were any differences in ascetic types between men and women.[29] Therefore he introduces his models as general types. However, if we look at the material from a gender perspective, we find that this pilgrim type of ascetics fits the description of male followers of Jesus in the gospel narratives. It is the men who break up abruptly and leave their households. Pilgrimage is one form of being in a liminal stage. In our study, however, we did not find women addressed in exhortations to leave household and to enter into a liminal stage. At the same time, other narratives indicate clearly that there were women in the Jesus movement. The description of women followers appears to correspond to a different ascetic type, which Valantasis calls the "integrative model."[30] This is a type in which the "ascetic subject remains substantially the same as the socially constructed subject of the dominant culture, but . . . achieves a transformation or enlightenment that enhances and enriches the subject's life within the dominant culture." The emphasis is on the maturing of the subject over time, without a conflict between old and new identities.

The culturally conditioned descriptions of women in the gospels appear to fit this model. There are no calling or conversion stories, and there seems to be continuity in their attitude. The ascetic subject "woman" remains substantially the same as the socially constructed subject "woman" before she encounters Jesus. Power here emerges as empowerment. For several women the result of their meeting with Jesus can be described as being empowered (Mark 5:24–34; Luke 7:36–50). Moreover, the ascetic type that grows in insight within one's culturally defined position might also explain why there seems to be such continuity in the description of women in the gospels. They served in their position as women in household and family, and they continued to serve and to support in their position in the community of followers of Jesus (Mark 1:31; Luke 8:3). And the irony that modern readers see in the way in which "to serve" was made an ideal and metaphor for life in that fellowship, while at the same time keeping the women who served in their servant role, might not have been so problematic to ancient readers. Thus, I think it is at least possible that the authors of the gospels have given priority to one type of narrative and one type of disciple, the typically male, which pushed women to the margins.

But if we imagine that men and women actually followed Jesus in an unorthodox fashion, in one group, breaking with traditional patterns of behavior, how and why could that happen? I suggest that Victor Turner's views on liminality and *communitas* may provide ideas to explain the composition of this group.[31] Turner proposed that there are similarities between three different aspects of culture: liminality, outsiderhood or marginality, and structural inferiority. Liminality describes a situation in which full members of society are divested of the attributes associated with their structural position. For instance, men move out from their previous, privileged position. Outsiders and marginals are a different case. Outsiders are outside the structural arrangements of society, temporarily or even voluntarily. They include, for instance, shamans and monks, but also hippies (Turner wrote in the 1970s!) and gypsies. Marginals come from inferior groups, but aspire to a higher position. Examples are immigrants, migrants from villages to the city, persons of mixed origins, and women in nontraditional roles. The third group is composed of those who are structurally inferior. These persons are of the lowest status, outcasts and the poor.

Like Valantasis, Turner does not raise the question of gender and possible differences between men and women. Therefore, he may have generalized and universalized his models in an unacceptable way. His theory of liminality, which includes social drama, conversion, and reversal, may fit men's religious experiences, but not so much those of women.[32] In the material that we have studied, liminality was not a universal experience, but characterized the experience of male followers of Jesus. Young men who had left their household had entered a stage of liminality. They were eunuchs, at least in a social sense, as far as their place as men without a household was concerned.

But Turner's suggestions about the possibility of community between people in different situations may still be helpful within a gendered analysis. If men are described as being in a *liminal* position, the women who were part of the Jesus group may have been *marginal* in society. Ross Kraemer makes the observation that "few women in the early Jesus movement appear to conform to the most socially acceptable categories of virgin daughter, respectable wife, and mother of legitimate children."[33] They were most likely not bound in marriage, or they had some freedom within this relationship to leave their husbands. They were not childbearing, or had reached the stage of life when they were free because of their age. Thus, their sphere of possibilities had opened up. In several stories widows are mentioned, who, although it is not explicitly stated, could have become followers and were in a position where they had little to lose in doing so. With a couple of exceptions, we do not know even the names of the husbands of the women who accompanied Jesus. And while we hear about mothers of disciples who became followers, no fathers are mentioned.[34] Thus, the women are characterized as being without children or husbands, maybe widowed or maybe divorced, and as women who did not want to remarry. The women we glimpse in the gospel narratives appear to be prototypes of the "irregular" women that we meet through the suspicious eyes of Paul or the author of the Pastorals.[35] That is, in Turner's categories these were women in nontraditional roles, and therefore already in marginal positions.

Why should there be an affinity and bond between members of these various groups? Since liminality represents a divesting of all external attributes of position and hierarchy, those who experience it, Turner says, come close to the position of those who are outside of or on the margins of structure, or those on the very bottom. They are all in an outside space, not within the hierarchy of power. Instead they share an undifferentiated space. There were structural similarities between the young males who identified with the kingdom of heaven and the women who followed Jesus. They inhabited the same space outside of the household, and thereby outside of the village system based on households. Their group did not correspond to traditional households. There was probably no sexual involvement between men and women in the Jesus movement, both because of the emphasis on an ascetic lifestyle, and because there was a difference in age. Several of the women appear to have belonged to the mother generation. This made it possible to establish a common space, something that had not previously been possible for men and women from different households.

The reflections in the Jesus tradition about this common space used household imagery, but used only images of some selected parts of the household. Jesus' words about "mother and brothers" (later tradition includes also "sisters," Mark 3:34) suggest a household without a father, that is, without the patriarchal head. This does not necessarily mean that the group was egalitarian. Mothers and sons, or brothers and sisters, inhabited different places within a household. But another saying from the early Jesus tradition emphasized that this was a space that was not defined through a patriarchal, male head: "And call no man your father on earth, for you have one Father, who is in heaven" (Matt 23:9).[36] The father was at the center of the household; he also defined it as a hierarchical space. If the saying meant that Jesus' followers should not call anybody father, this signified more than the absence of a father within the group. It also meant that the place itself, the mental and social space that the group occupied, was structured differently. I spoke of it as "no-man's-land," not in the sense that there were no men in the space, but in the sense that it was not dominated by a male head.

EATING OUT OF PLACE

Sayings about renunciation of sexuality and gender roles provide insight into the symbolic and social structures of the Jesus movement. Discussions of the related topic of renunciation of food have a similar function. Food and sexuality both belonged to the items that ascetics should renounce. In both pagan and early Christian writers there was a link between control of the bodily appetites of eating and control of sexuality.[37] It was part of the masculine ideal that a man should be able to control his body with regard to sex and food.[38] Therefore, a saying that criticizes Jesus for excessive eating and drinking may be another challenge to Jesus' masculine virtues. In this Q saying Jesus is compared to John the Baptist: "For John came neither eating nor drinking; and you say: 'He has a demon.' The son of man came, eating and drinking, and you say: 'Look, a person [who is] a glutton and a drunkard, a friend of tax collectors and sinners!'" (Q 7:33–34). The context of this saying is the question from John the Baptist in prison, and Jesus' response (Q 7:18–23) and his praise of John and accusations against those who would not listen to John, nor to himself (Q 7:24–35).

Eating and fasting are, in addition to their nutritional aspects, also forms of social communication with bodies and food.[39] The physical body replicates the social body, so that what one does with one's body is a way to speak to the social body to which one belongs.[40] Fasting as nonconsumption does not allow food to enter into the body, and thus focuses on the boundaries of the body. As a form of communicative nonconsumption, fasting means a negation of the reciprocities that make up social interaction. Fasting, therefore, places the one who performs the fasting outside social bonds, in a liminal position. It may be for only a period, and it may actually be in order to strengthen bonds and boundaries in the community. To fast may be a way to focus attention on something that is wrong with the community, and to express repentance and ask for forgiveness in relation to God.

These reflections may help us better understand the accusations against John the Baptist—that he was neither eating nor drinking, and that he "had a demon," that is, that he was possessed. In a society in which fasting was known and practiced, this accusation could imply that he was fasting too much or that his fasting had an evil source. The gospel narratives about John tell that he lived in the wilderness, and proclaimed justice and judgment over people and a baptism for repentance of sins (Mark 1:4–8; Matt. 3:1–12; Luke 3:2–18). In this context John's fasting takes on the aspect of a symbolic act, communicating to people that they were in a state of sin that made repentance and fasting necessary. His own fasting was a form of speech through his body, pointing to what was right, and signaling judgment over those who did not repent. His critics, however, who might have been Pharisees and scribes (Luke 7:30), would not see it that way. They would ascribe his fasting not to a prophetic speech-act, but to possession by a demon. From this perspective, John's fasting was not a position of representative liminality on behalf of the group, but rather a proof that he was "out of place," possessed by a demon. His fasting was considered dangerous.[41]

In Q's rendering of the saying, the point may be to show how unreasonable the accusations were, in light of the presentations that Q gives of John and Jesus.[42] The accusation against Jesus was of a different kind: that he was a "glutton and a drunkard, a friend of tax collectors and sinners." This was an accusation of being "out of place," on the opposite side of the spectrum, not fasting but feasting in the wrong place, together with people who were outside the social order.[43] In light of what we said about the body and the social body, I think that we should see the two parts of the accusation together. Jesus is accused of lack of control of his own body, and of not keeping proper control of the boundaries of the social body concerning meals.

In discourses from antiquity about self-mastery or self-control (*sōphrosyne*), eating and drinking are frequently mentioned as areas in which it was necessary to have self-control (Aristotle *Eth. nic.* 3:10.1117b.23–26). Together with sexuality and property they made up the central areas of concern. Gluttony and excess of drink were prime examples of a lack of self-mastery. Therefore, excesses in these areas were no innocent matters; they reflected what kind of person you were.

Socrates encouraged self-mastery over the passions for food and drink as something with which the upbringing of children should be concerned (Xenophon
Mem. 2.1.1–4). It was taken for granted that exhortations to self-control were primarily addressed to men. Consider how Seneca discusses drunkenness in relation
to different types of men: "How much better to arraign drunkenness frankly and
to expose its vices! For even the middling good men avoid them, not to mention
the perfect sage, who is satisfied by slaking his thirst; the sage, even if now and
then he is led on by good cheer which, for a friend's sake, is carried somewhat too
far, yet always stops short of drunkenness" (*Ep.* 83.17).

In ancient Israel also excessive eating and drinking was regarded as an offense.
With "he is a glutton and a drunkard," Deut. 21:20 gives an example of the
behavior of a son accused of being stubborn and rebellious against his parents.
But the main moral point of the story is disobedience to parents; there is no independent reflection on the dangers of excessive eating and drinking. In the warn-
ings against gluttony and drinking in Prov. 23:21 the point is also practical: "For
the drunkard and the glutton will come to poverty." The accusation against Jesus
in Q 7:34 seems to be more along the lines of Greek and Roman moral philosophy: excessive drinking and eating reflects a personality that lacks moderation.
Lack of constraint in one area is reflected in others as well—and when it comes
to eating and drinking, the company in which this takes place is the most obvious parallel. To cast Jesus as a friend of tax-collectors and sinners obviously was
part of the accusation that he was beyond the pale. Food has a social dimension;
at meals it communicates social inclusion or exclusion, transgression or maintenance of boundaries.[44] It can be either a "sustaining, or a destroying mechanism
of sociability."[45] The accusations against Jesus must have come from groups who
were concerned with purity of food and the boundaries around meals. In this
respect the Pharisees were the most likely source.

But similar to the eunuch saying in Matt 19:12, Jesus may have consciously
accepted this accusation, "friend of tax collectors and sinners," and turned it into
a positive proclamation.[46] That Jesus had meals with tax collectors and sinners is
a common thread throughout the gospels, an important part of the picture of
him and one that has great credibility. It is possible that Jesus has taken up
the accusation "a glutton and a drunkard" defiantly, in combination with "friend
of tax collectors and sinners," to make his point about open boundaries. It is
a saying that invokes images from other narratives about Jesus at meals with
tax collectors and sinners, of a house that is open to visitors, in which outside
groups are not denied access to the table (e.g., Mark 2:15–17 par., Luke 15:1–2).
In a similar way, Jesus' response to the question why his disciples did not fast
(Mark 2:18–20) shows how Jesus could use images about celebration and feasting in a positive way.[47] The saying about how the male attendants of the bridegroom cannot fast while the bridegroom is among them explains why fasting
is unnecessary or even impossible at this stage of the Jesus movement. Read in
light of other stories about weddings or celebrations, this image suggests an inclu-
sive celebration.

Fasting, in these words of or about Jesus, is not just about self-mastery or control of the body, it is about body and food as expressions of a social map. The emphasis has moved from keeping the boundaries of the body intact toward the symbol of meals as a way to challenge boundaries. The images of feasting, maybe even of gluttony and drinking, were also put to use for social inclusion.

There is a similarity between the accusations against Jesus that he was a eunuch and that he was a glutton and drunkard. In both instances he was accused of breaking with central aspects of the masculine role and self-control. The accusations were a way to push Jesus outside the order of the household. Being a eunuch or a drunkard and glutton meant to transgress the boundaries, to place oneself outside the social map. Jesus appears to have accepted these accusations. His nonfasting was a transgressive act. Not only did Jesus not fast, he actively engaged in feasting and commensality with people who were beyond the boundaries, in the same way that he included eunuchs in the kingdom. Thus, he altered the order of society and changed the social map. Jesus' feasting was therefore not ascetic in terms of renunciation of food, but as an activity that transgressed the existing order and created something new, it represented a form of asceticism.[48]

WHERE IS QUEER SPACE?

This and the preceding chapter have dealt with issues that are often discussed in terms of Jesus' asceticism, his and his followers' renunciation of household, family, and sexuality. But, in contrast to most others who have discussed this topic, I began by qualifying the question: what did it mean that asceticism entailed leaving a *male* space? With that we meant not just the location of the household, but the way it was structured as a patriarchal social order. Moreover, the household also conveyed a sense of place, a system of meaning that supported its social structures and defined its relations to the outside world. This system of meaning was defined in binary terms: for instance, "male" and "female," "we" and "them," "inside" and "outside," "central" and "marginal." In this structure of binary opposites, the first element in each pair was privileged, for instance, "male" versus "female." The household was a place where everyone knew his or her place and had a sense of limits and boundaries. And the household structure and sense of meaning replicated that of the larger community, from the local village to the people or nation. Thus, we may say that the social entity of the household and the meaning associated with it has its place in the house as a geographical location, situated in a specific area. Therefore, to leave the household meant not only to leave the immediate social group, but also a geographical area—and to question the household as a place of meaning.

Among all the sayings in the Jesus tradition that speak about leaving the household for an ascetic life, I chose to start with the eunuch saying. The eunuch as a liminal figure is interesting just because the discussion of the eunuch is important for defining the norm for what a man in a household should be. There-

fore Jesus' eunuch saying, "[Some] have made themselves eunuchs for the sake of
the kingdom of heaven," is important in the way it signals what type of place the
kingdom is. In Jesus' sayings the kingdom has aspects of social relations and
power structures, but it is also imagined as place. The controversy around the
eunuch saying of Jesus, both in the society contemporary to Jesus and in the social
and cultural context of later interpreters, suggests that the saying exposed
topographies of masculine power. This power was located in specific places of stability and continuity, and within social relations that were considered "natural"
or "given." Wandering groups of men who had left their homes threatened this
stability and put question marks around "natural" relations, and specifically
around the male householder as the ideal figure in society.

This controversy over the household is reflected in Jesus' kingdom sayings. It
is noticeable that despite the dominant role of the household in the social world
of Jesus, its traditional form was not reflected in these sayings. Instead, they introduced a strange world, peopled by eunuchs, children, and barren women. Jesus'
symbolic world did not resemble that of married couples and their households;
instead, marriage was explicitly barred from the heavenly world. The eunuch
breaks with the masculine role, the barren woman with the role of the ideal
housewife and mother, and the single child with the child integrated into household structures of obedience to parents.

This transgression of the roles and order of the household did not mean the
abolition of place, however, but its transformation. Transgression always presupposes that some sort of spatial ordering exists.[49] In a saying attributed to Jesus,
he contrasts his own household with the group of followers around him. They
are described in household terms as "brother, and sister, and mother" (Mark
3:34–35), but it is significant that there is no father in this household. There are
no images of a complete, patriarchal household in sayings about the followers of
Jesus or about the kingdom household; "father" and "wife" are often missing. The
relations of authority and procreation are not included. These were the relations
that were most closely associated with the normative structure of the household.
The kingdom was not a mirror image of the patriarchal household, it transgressed
its boundaries, it had a different composition, and it lacked its hierarchy. Therefore we may say that the household in the kingdom has been "queered." The traditional order has been questioned and twisted. This term *queer* is quite similar
to the other terms we have used—transgression, asceticism, and liminality—in
that it does not represent a new identity or a fixed position in place. Rather, it
challenges definite identities or normative ways of situating persons in places and
social structures.[50] By not fasting, but instead explicitly feasting with persons who
were outside the social order, Jesus challenged its boundaries and the way they
created divisions among people. Jesus was an ascetic who transgressed the boundaries of what it meant to be male in first-century Palestine.[51] Moreover, he introduced that transgression as characteristic of the kingdom.

In antiquity, asceticism could be a way to strengthen social order and control.
Asceticism could be used to heighten masculinity, and so renunciation was then

an expression of male strength and control over the body. But Jesus' asceticism was of a different kind. The eunuch saying explicitly challenged masculine ideals and the order of the patriarchal society. Likewise, the inclusion of barren women and children together with the eunuchs in the kingdom challenged the old order based on household and family. This was an asceticism that transgressed the given structures of society and set up a vision of a new symbolic order.[52]

This symbolic world does not necessarily tell us about the actual practice of the Jesus group, but it created images that could serve as points of identification for Jesus' followers. The cemetery in the old Moravian colony in Old Salem, North Carolina, may illustrate my point. A visit to Old Salem provides an impression of everyday life in the colony. Some members of the settlement were unmarried and lived in communal houses, but most members lived as families. Visitors to the church are told how the Moravians were divided for worship into different classes, as well as about the theology that undergirded their life. But it was not till I saw the cemetery that the importance and power of this theology became visible. The cemetery reflected an ideal reality. There were no family burials; each person was buried according to his or her "class," into which the members were divided for Sunday worship. Thus, there are long rows of graves for boys and young men, adult or old men, and similarly for different classes of women. The cemetery was a picture of the heavenly world that represented the real identity for these church members. It was not their ordinary family life in the colony that expressed their true identity, but rather their burials in preparation for resurrection.

In a similar way the symbolic world of the kingdom of God in Jesus' sayings is not a social map. But it is possible that its structure in some form was reflected also in the new social relations among Jesus' followers. We may speak of "seeds of new spatial orderings."[53] Applying Turner's models of liminality and marginality, it is possible to imagine how men and women in the Jesus movement shared a position outside the societal order. This shared position made it easier to come together as a group that defied rules of behavior between the sexes. In this way relations between men and women in the social group of Jesus followers at least partly mirrored the symbolic universe in Jesus' kingdom sayings.

In the previous chapters we have emphasized how important household was as the geographical, social, and ideological location for identity in Palestine at the time of Jesus. Only when we understand that can we realize what dramatic implications leaving household had for identity and social integration. Our discussion in chapter 3 pointed to some of these consequences, but also to the strange situation wherein no new locations became visible in Jesus' calls to leave. Disciples were called into "no place" or liminality. In this and the preceding chapter we have come closer to an understanding of this "no place" or liminality. Our starting point was how Jesus identified with the liminal position of the eunuch. We then attempted to see how Jesus challenged and transgressed the geographical, social, and ideological structures of the male-dominated household. As ideology, a kingdom of eunuchs, barren women, and children clearly presents a queer image, a break with the social model of the ideal household. As a social group, the community of men and women can best be understood as a coming together of those who were outside the gender and power structures of society.

Until now we have focused on sayings of Jesus that have emphasized criticism of established positions and order where we do not find a resocialization into a new location. But other of Jesus' sayings about the kingdom seem to be addressed to displaced persons with the purpose of providing new places, of integrating them into a different order. In the next chapter we shall look at some of these kingdom sayings of Jesus.

Chapter 6

Kingdom Returns Home

In this chapter we shall investigate how Jesus' kingdom sayings addressed the situation of his first followers. We shall focus on some of the kingdom sayings that appear to follow up his calls to leave house and household. These kingdom sayings address a situation of liminality, of being outside the order and structure of society. My hypothesis is that the kingdom sayings function to strengthen the followers of Jesus in their critical attitude toward the social order, but also to compensate for some of the losses they have experienced, first of all their dislocation from house and household.

But in what way do Jesus' kingdom sayings manage to do this? The most striking element in these sayings, and even more in parables about the kingdom, is Jesus' evocative use of images. The parables and sayings present a visual language that speaks not only to intellect and reason, but also to emotions and fantasy. This form requires that modern interpreters and readers receive them in the same way. We shall start, therefore, with a little exercise in imaginative reading.

KINGDOM AS IMAGINED PLACE

A kingdom of eunuchs, barren women, and children is a strange entourage! It brings to mind other strange pictures of lands and societies, originating in well-known works of imagination like *Wonderland, Lilliputland,* or *Utopia.* These are just a few of the many entries in a wonderful book called *The Dictionary of Imaginary Places.*[1] The authors write of their entries: "The imaginary universe is a place of astonishing richness and diversity: here are worlds created to satisfy an urgent desire for perfection, . . . others, . . . brought to life to find a home for magic, where the impossible does not clash with its surroundings."[2]

There is a long tradition of writings about imaginary places, stretching at least as far back as Plato and historians like Homer, and continuing with Hellenistic moralists and natural history writers like Pliny the Elder. In both the medieval period and in modern times this has been a very popular genre. In recent years we may think, for example, of the success of films based on books by C. S. Lewis and J. R. R. Tolkien. Descriptions of imaginary places have different purposes and functions. Some may indeed have as their primary goal to "find a home for magic, where the impossible does not clash with its surroundings." This is something we recognize from Lewis Carroll's *Alice in Wonderland* and *Through the Looking Glass.* Others may have a more serious purpose; thus the authors of the *Dictionary of Imaginary Places* speak of "worlds created to satisfy an urgent desire for perfection." These worlds may be created from a desire to control and to rule, but they may also have another motivation—to create an ideal place that serves as a criticism of the present world. That, for instance, was the purpose of Thomas More's *Utopia* (1516) and Jonathan Swift's *Gulliver's Travels* (1726). In criticism of the English society of their respective times, More and Swift created imagined societies that exemplified all the ideals they found lacking at home.

The kingdom of God is not listed in this dictionary, nor does it include heaven or hell. However, I want to place the kingdom of God alongside these "imaginary places" to stimulate our imaginations. I prefer to use the term "imagined place" for the kingdom, to indicate that it might not just be "imaginary," but also a vision of how a real place might be imagined differently. To read Jesus' kingdom sayings as sayings about an "imagined place" may open up new perspectives for us, both in terms of thinking about the kingdom as place, and in terms of the creative and critical function of imagination.

Such ideal "imagined places" represent that third perspective on place in the model of Harvey and Lefebvre that we discussed in the first chapter of this book. The first perspective is "material spatial practices," what actually takes place in a location. An example could be the practices of Galilean households or Herod Antipas's building projects. The other is "representations of space," the ideological underpinning under those practices, that represent them as "natural," as part of "the given order." This ideological level represented the power of the elite. In Galilee, the Torah as well as tradition represented this ideological level. Finally, the third dimension of place presents the perspective from below, from the nonprivileged position, often as a protest against a practice and an ideology dominated by the elite. This dimension is called "spaces of representation" or "imagination," what I call "imagined places." These imagined places present visions or plans for alternative ways to use and structure places and material practices.

I suggest that we read Jesus' kingdom sayings within this tradition of "imagined places," both as visions of magic, or strange, places and as poignant criticisms of present conditions. This perspective on the kingdom as an "imagined place" stands in contrast to much scholarship on the kingdom of God in the teaching of Jesus. In the history of the study of the kingdom of God, we can clearly see how biblical studies has been influenced by modern historicism and its emphasis on *time*.[3] It was this concern for time that made eschatology the almost exclusive context for discussion of the kingdom of God.[4] "Eschatology" (the study of the last things) is a term that was created early in the nineteenth century.[5] It signals a modern interest in the future,[6] but was used in studies of Judaism and early Christianity to characterize ideas about the end of the world. It was Johannes Weiss[7] and Albert Schweitzer[8] who first combined eschatology and Jesus' preaching of the kingdom of God. They argued that Judaism at the time of Jesus was filled with eschatological expectations and that Jesus' proclamation of the kingdom of God was totally eschatological. Especially since Schweitzer, this context of eschatology and concern with time has determined the interpretation of the kingdom. Even when his focus on future eschatology was criticized, the time reference for the kingdom was accepted, as, for instance, when C. H. Dodd argued that it should be understood in terms of present eschatology.[9] This inheritance from Weiss and Schweitzer has been questioned again more recently, by a growing group of scholars who argue that Jesus' proclamation of the kingdom was not eschatological in the (narrow) sense of an expectation of the imminent end of the world.[10] This criticism of the eschatological understanding of the kingdom is helpful. It takes the study of the kingdom away from the focus on *time* that has totally determined the interpretation. Thus, this criticism is parallel to similar reactions against the dominance of time in many other areas of study. But unlike many other academic disciplines, kingdom studies have not have experienced a "spatial turn." The criticism of an all-dominant interest in time has not been followed up by a focus on place.[11]

Thus, we may say that from the end of the nineteenth century, the paradigms for the interpretation of kingdom followed the common paradigms for historical or social studies, in which place played a subordinate role.[12] In the second part of the twentieth century, newer studies of the kingdom reflected a growing interaction with the social sciences, in particular sociology and psychology, but even these disciplines had little interest in place. As a consequence, a one-sided focus on time has marginalized the question of place. It is this neglect that has to be redressed, and it is therefore the spatial aspects of kingdom that we shall emphasize in what follows here. We shall start with a parable, where a reading in terms of place presents unexpected images.

One type of place included in the *Dictionary of Imaginary Places* presented readers with a strange, magic world. Some of the images of the kingdom in sayings of Jesus seem to belong to this type. In our last chapter we found an unorthodox range of persons identified with the kingdom of God: eunuchs, barren women, and presexual children. I suggested the term "queer" to characterize this image of the kingdom, since it set itself up against that which was established wisdom and forced listeners or readers to imagine the kingdom in a different way.

This is also what happens through many of Jesus' parables of the kingdom. One of them is the parable of the mustard seed (Q 13:18–19). It is one of the parables of the kingdom that has been interpreted primarily in *temporal* categories. It has been interpreted together with a group of parables as "parables of growth."[13] The emphasis of interpretation has been on various aspects of the growth process—either the inauspicious beginnings, the growth process itself, independent of human activity; or the end result of great magnitude. The interpretation has focused on progress along a linear development, and with a diachronic pattern it moves from small to large.

Joachim Jeremias represents a typical example of this interpretation oriented toward time and growth when he says: "Their meaning is that out of the most insignificant beginnings, invisible to the human eye, God creates his mighty Kingdom, which embraces all people of the earth."[14] But this emphasis on growth, based on a temporal paradigm of eschatology, may be derived from outside the parables themselves, and may overlook the symbols and metaphors that make the parables work.[15] Sometimes the images in the parables seem strange or unfit to serve as metaphors for the kingdom.

The strange side of the images in the parable of the mustard seed becomes especially visible in the version in Q:

> What is the kingdom of God like, and with what am I to compare it? It is like a seed of mustard, which a person took and threw into his [garden]. And it grew and developed into a tree, and the birds of the sky nested in its branches. (Q 13:18–19)

This is one of the best-attested parables of Jesus, with three independent attestations: Q 13:18–19 (Matt. 13:31–32); Mark 4:30–32; *Gos. Thom.* 20.[16] Mark and *Thomas* explicitly tell that the mustard seed is the smallest seed there is. This sets up the contrast between the inauspicious beginning and the marvelous end. In Mark that is expressed as ". . . it grows up and becomes the greatest of all shrubs, and puts forth large branches"; in *Thomas,* "it produces a great plant." The end result is extraordinary; the smallest seed becomes the greatest of all shrubs! This makes it possible to read the text as a "from small beginnings to great results" parable. That would be an ordinary story of reversals, within a common set of expectations. God would come in as the mighty king to make his (predictable) miracle.

But that is not what happens in the parable in Q; in its version, this sort of expectation is destabilized by the parable rather than supported by it.[17] The Q version has some distinctive features that set it apart from the linear development in the other versions. The agent of the sowing of the mustard seed is named, he is "a person," and he acts rather strangely, "throwing" the mustard seed into his garden. And there are marked differences in the description of the mustard seed. That it is the smallest of all seeds is not mentioned, and thus Q does not employ the contrast in size between "smallest" and "greatest of all shrubs."

Instead, Q speaks of a contrast in kind: the mustard seed "grew and developed into a tree." The strange behavior of the man and the even stranger transformation from a vegetable seed into a tree suggests that more than a small beginning and large result is at stake. There is something strange going on.

It is not adequate to say that the kingdom is like a small beginning, which over time miraculously becomes a large end result. Rather, what the kingdom is "like" is presented in a combination of ambiguous and contrasting images of "mustard seed in a garden" and a "tree." The story of the mustard seed takes place in a vegetable garden. This is the familiar scene of house and household. But then the image shifts to that of a tree. And the tree moves by biblical associations into another space, as we shall see—the tall tree is a political symbol that stands for the power of the people or of a ruler.

But even the first picture, the mustard seed in the garden, is strange; it is a picture of something "out of place." It was well known that the mustard seed multiplies easily, so that if sown in a garden, it spreads famously. That may be one of the reasons that there were regulations against sowing it in a garden; it was regarded as impure. The strange image of the man in Q 13:18 who throws the mustard seed into the garden may be related to that. It suggests that he does so furtively—that one was not supposed to put mustard seed in one's garden. To sow mustard might go against rules not to mix seeds. So mustard seed was actually from the very beginning impure, and the kingdom of God associated with the impure that which was out of place.[18]

Thus, the Q version signals that there is something strange here. And the strangeness increases with the picture of the end result. The final picture of what had become of the mustard seed, the tree, seems to be patterned according to its purpose, "The birds of the sky nested in its branches."[19] That appears as a simple picture, still within the house and farm setting. But there is more than just an image from the garden here; the picture is loaded with associations. Here is a metaphor that would be recognized as belonging to the picture of the large tree, mythically, "the world tree." In biblical tradition, the large tree symbolized nations. The most telling example was the large cedar of Lebanon, which, because it was proud, would be destroyed. In Ezek. 31:2–6 it is used as a metaphor for Pharaoh. It is within a similar set of images in Ezek. 17:22–24 that a little sprig that God will take from a large tree becomes a symbol for Israel. God will plant it on the mountain heights of Israel. It will become a "noble cedar" and "in the shade of its branches birds of every sort will nest." Thus the place of the tree is no longer farm and household. The tree is situated in a political context. The large cedar tree with many birds nesting in its branches was thus a fitting picture of the kingdom of God.

But the listener who tries to find what the kingdom is like in this parable has to deal with at least two very different places: the small mustard seed thrown into the garden made impure, and in contrast the tall tree of the nation, a protector of the birds of heaven. It is obvious that the last picture was the more fitting for the kingdom. But in the parable these contrasting pictures stand side by side. The result of the parable is that the kingdom of God is like both the mustard seed and the tree. The contrast between the images remains, not only in an ironic, but also in a destabilizing, way. To put the mustard bush in the role of the tree makes fun of the cedar; it becomes a burlesque picture.[20] The cedar was a symbol of Israel's ambitions, the hopes of a people. In that respect it was a political picture. That role was now challenged by the association with the mustard seed in a garden made impure.

The two places, house and garden as well as the tree and politics, are preserved, but played out against one another and combined in an unexpected way. The parable does not play along the lines of the dialectical opposition of small versus tall; the dialectic is disturbed by a transmutation into a third alternative: an impure seed in a garden that becomes the tree of salvation.[21] As an "imagined place" this is a strange kingdom; it is queer in the sense that it questions identities and blurs distinctions between the impure and the proud, the private and the political.

It is only in the magic, strange world of an "imagined place" that this can happen. An interpretation in terms of a temporal paradigm with its dialectic between "small" and "large" does not grasp this strange combination of place images. A temporal interpretation focuses on the process of what the kingdom will become, and as a result the meaning of the kingdom itself stays unquestioned and therefore remains traditional. But read in terms of spatial images that are contrasting and simultaneous, the parable functions differently. It presents the kingdom in an unconventional, countercultural way, which both questions the purity of the household garden and ridicules the political image of kingdom as the tall tree. In this way the parable of the mustard seed presents a suitable context for a kingdom made up of eunuchs. This and other parables of Jesus present a kingdom with queer qualities, by means of images that represent a number of different "imagined places."[22] Many of these images were not immediately associated with kingdoms, but brought new places into the imagination of what the kingdom of God was like. The unpredictable and the overturning of conventions made the kingdom into something that followers of Jesus in a liminal position could identify with.

KINGDOM BECOMES HOUSEHOLD

In seeming contrast to the political image of kingdom, one of the "imagined places" for kingdom was that of house and household. This image of kingdom as household appears to be part of Jesus' response to the dislocation that at least some of his followers experienced. In the material that we analyzed in chapter 3, Jesus' exhortations to leave the household were characteristic. We noticed that in the earliest tradition of Jesus' sayings there were few traces of integration into a new location of identity. This was apparently problematic for those who transmitted the Jesus tradition. They could not imagine a life that was not rooted in a household. In his gospel, Mark therefore established a new location for the fictive kinship group of Jesus' followers in houses and households. In his narrative, Jesus is placed in a house and those who have left their households are promised new households (Mark 10:30).[23]

Those who transmitted the Jesus tradition in Q did not choose this solution. The compiler of Q did not offer a substitute for the households that his followers left. But we may say that even this tradition presented an alternative in terms of a new location. My hypothesis is that in Q it was the kingdom sayings of Jesus that served to establish a new location for his followers. This was not a location in the same sense as the original household, however, but in the form of "imagined places." It is striking that so many of the kingdom sayings address a situation in which the addressees experience deprivation and need as well as alienation from their previous household situation.

We find a typical example in the beatitudes in Q 6:20–22. The beatitudes probably reflected the situation of the early followers of Jesus.[24] They were ostracized from the households and villages they had left, and therefore they were without support to cover their needs for food and drink. The beatitudes promised them a reversal of their fortunes, summed up in the beatitude to the poor in 6:20b: "for God's kingdom is for you." These early followers must have found alternative sources of support when they left their households. Q 10:2–10 describes possible sources of support for itinerant followers of Jesus: when they entered a town they might experience hospitality or rejection. This passage suggests that there were local groups who supported these followers.[25] Another possibility is mentioned in Luke 8:1–3, which speaks of wealthy women who provided for Jesus and his male followers. This support may have been based on a bond of fellowship and sharing similar to that between brothers and sisters (cf. Mark 3:34–35). This is what we call fictive kinship, that is, it has the function of a kinship group, but its members are not biologically related. However, a fictive kinship group also operates in the real world and takes up functions similar to those of a biological family group.

In Q we hear very little about such groups. The earliest Jesus sayings are strangely silent about the social form of the group of Jesus' followers. However, Jesus does say that they will receive sustenance, and speaks of what they need. There are two clusters of sayings from the Q material that are especially relevant. One cluster starts with the "Our Father," Q 11:2–4, with petitions for the arrival of the kingdom as well as for daily bread. In Q this prayer is followed by two additional sayings on trust that prayers will be answered, Q 11:9–10 and 11:11–13. The first saying (11:9–10) presupposes a location in a house, and the last saying (11:11–13) explicitly draws a parallel between the father-son relation in a household and the relation between God and needy followers. Another cluster of sayings, the admonition "On cares," Q 12:22–31, belongs thematically in the same context.[26] These sayings share a concern for the needs of daily life. They portray the needy and God in terms of a father-child relationship, and, finally, the fulfillment of these needs is associated with the kingdom of God.

In this early Jesus material we can distinguish between two related types of sayings.[27] The passages we discussed in chapter 3 represent sayings about leaving households, giving up one's life—that is, sayings that will bring the hearers out from that which gives their life security and identity. The other type, represented by the sayings mentioned above, addresses a situation in which the hearers have become displaced or are moving toward that position. These sayings will promote a new ethos for the group, of living in a marginal situation without fear or anxiety.[28] In order to make this ethos and lifestyle possible and plausible, it is legitimated in various ways, for instance, by reference to nature. But most importantly, Jesus undertakes this legitimating by conjuring up a picture of a household with God as father and the followers as children or dependents. These sayings present the household of God as an imagined place in order to support the exhortation "do not be anxious" (Q 12:22, 25, 29). Thus, these sayings have a paraenetic or hortatory goal. Jesus will instruct the hearers and motivate them to adopt an ethos of confidence and trust despite their marginal position. This purpose also determines the use and meaning of statements about the kingdom. We should read them not as "information" about the kingdom, as "facts," but rather with a concern for the function of these statements, what they want to create in the hearers in terms of imagination and motivation.

The address "Our Father" in the prayer in Q 11:2–4 immediately places the petitioner within the "imagined space" of household relations. It signals a relationship of father and child. But this prayer also shows clearly two ways in which Jesus spoke of God, and how they are linked. One was God as father, the provider, who cares for his household. The other one was associated with the kingdom, in the second petition "let your kingdom come" (Q 11:2).[29]

For a long time it was held that the address "Father" (Abba), used by an individual speaking to God, was unique to Jesus and expressed an especially intimate relation to God.[30] This theory has now been disputed in light of material that shows it to be used in other sources as well.[31] It is still possible, however, to say that to use "Father" to address God was characteristic for Jesus, and it is possible to address the question of how he used it. To speak of God as both king and father was common in ancient religions. For instance, the Greek philosopher Dio Chrysostom (early second century C.E.) says of Zeus that he "alone of the gods is named 'father' and 'king.' He is named 'king' according to rule and power, 'father,' I think, according to providence and mildness."[32] This perspective on God as father could be a comfort especially to those in need. From the perspective of slaves, Epictetus says, "To have God as our maker and father and guardian—will this not deliver from pain and fears?"[33] Closer to home, in Jewish literature God was also spoken of both as king and as father, and sometimes the two titles were combined.[34] In this literature God is spoken of primarily as father to the people, Israel, and to the king.[35]

We may therefore say that Jesus uses a commonplace when he speaks of God as father as well as king. However, compared with the Jewish material there is a remarkable imbalance in the way that Jesus uses these terms. In the gospels the use of "Father" for God is very frequent, but the use of "king" is extremely rare.[36] Instead Jesus speaks of the kingdom of God (or Heaven), a term that he uses frequently. This is a reversal of Jewish usage, in which God is often spoken of as king while the term kingdom is very rare.[37] Moreover, even in contexts where he speaks of the kingdom, Jesus does not speak of God as king. Instead, Jesus combines sayings about the kingdom with sayings about God as father in a household. Jesus moves away from political terminology for God, which was associated with power and rule, and emphasizes a paternal, providential role. Jesus portrays God in analogy with a father in a household; it is primarily the ideal role of a father and householder in the world of Palestinian society that Jesus applies. He may use various aspects of this role, according to the context. The main aspects seem to be: (1) the father is the source of origin of a family and gives inheritance to his children; (2) the father provides for his children and protects them; (3) the father has the right to claim obedience and honor from his children.[38] In the following texts about the kingdom as household, it is primarily the role of provider for his children that Jesus emphasizes.

In the Lord's Prayer we should read the petition "let your kingdom come" in light of the following petitions.[39] God is addressed as "Father" and the petition for bread gives an example of how he acts as a father. It is this household activity that becomes the primary context for the kingdom. The petition: "Our day's bread give us today" (Q 11:3) shows the relation to the everyday needs of subsistence, that is, the special needs that must be covered within the household. The term *epiousion* points to the daily ration that is needed for life, and places the petition within the present experiences of the followers. This petition is therefore linked in a special way to the initial address to God as father. Here the household picture of the father who provides for those entrusted to his care comes to the fore. At the same time, we see here how the image of God as father of the household and the image of the kingdom are connected. The image of a close relationship between father and child and of concern for hungry children merges with that of a kingdom.

Jews under Roman dominance experienced the contrast between the small world of household and kinship and the large world of the politics of empire. In this prayer these two worlds become one, or a third space. The images of the household and the kingdom are combined. They merge, so to speak, so that the kingdom is characterized by the qualities of the ideal household, and household support takes place in a kingdom.

Two sayings on prayer that support the Lord's Prayer use the same imagery of house and household.[40] Q 11:9–10[41] builds on the visual images of houses and households that practice hospitality: "I tell you, ask and it will be given to you; search and you will find; knock and it will be opened to you. For everyone who asks receives, and the one who searches finds, and to the one who knocks will it be opened." To "ask, search, and knock" refers to the needs for subsistence.[42] The image is that of a person in need who seeks help in a household by knocking at the door of a house. Within the immediate context in Q, the "mission speech" in 10:2–12 pictures the followers of Jesus as itinerant beggars knocking at doors to seek food and hospitality. In this context Q 11:9–10 promises confidence in the relationship between petitioner and provider. For those who had broken away from their household, such confidence could not be taken for granted. Q 6:22 spoke of situations "when they insult you and persecute you, and say every kind of evil against you because of the son of man." Thus, Q 11:9–10 was not a word spoken out of common experience. It had more the form of a promise. It envisaged a new material practice, in that the structures of support typical of a household are to be reconstituted, not in one's own household, but in other houses and households.

The passive form used here indicates the "divine passive": it is God who will give and open, and so on. It is noteworthy that those in need are asked to trust God, and that there is no mention of other humans who might give or open doors. This points to an interesting distinction in the way Jesus addresses different groups, and how he thereby indicates their social relations. When he addresses those with resources, and encourages them to share and to give to the poor, it is with the understanding that they will not receive anything in return from the recipients (Q 6:34; *Gos. Thom.* 95). However, God will reward them. Within the social context of reciprocal relations[43] this is significant. Gift giving and exchanges of services bound two parties together in a mutual dependency. In the case of giving from a more resourceful person to a poor one, the result would be a patron-client relation in which the poorer was bound in loyalty and subservience to his patron. When Jesus emphasized that the poor did not have to reciprocate, but that the patron would instead receive a reward from God, the poor was not put in place as a client, and he or she was not bound to return in kind.[44] Likewise, when Jesus addresses the poor, those without resources, he urges them to trust that they will be answered, that it will be opened for them. It is God who will respond. Once more, the poor are not bound to human patrons.

In the saying that follows, Q 11:11–13, an idealized household scene is the model for relations between God and the petitioners. Jesus poses a rhetorical question that takes its image from household life: "What person of you, whose child asks for bread, will give him a stone? Or again if he asks for a fish, will give him a snake? So if you, though evil, know how to give gifts to your children, by how much more will the Father from heaven give good things to those who ask him!"[45] Two households are described, one with a "real" father and his son, and another with God as father "from heaven" and the petitioners. These two images are based on a common norm: the obligation of a father to care for the maintenance of his household. The point of the statement must therefore be how this norm is applied to the second part of the comparison. It is addressed to the followers of Jesus, who are in need, to give them confidence that God will act toward them as a father who honors his obligation to provide for his household.

The father image of God is used here with a purpose. There is a clear parallel between the expectations about how a father in a household will behave toward his children and the expectations about how God will act toward the followers of Jesus. God will give "good things," which we must understand here in parallel with the first part of the comparison: what is needed to sustain life.[46] The addressees are relocated into a household and in a dependent relationship as children vis-à-vis a father, not within a human social scene, but in an imagined place. The addressees now participate in a household in which God is the father. This household with God as father is brought in as an "imagined place" imposed on the actual lives of the Jesus followers. There is no direct mention of kingdom in this passage, but it combines the content of the two petitions about "bread" and "kingdom" in 11:2–4. When bread is provided, even if it comes from sympathizers, it is because God can be trusted as the father of the household.

The combination of kingdom and household sayings makes up an imagined space, which at the same time speaks directly to the actual situation of the addressees. The addressees are, so to speak, transported into the space of the kingdom. This kingdom is visualized as a household, with God as the father and the addressees as his children. This is not totally fictitious, however. Relations within this imagined place are meant to influence the material practice of the place in which they find themselves. It is because God is their father in heaven that they can hope to experience ideal household practice in terms of material support in their daily life. Thus, the imagined place of the heavenly household influences the experience of their present place and turns it into something else, a more familiar place.

The portrait of God as father also makes up the main argument in sayings about not being anxious in Q 12:22–31. For most people in the ancient Mediterranean area—as in many places today—life was first of all centered on the needs and the ills of the body. Peasant economy was based on subsistence. The picture of peasants in Galilee that the gospels give is of an economy that was basic, concerned with houses for shelter, clothes for protection, and food for nourishment.[47] Debts, rents, and taxes were threatening. They could put the life of a peasant family at risk. The line between subsistence and outright poverty could be thin, depending on the harvest. Very few had more than they needed. This elemental existence was a general fact of life, and it is well described in the gospels. Illness was a constant threat and, in situations where only the few could afford doctors, the question of health and healing was a question of life and death. Life expectancy was low, as it is for the poor in many countries today. Thus, a saying like "Do not be anxious" is understandable as an exhortation that addressed a general situation.[48]

But the statements in Q 12:22–31 may be more specific. Jesus probably addressed a special group, those who had "left everything to follow him."[49] We should therefore have in mind the followers of Jesus as displaced persons who, by acting on the words of Jesus, had been dislocated from their households and their village community. These sayings address the same concerns for the basic necessities of life as the Lord's Prayer and the following sayings in Q 11:2–13.[50] Primary among these necessities is food and clothing (Luke 11:3, 5, 11–12; 12:22, 29). Thus, I think that the purpose of the exhortation "do not be anxious" in Q 12:22, 29 was to create households as "imagined places" and to place the addressees within these new household relations. This was a way to speak of their daily lives and social contexts, but also a way of moving them into a different space.

In their present form, the sayings on anxiety in Q 12:22–31 and Matt. 6:25–34 are integrated into each gospel and reflect the main motifs of that gospel. Both in Luke and in Matthew the discussion of anxieties reflects the changing social locations of their audiences. They situate the sayings in a context of the danger of riches, and thus have removed them from an immediate situation of pressing needs.[51] But in Q the sayings seem to be addressed to followers of Jesus who actually faced a situation of basic need.[52] That would also have been the situation that Jesus addressed, speaking to followers who had left everything. The context is different from that of "riches" (Matt. 6:19–21). Freedom from anxiety is not a matter of spending wisely what one has. Nor is it a matter of acting in such a way that one overcomes anxieties by working, and thereby providing what one needs. There is no moral argument about the value of work in Q 12:22–31 and no reintegration into the working community of household that the followers had left. Instead, the hearers are encouraged to be integrated into the household of God, where they are provided with all that they need.

The main concern and the cause for anxiety was the need for food and clothing. The necessities of life are summed up as what the hearers need (Q 12:30). The basic exhortation "do not be anxious" is repeated in two major cycles in this passage, in Q 12:22–24 and 26–28, and in 12:29–31.[53] The first cycle starts with a general exhortation not to worry about what to eat and to put on, 12:22. It is followed by a thesis in 12:23 that has attracted criticism for being such a platitude: "Is not life more than food, and the body than clothing?" This thesis has two supporting arguments, and each argument concludes by giving a reason to trust in God's care. The first argument concerns food (12:24) and points to the carefree existence of the ravens, concluding with "and yet God feeds them." This section ends with an *a minore ad maius* argument: "Are you not better than the birds?" (12:24c). The next argument takes up the question of clothing (12:27–28),[54] and starts by pointing to the lilies of the field that grow without toiling and spinning, so that not even Solomon in his well-known royal splendor could compare with them. And another *a minore ad maius* argument claims that God, who clothes the perishable grass, will also clothe the hearers of this saying (12:28).

The second cycle (12:29–31) is shorter, and starts with a repetition of the exhortation not to worry about what to eat or drink, 12:29. The supporting argument follows in 12:30. First the Gentiles are characterized as those who "seek" such things, and in contrast to the Gentiles the hearers are assured that "your Father knows that you need them [all]." And then, in a positive contrast to what the Gentiles seek, follows an exhortation about what they shall seek: "Seek his kingdom," and finally a promise: "and [all] these shall be granted to you" (12:31).

The reason that the followers of Jesus should not be anxious about their lives, and about food and clothing, is repeated throughout this passage. They are asked to look at nature, not just at animals but also at plants, and to see in nature God's care. And then, emphasizing that human beings are much more than birds and plants, they are reassured that God will feed them and clothe them. The comparison with the Gentiles and their worries does not put down the need for food and clothing as unnecessary. On the contrary, the point of contrast is that the followers of Jesus have a father who knows what they need, and who has shown that he provides what they need (Q 12:30). The proofs from nature about how God provides food and clothes to all creation, humans included, are here summed up with a reference to God as father. Again, it is the image of the father and the household that is used. It is not just God's care for his creation that gives reassurance, but his role as father that secures a special relationship to Jesus' listeners.

There is a great contrast between this picture of trust in household relations and in nature, and the exhortations to leave behind household relations as "dead" and human existence as a negative counterpoint to nature in Q 9:58–60 (see chap. 3 above). This suggests that the statements in 12:22–31 are not general wisdom sayings. In contrast to the negative experiences that are presupposed in Q 9:58–60, they establish a location in which there is not conflict, but harmony between nature and human life. And in contrast to tensions within households and conflicts with fathers, Jesus' words in 12:22–31 portray a household of a different kind.

The image of father carried with it the notion of someone who "knows that you need them all," and this was the main content in Jesus' use of this metaphor for God. This tradition is summed up in the saying that introduces the Lord's Prayer in Matthew: "Do not be like them [i.e., Gentiles], for your Father knows what you need before you ask him. Pray then like this" (Matt. 6:8–9). In a situation in which the addressees were homeless, without households to provide food and shelter, Jesus speaks to them about God as one who includes them in a household. The family relations that were broken are re-created, but not with the same household members. Rather, the familiar form of household relations is described as relations to God. But it is not the full range of household relations that is re-created; only God as the father of the household is mentioned. It is only a splinter of a household relation between father and sons that is introduced,[55] and it is the primary relationship of provider and recipient that is reestablished.[56]

Many commentators take it for granted that "kingdom of God" is oriented toward future time, claiming that the term in itself introduces a time perspective, commonly called eschatological.[57] But can we presuppose such a strong meaning to the saying "seeks his kingdom" in Q 12:31?[58] The kingdom is not used in the previous argumentation in Q 12:22–30, which was based on conventional wisdom. Nothing requires an expectation of the immanent inbreak of the kingdom, and there is no mention of it. Instead of the "coming of the kingdom," Jesus speaks of "seek his kingdom" (Q 12:31). But it is unclear what "seeking" his kingdom means. The form of argument in this passage has been (a) "do not be anxious," . . . (b) because God is the one who gives and provides, and so on. The final exhortation in Q 12:31 turns this around. It is a positive exhortation about what they should do: first, seek his kingdom, and the result follows—these things will be given you, that is, by God. Thus, the illustrations of God's care from nature and household are not general observations. They require a decision. The followers must place themselves, so to speak, within this picture of nature and household where God provides, and then they will also be given what they need.

This meaning of "seek his kingdom" makes good sense within the context of the passage. The term "God's kingdom" receives its meaning from the images that are provided from nature (the world is created and every day supported by God) and from household (God is the father who cares). In itself "seek his kingdom" is an empty term, that is, it is not explained or elaborated on. Consequently, it makes most sense to read it as a metaphor that sums up the preceding images of God as creator and father.[59]

In light of the purpose of the whole argument, not to be anxious, one may argue that the last part of the verse with the kingdom saying is most important: "and [all] these shall be granted to you" (Q 12:31b). The bottom line of the argument is that the needs of those who seek the kingdom will be met.[60]

The argument from nature, concluding with "seek his kingdom," is quite similar to the kingdom saying in *Gos. Thom.* 113: "the kingdom of the Father is spread out upon the earth, and men do not see it." The pointers to birds and flowers carry weight only if people can see that it is God who is at work, that it his rule and care that spread out over the world. The statement in *Gos. Thom.* 113 is Jesus' response to the question from the disciples about *when* the kingdom will come. In the *Gospel of Thomas* this question about the time of the kingdom is rejected, and Jesus' reply is instead given in terms of its spatial extension. The kingdom is not presented as a different space, in contrast to the world, rather, "it is spread out upon the earth." That is, kingdom and the world are not contrasted, but combined. There is not a dualistic view of the world here. Although there is a distinction between the kingdom and the world, they exist together,[61] and the earth is imagined as a place where the kingdom is spread out.

The way in which the world and the kingdom exist together in the *Gospel of Thomas* suggests that the same might be the case in Q 12:22–31 as well. In this passage "kingdom" is not a separate space, in addition to the "natural" world with its birds and flowers or to the human world of house and household. Rather, the kingdom is a transformation of these spaces, visible for those who "seek." For those who "seek," the world will become a place like perfect nature or like the household with a father who provides. Kingdom is that "imagined place" that they may seek.

A RETURN OF MALE SPACE?

Compared with the image of God as king, the presentation of him as father who provides for his household seems unquestioningly positive. But the father also represented patriarchal power, and we discussed in chapter 4 how Jesus and his followers left the "male space" of patriarchy and masculinity. Was patriarchy now reintroduced, not on the human level but on the divine level, so that Jesus and his followers were reinscribed in male space? This has been a criticism from many feminist scholars. Some male scholars have tried to read Jesus' use of the father image for God in a different way, as a criticism of patriarchy. One such attempt says: "He [Jesus] relativized what in the patriarchy were absolute obligations to father and family, in the name of the heavenly father. The effect of Jesus using it was to deprive the patriarchy, along with everything else that is compared with the sovereignty of God, of absolute power. The fact that Jesus chose the 'father' symbol for this purpose suggests that he intended to direct his message especially at the patriarchy and to reorganize it by freeing people from its clutches."[62] However, this attempt at a reinterpretation of the father image was effectively blocked by feminist criticism: "To the extent that Jesus disavowed the earthly father in the name of the heavenly father . . . , to that extent Jesus re-inforced patriarchy by absolutizing the rule of the father. To transfer male dominance from earth to heaven is not to eliminate but to exacerbate it."[63]

There can be no doubt that the image of God as male and as father did serve to form masculine ideals and to support male leadership in Christian communities.[64] In many instances it was also directly used in that way, for instance, when Paul argues for the superiority of men over women on that basis (1 Cor. 11:1–16). Also modern readers, and in particular male interpreters of Jesus and the gospels, ought to reflect on their own conceptions. In many of her books Elisabeth Schüssler Fiorenza has explored these conceptions and how they are inscribed in language itself.[65] Instead of the analytical category patriarchy (the domination of the father/male over women), she has coined the term "kyriarchy" to grasp the multifaceted forms of power and domination in the modern world.[66] Male domination is articulated in language and philosophy and determines the way in which we construct and label the world. This construction is not a "fact," but characteristic of power relations.[67]

It is obvious that the image of God as father and householder inscribes him in a gendered relationship where males were regarded as superior. But does Jesus' image necessarily authorize a male superiority? When we reflect on Jesus' way of speaking about God, I think it is significant that he did not speak of God as king. And when he used the father image, it was primarily the aspect of the father who provided for his children and protected them, not the father as an authority figure (see above). Thus, the image of God who provides in Q 11:2–13 and 12:22–31 does not have an aspect of authority that is transferred to males in the group. Rather, Jesus' sayings about God's care as father in his household seem to be addressed to a situation described as one of loss, of lack of power and of resources, as a commonly shared situation for the followers of Jesus. There is at least a possibility that the image of father did not necessarily encourage male supremacy in the group, but rather put all—young men, older women, and children—into the same category as dependents in the household. Moreover, a later saying in the Jesus tradition explicitly denies that the authority of God as father is transferable to the fellowship of followers (Matt. 23:9).

In other instances Jesus' use of the father image for God seemed to destabilize and to decenter a traditional image of the patriarchal father. This becomes particularly visible in two parables about the relationship between a father and his two sons. In these parables the authority structure is presupposed—the father has the right to obedience and honor from his sons. But it is exactly this aspect of the father-son relationship that is challenged in these parables. One is the narrative of the father who asked his sons to go and work in his vineyard (Matt. 21:28–30). One of them said no, but repented and went. The other son said yes, but did not go. Here the household imagery for the kingdom is used with an ironic twist. This is a household in conflict. In one instance the father was privately shamed and publicly honored, since the son repented and went to the vineyard. In the other instance the father was privately honored, but publicly shamed, since the son did not go after all.[68] Also, in the parable of the two sons in Luke 15:11–32 the authority of the father is challenged when the younger son claims his inheritance. But the father does not rise to this challenge; instead, he is portrayed as breaking the village codes of honor in his relation to his younger son. The father is too weak vis-à-vis his son, and in showing too much affection at the return of his son, he does not behave properly, and therefore brings shame on his family.[69] In parables like these Jesus portrays fathers and householders who do not conform to socially honored masculine roles, who are made to look weak and "unmanly," who choose compassion and love over honor. In this way Jesus must have made his audience reflect on their conceptions of fathers and of God as father.

Since the father is identified as male, in a position of domination and authority, we may not be able to grasp what it means that he is described as lacking in power and honor. Our mental and linguistic structures of male domination may be so strong that we cannot grasp a father figure who is "out of place."

CONCLUSION

There is something strange in the way Jesus speaks of the kingdom, both in the parable of the mustard seed and in the sayings on "cares." The kingdom is portrayed through contrasting images. In the ancient world, kingdom was above all a term that referred to politics, to the area of emperors, kings, and rulers. In particular, when speaking of the kingdom of God this would seem to be the appropriate context. But in the parable the proud tree as a symbol of the kingdom is contrasted with a mustard seed in an impure garden. In this way the kingdom becomes something new, a "third space" that parallels its queer members. And in Jesus' sayings "on cares," kingdom is located not in an empire, but in a village and a household.[70] God is portrayed not as a king, but as a "paterfamilias of rural Galilee."[71] Therefore, we may characterize the images of the kingdom of God as a household as countercultural.[72] The images broke not only with expectations of God as king, but also with the traditional picture of a householder. The image of the father who provided for his children was emphasized, while the role of the patriarch was downplayed. He was even portrayed as a father whose authority was questioned, who was denied honor.

Jesus speaks to his followers of kingdom as a household, with God as father and the addressees as his children. But the practices of this household, for example,

God's support and provisions for his children, do not happen only on a heavenly level. They take effect in the experience of the followers of Jesus, in the support given to them by householders and resourceful women, for instance. In the sayings of Jesus these effects are spoken of as taking place within the household of God, with God as the father and source of support. In this way these sayings create a new space for the listeners. The kingdom and the household, with God as father, are combined with the world of experience for the listeners, and create a space in which the support of the household of God is experienced in the world.[73] In this way an "imagined place" becomes part of their experience. But this space of experience is not that of the real households that the addressees of the sayings of Jesus have left behind. There is no immediate relation between the household of God, of which they are now members, and their household of origin. The image of household is applied not to real households, but to the followers of Jesus, who were in a precarious and disadvantaged position. Thus, the ideals of household relations, especially the father-son relation, are fulfilled in a space that is outside of and in contrast to "real" households. The actual space in which they found themselves was transformed by means of these sayings of Jesus.

It seems to me that the expression "the kingdom returns home" is an appropriate expression for what was happening. For those who had left households, Jesus' sayings about the kingdom imagined it as a new home place. Jesus' sayings about the kingdom were a way to turn the displaced and homeless existence of Jesus' followers into a household; it was a way of speaking about the unfamiliar in a familiar way. With a subversive form of rhetoric, Jesus turned the life of the wandering disciples into households of God. The sayings of Jesus subverted the traditional meaning of household, since it was the homeless who now made up the household of God.[74]

Jesus' sayings about the kingdom were not only about the kingdom, but also about the addressees of and listeners to his message. For hearers who had been uprooted from their place of identity, the sayings about the kingdom also served to reinstate them in a location that could give them a new identity. And kingdom as household provided a familiar place for identity. This was an internal function of kingdom sayings, to provide a "home" for the Galilean followers of Jesus.

But Jesus' kingdom sayings also had an external function. In conflicts with opponents, Jesus' kingdom sayings could take on a political meaning and participate in a competition over power.[75] In chapter 7 we will see the critical aspects of the kingdom sayings become much more pronounced, as do the political perspectives of kingdom as rule over a territory.

Chapter 7

The Power of Place

The Exorcist and His Kingdom

The Kingdom sayings of Jesus not only created alternative households for his followers—some of them moved out from the household setting into the political realm and challenged the symbolic and political power over Galilee.

An appropriate starting point is the Jesus saying in Q 11:20, in response to the accusation that he practiced exorcisms by the help of demonic powers: "But if it is by the finger of God that I cast out demons, then there has come upon you the kingdom of God." This saying is significant in that it gives an interpretation of Jesus' exorcisms from the early Jesus tradition. Therefore, what we want to study in this chapter is not so much possessions and exorcisms as such, but rather discourses about them, how they are talked about and what meaning they are given. We shall study conflicting interpretations of the same facts, in particular the accusations directed at Jesus that he was possessed by demons. Such accusations were a common way to question the legitimacy of an exorcist. It was in response to this type of criticism that the Jesus saying in Q 11:20 presents an interpretation of the exorcisms that he performed. It is remarkable that in this saying exorcisms are introduced not as healings, as part of medical care, but in terms of God's kingdom and control over space. By linking exorcisms with the kingdom of God the saying places exorcisms in a spatial context. This saying is an example of how discourse can provide or uncover a spatial meaning where it has not been recognized. This function of language is called "social spatialization."[1] When we study this function of Jesus' sayings, we also become aware of the spatial implications of our own discourse. Often there has been little awareness of this spatial character of language, so this chapter is also an attempt to bring back that insight.[2]

Most New Testament studies that have discussed exorcisms have done so in a rather narrow way, based on an internal reading of the gospels and their world-view.[3] Few studies have tried to place the question of demon possession and exorcism in the social and political context of Palestine in the first century, or to interact with studies of exorcism within other disciplines.[4] Exorcisms have also been marginal to most discussions of the historical Jesus; they do not seem to fit the picture of him either as prophet or as teacher of wisdom.[5] One notable exception is the attempt by Geza Vermes to describe Jesus as a Jewish charismatic from Galilee, one of the Hasidim from that area.[6] But for the most part, healings and exorcisms have been put into a "private" sector of illness and healing. They have been viewed as forerunners to what in modern times is the medical sector.[7] Consequently, it has primarily been modern and Western conceptions of illness and healing that have determined the interpretation of the miracles dealing with illness and possession. In the Western world, illness and health have become secularized, bereft of symbolic and cosmological significance. And the medical profession has been very concerned to guard its privileges against a folk sector of alternative medicine. As a result, cure for illness is regarded as a medical issue, and exorcisms have been discussed within these medical and natural science paradigms of understanding the world. The most common question regarding the healings and exorcisms of Jesus has been whether he actually did perform them. Was it possible for Jesus to break with the laws of nature (or of medicine) and to expel demons—that is, if they existed in the first place?

That this is a limited perspective becomes obvious when we compare these attitudes to the cultural context of illness and healing in non-Western societies.[8] Africa, in particular, is a good example of many societies that share a very different view from the Western one. Illness and healing are in many cultures viewed in a more holistic perspective when it comes to the individual person. Not only "Western" medicine may help, but healing may also come about through traditional medicine men or church healers and healing sessions. Moreover, health and illness have cosmological dimensions; possessions and exorcisms are therefore part of a cosmological battle in people's lives. "Healing" in an African context, therefore, has much wider implications than cure of illness in the West—it may not only refer to individuals, but to society at large; it represents a restoration of society to health and balance.[9]

This example shows that in the case of exorcisms, our own perspective in interpretation is very important; to a large degree it is this perspective that determines what questions we ask and what we see. In this chapter, I shall apply a *spatial perspective* to the discussion of the exorcisms and accusations of possessions regarding Jesus, to see them as taking place in a spatial location, and with implications for the control and domination over place in Galilee. This is not a common perspective. Therefore, I will point to a recent example of such a reading of present-day Colombia that suggests that this is a possible and indeed helpful perspective.

SHAMANISM AND CONTROL OF THE LAND

In the discussion above, we mentioned that in modern Western societies medicine and cure belong to a medical sector and not, for instance, to a religious or political sector. This compartmentalization is a result of the way in which our minds work, as they are formed by modern societies, and the way in which we divide the world neatly into different sectors. It is also reflected in academic writings that faithfully reproduce these divisions. But sometimes we come across books that jolt us out of our compartmentalized existence and make us see how the issues are interrelated. The result of Michael Taussig's anthropological studies in Colombia in the period from 1969 to 1985 is such a book. The title, *Shamanism, Colonialism, and the Wild Man: A Study in Terror and Healing,*[10] bears out that it combines medicine, politics, and the study of mentalities. Taussig gives a fascinating picture of the relations between Spanish colonizers and their descendants and the colonized Indians in Colombia. In order to grasp the complex and multifaceted relations, he combines historical studies of colonization and studies of modern Indian shamans and their relations to white Colombians. At the center of the relations between colonizers and colonized is the occupation of space by the colonizer. But this occupation of the land is not a clear-cut or unambiguous situation. Taussig speaks about the experience of traveling through a landscape, and raises the question of what it means. There is a connection between the land and the medicine men; and Taussig says that the Indian medicine men see the symbolic meaning of the land when they "arouse the slumbering meaning of space long colonized by the white man and carry him through it to uncover the hidden presence not only of God but of the sorcerer."[11]

There was an everyday relationship between whites and shamans, or sorcerers, in that whites also came to ask for healing. In many cases they had a very ambivalent view of the Indians, but nevertheless asked the Indian sorcerers for protection against the effects of the envy that affected their land, their houses, and their businesses. Taussig's review of histories from colonization places the present relationship against this history of colonization. That was a history of terror, excessive and cruel use of power, but Taussig also points to ambiguities in the relationship. An illuminating example is a chapter called "on the Indian's back." Quite literally, to be able to travel in the dangerous and steep mountain regions of the Andes, white administrators had to be carried on the back of Indians. This was a situation of both power and dependence, with the oppressed Indian as the superior in terms of mastering the landscape. The landscape itself served to "unbalance" the relations of power.

Against this background, the healings of the modern Indian sorcerers were a way to take back power or to gain access to a world of meaning that lies underneath the obvious, visible world with its white power. The land was under the dominion of spiritual powers, good and evil, and the sorcerers had access to this world. An economic or political dominance of the land could not guarantee control. The distribution of power over land, over houses and other properties, as well as over one's own body, was always threatened. There were evil powers at work that could be activated by other people's envy, by those who wanted their goods. The assistance from sorcerers was directly related to these issues related to individuals, their health, well-being, and property. With their sorcery, the shamans acted within the context of a shared cosmology, a world ruled by spirits.

Taussig's study shows that in this colonized society, sorcery and healings by Indian shamans must be understood in the context of a colonial history; its complex relationships are part of the politics of control over space. To colonize meant to take control of the land of the Indians, and therefore all conflicts were related to this control of land. Although the white colonizers and their descendants had the political control, the Indian sorcerers had a more subtle power, that of the deeper meaning of the land, governed by spiritual powers. But the sorcerer was always an ambiguous figure, needed by the white colonizers, but also contested and criticized.

EXORCISMS AND ACCUSATIONS OF DEVIANCE

Taussig's book suggests a new, spatial perspective in our discussion of the exorcisms of Jesus. The discourse about demon possessions and exorcisms took place within the context of social and political control of land and resources in Galilee. Jesus' saying in Q 11:20 makes it explicit. By linking exorcisms to kingdom and speaking of the kingdom of God in spatial categories (as we shall see in the exegesis of Q 11:14–20), Jesus expresses his spiritual meaning of the land. But this was apparently not universally accepted. The reports of Jesus' exorcisms participate in an ambiguous context of accusations as well as acceptance.

I repeat that I do not aim to discuss possession and exorcisms as medical facts, but am interested in their cultural meaning, and in the function of the discourse about possessions and exorcism. Such discourses suggest that possessions and exorcisms belong in a context of conflicts and competing interests. In a study of how to interpret demonic powers in Hellenistic and Roman antiquity, Jonathan Z. Smith has suggested that "demonic" is primarily a locative category, that is, a category concerned with "placing"[12]: "The demonic is a relational or labeling term which occurs only in certain culturally stipulated situations and is part of a complex system of boundaries and limits." Therefore, says Smith, "demons serve as classificatory markers which signal what is strong and weak, controlled and exaggerated in a given society at a given moment." He argues for the need of a "shift from a logic of identity to a logic of relations," that is, from discussions of what demons "are," to what discourses about them tell us about relations and boundaries of a society.

Belief in demons, possession, and exorcisms in first-century Galilee may say something about this society, what it felt about its boundaries, about internal and external pressures. The sociopolitical situation of Palestine at the time of Jesus was probably conducive to creation of an atmosphere where possession and witchcraft accusations would proliferate. Likewise, the same might be true for the first Christian groups in the early period of the transmission of the Jesus tradition. It might very well be that experience of possession was a result of and partial response to critical life situations, increased by Roman rule and the economic and political pressure on village life with the rise of a Hellenistic economy. A growing number of accusations of possessions and witchcraft are often a sign of social pressure, social breakdowns, and political oppression.[13]

Historically, in the context of Palestine in the first century, it was not the modern question, whether Jesus could do miracles and exorcisms, that was on people's minds. Rather, the main question was by what power he performed these exorcisms. Therefore, we should take into account that Jesus' exorcisms were surrounded by ambiguity. Sources from antiquity tell us that the exorcist was an ambiguous figure, and that he himself could suffer the accusation that he was possessed. Popular opinion held that to have the power to cast out evil spirits or demons that had taken possession of a person, the exorcist had to be in contact with more powerful spirits and demons. This included the risk for the exorcist himself to be accused of being in alliance with evil sources. Typical social forms of such accusations were witchcraft accusations and labeling.[14] Studies of such accusations do not take for granted that something called witchcraft or demons exists, but through these accusations they look at the social sources and functions for such accusations. Thus, it is not an "objective" fact of witchcraft or "deviance" that is regarded as the problem, but through these accusations one looks at the social process by which witches and deviants are created.

Witchcraft accusation is a term from social anthropology, and labeling a term from the sociology of knowledge. Beliefs in witchcraft are part of cultural cosmology, and are characteristic of (small) societies that may have clear external boundaries, but confused internal relations.[15] Interaction between persons in such societies may be close, but there are no, or underdeveloped, techniques for releasing tension. Authority is weak, and there is an intense competition for power and leadership. Accusations that somebody is a witch or performs witchcraft function as a means to gain control in a situation of competition over leadership.

In the New Testament world, such accusations and labeling were common, reflected, for instance, in the form of interaction—challenge and riposte—that have many examples in the gospels. It has been regarded as plausible that many of these disputes are later than the time of Jesus and that they reflect conflicts between followers of Jesus and the Pharisees of the next generation. However, the cultural form in itself is traditional, so it is, rather, a matter of content whether the actual conflict goes back to Jesus or should be ascribed to a later stage of the Jesus tradition.

The witchcraft model may help us to see the cultural context better, while the labeling and deviance theory may better explain the actual working of accusations and their function. That is, this theory does not so much explain why Jesus was accused of being a witch, but it explains how accusations work and what they do. To label somebody as "deviant" means to define a person as being out of normal place. This labeling is not based on individual acts, but on a definition of a person as deviant, that is, "a person perceived to be out of place to such an extent or in such a way as to be redefined in a new, negative place."[16] A person who is perceived as deviant must be removed from the ordinary to the "out of the ordinary." As a reaction to such labeling as deviant, a person may respond in various ways—for instance, by repudiation, by evasion and denial of responsibility, or by a redefinition.

EXORCISMS AND THE KINGDOM OF GOD

To study the exorcisms of Jesus in their ambiguous setting of accusations and labeling, I shall focus on Q 11:14–20 and the accusation that Jesus received his power from demons. This saying of Jesus is part of a larger passage of challenge and riposte between Jesus and his adversaries. The so-called Beelzebul story has two main forms, one in Mark 3:22–27 (28–30) and another one in Q 11:14–23.[17] It is only Q that has the famous saying of Jesus in 11:20, and therefore we shall pay most attention to the Q version of the story.

We shall first look at the spatial dimension of the relations between exorcisms and kingdom in this exchange, to establish the worldview behind this passage. In a next step we shall attempt a historical analysis of the role of Jesus' exorcisms within the spatial context of Galilee in the Herodian period. At this point it is useful to introduce the main text we shall discuss, Q 11:14–20:[18]

> 14. And he cast out a demon which made a person mute. And once the demon was cast out, the mute person spoke. And the crowds were amazed. 15. But some said: "By Beelzebul, the ruler of demons, he casts out demons!" 17. But, knowing their thoughts, he said to them: "Every kingdom [*basileia*] divided against itself is left barren, and every household divided against itself will not stand. 18. And if Satan is divided against himself, how will his kingdom [*basileia*] stand? 19. And if I by Beelzebul cast out demons, your sons, by whom do they cast them out? This is why they will be your judges. 20. But if it is by the finger of God that I cast out demons, then there has come upon [*ephtasen*] you God's kingdom [*basileia*]."

The basic outline of the story in Q is as follows:[19] The introduction in 11:14 is a very brief narrative, almost in skeleton form, which contains the basic motifs in a miracle story:[20] identification of illness, healing, confirmation of healing, and astonishment of crowd. The accusation from his opponents that it is by Beelzebul that Jesus casts out demons (Q 11:15) is the starting challenge in this exchange of challenge and riposte.[21] It is followed up by a riposte from Jesus in two parts. The first part, in 11:17–18a, does not respond directly to the accusations, but employs the

image of the divided kingdom to show how unfounded the accusation is. Then in
11:19–20 Jesus' response moves on to address directly the accusation against him,
by pointing first to the exorcisms of the Jewish exorcists, and finally by combining
exorcisms with a statement about the kingdom. The exchange is followed up by the
parable of the strong man who is defeated by a stronger one (Q 11:21–23).[22]

In what follows here I will argue that the saying in Q 11:20 must be read
within the passage as a whole, as part of a discussion that places Jesus' exorcisms
in the spatial context of the kingdom of God versus the kingdom of Satan. This
goes against a long tradition of interpretations of this saying. Q 11:20 was for a
long time almost universally accepted as a secure word of the historical Jesus.[23]
Most scholars viewed it as a logion that was independent of its present context.[24]
That was partly from theological reasons; the comparison with Jewish exorcists
in 11:19 appeared to threaten the uniqueness of Jesus.[25] Severed from this textual context, this logion was interpreted within the context of the eschatology of
Jesus, and in particular within the discussion of future versus realized eschatology.[26] Thus, it has been the *time* dimension of the kingdom of God that has been
at the center of interest, and the discussion has focused on the temporal aspect
of the verb *ephtasen* (to come, to draw near).[27]

It is obvious that even when viewed as an independent logion, interpreters
must provide a context for their interpretation of Q 11:20. All sayings of Jesus
must be interpreted within a cultural-religious and social context to give meaning. When Q 11:20 was regarded as an independent logion it was the general
notion of the eschatology of Jesus that provided the context. But recently the consensus that Q 11:20 was a secure word of Jesus and independent of its present
context in Q has been seriously questioned.[28] The parallelism in form and vocabulary between 19a and 20b is so strong that it points to mutual interdependence.[29] And both verses seem to depend on 11:15 for their terminology. This
interdependence through a large section of the text in Q 11:14–20 suggests that
the logion in 11:19–20 was part of the original Q narrative, and that Q 11:20
cannot be singled out as a Jesus saying independent of its present context. The
context in Q, made up of a controversy setting with challenge and riposte, represents an old level of the Jesus tradition. Since Q 11:20 makes good sense in its
present context in 11:14–20, it is on that basis that we shall establish the relationship between the kingdom and exorcism.[30] I do not claim that every part of
Q 11:14–20 goes back to the historical Jesus, but that the passage represents a
plausible context for the saying in 11:20, and that it "echoes a Palestinian debate
between Jesus and his Jewish peers."[31]

Q 11:15: THE CHALLENGE:
PUTTING JESUS OUT OF PLACE

What was the meaning of the accusation against Jesus that he expelled demons
with the help of Beelzebul? An exchange of challenge and riposte is part of a

competition for honor and social power. The brief mention of Jesus' exorcisms in Q 11:14 functions in the narrative to introduce Jesus' claim to honor. The criticism of his exorcisms in 11:15 serves as a challenge to that claim and is the starting point for the controversy reported in Q 11:14–20. Jesus is challenged through the accusation that he was a sorcerer, that it was through demonic powers he expelled demons. Thus, in this story we have to do not only with people who were possessed by demons and with exorcisms, but also with accusations against the exorcist that he worked with the help of witchcraft or sorcery. In Q the accusers are listed only as "some." In other versions they are people in authority, Pharisees or scribes coming from Jerusalem.[32] The question of Jesus and exorcisms takes us into a complex social situation, with many players and many different types of actions. Therefore, we must start with an attempt to analyze the social and cultural situation of which possessions and exorcisms were part.

This story does not say much about being possessed or about reasons for being possessed. We shall return to that issue. It may be that experiences of being possessed were a result of and a partial response to critical life situations and societal pressures. But the story focuses primarily on the accusations directed against Jesus—that it was with the help of Beelzebul, the ruler of demons, that he cast out demons. With this accusation his critics have placed Jesus outside of civilized society. The episode illustrates how discourses of the demonic or of devil worship function "primarily as a locative term which establishes outer limits or distance much as wild men or monsters are depicted as inhabiting the borders of antique maps."[33] The use of the name Beelzebul for the leading demon may point in the same direction. It is not absolutely clear to whom the name refers.[34] One possibility is *zbl b'l-'rs*, "the prince, lord of the earth," a local Syrian representation of a major god. If it was a reference to this god that was behind the name Beelzebul, he had become demonized, since all foreign gods were regarded as demons.[35] And if Beelzebul were associated with a foreign god, this would heighten the accusation that Jesus was an outsider.

Q 11:17–18: JESUS' FIRST RIPOSTE:
SATAN'S RULE AS KINGDOM AND HOUSEHOLD

Jesus' response in Q 11:17–18 is at first glance strange. Jesus does not directly counter the attack that he cast out demons with the help of Beelzebul. Instead, he appears to respond to assumptions about space and boundaries underlying the accusation. And he does it by the help of images that bring up the social and political context, by comparing the realm of Satan to a kingdom and a house: "Every kingdom (*basileia*) divided against itself is left barren, and every household divided against itself will not stand. And if Satan is divided against himself, how will his kingdom (*basileia*) stand?" The example of the divided *basileia* in Q 11:17 shows a knowledge of kingdoms as ruled areas.[36] *Basileia* has a spatial aspect; it indicates the area ruled by a king. Q 11:17 is one of only a couple of sayings ascribed to Jesus that explicitly uses the term *basileia* for a political realm. Other examples are his comments on Herod Antipas, the tetrarch of Galilee (Luke 13:31–33) and the saying about the *dēnarion* (Mark 12:13–17).[37]

We have earlier noticed how all-pervasive the image of the house and household is in the Jesus tradition.[38] Therefore, the house as a place for the household was an obvious setting to be mentioned as an example of a crisis of division (cf. Q 12:51–53). A similar example is used in the simile that follows our passage, in Q 11:21–22.[39] Satan is portrayed as a strong man, fully armed, with his house or even a palace (*aulē*), that is, a terminology that seems to make him a warlord or a king, and the conflict not a robbery but a battle. It is a picture more in line with that of the warring kingdoms in the preceding sayings.[40] In these small episodes that are provided in the supporting arguments in the Beelzebul pericope, we get an impression of common locations in a Palestinian or eastern Mediterranean scene in the first century: kingdoms and houses, even large, fortified houses or palaces. This picture is so common that it would be true of Galilee at the time of Jesus as well as of the later Q community.

With kingdom and house, Jesus has brought up the picture of the two main spatial referents that describe the situation for village Galileans in the first century. They correspond to two forms of spatial practice that we discussed in the introductory chapter. The practice that was associated with house and household was appropriation and the use of space. That referred especially to the role and function of houses and households and their activities on the level of village life. The practice associated with kingdom was domination and control of space, or what we might call politics. In Galilee, at the time of Jesus, this was represented by the rule of the Herodian vassal dynasty, their retainers, and the elite households (see Mark 6:21). They controlled the space that provided the livelihood for Galilean peasants and fishermen. Most of Jesus' addressees lived at the intersection of these two forms of spatial practice. Their life was a struggle between their own use of the land for subsistence and reproduction and the control and domination by the rulers—partly also the temple in Jerusalem and the emperor in Rome, through taxation. These are some of the cultural presuppositions that are brought to mind with these images in Q 11:17. And the picture of the fight between "strong men" in the following section, Q 11:21–22, illustrates the forms of power that members of the ruling elite could exercise, and that were threatening to ordinary villagers.

This image of *basileia* as a political and spatial unit, with personal and autocratic rule, is applied to the *basileia* of Satan in the saying in 11:18: "if Satan is divided against himself, how will his kingdom stand?" Here Satan is spoken of as a ruler over a kingdom, and the point of the argument is that it is impossible that a ruler will turn against himself. There seems to be a significant shift in the way to think of the demonic power compared with the accusation in 11:15, that Jesus cast out demons with the help of Beelzebul. That accusation built on popular notions of demonology that there were many demons of various ranks. In order to exorcise some of them, the exorcist gets hold of the power of a mighty spirit, which may drive out those who come from a position lower in the hierarchy.[41] In Jewish Scriptures, Satan is the name often used of the leading demon. But there were various views of the demons and their link with Satan, and therefore no unified perception.[42] This demonic world was pluralistic, the spirits were many and different, and there was no unity to them. Likewise, the pictures of Satan in postexilic Judaism are diverse. Only in the Qumran documents was there a consistent picture of Belial, the angel of darkness, within a dualism of light and darkness.[43]

The accusation against Jesus in Q 11:15 appears to represent a traditional, pluralistic Jewish view of the world of demons in terms of personal relations, with Beelzebul described as a leader of demons. Jesus' response, on the other hand, was based on a strictly monistic view of the world of demons, with Satan as the absolute ruler.[44] Moreover, it was a matter not just of "rule," it was the idea of a *realm* that became prominent in Q's version of the Beelzebul narrative. The demonic is described in terms of a realm, and there is a correspondence between the description of the powers of kingdoms in society and the descriptions of Satan. They are parallel structures. This places the demonic in the midst of political and social life. It may show an awareness of the sources of being possessed in social and political structures,[45] and in particular, it places exorcisms within the political realm. There is a spatial dimension to exorcisms. They have to do with control over space described as kingdom. The perspective in this exchange is not that of healing of ills. There is no description of the person who was possessed; there are no expressions of concern and care on the side of Jesus. The exchange of accusations and riposte centers on the question of power and control over areas and houses. Being possessed is an expression of the rule of demonic powers, of their control of an area, and Jesus argues that they cannot also be the source of exorcism. Exorcisms are described in spatial categories, in terms of establishing a rule over an area and setting up a different kingdom.

Q 11:19–20: JESUS' SECOND RIPOSTE: NOT SATAN'S BUT GOD'S KINGDOM

The second part of Jesus' riposte follows in Q 11:19–20, where he combines the defense of his exorcisms with the kingdom of God. Thus he continues the line of argument from 11:17–18, based on the logic of the kingdom of Satan.[46] Was it this logic of the image of *basileia* applied to Satan that led Jesus to use it also about God, and to speak of "the kingdom of God"? This may sound like a strange question, but we know that the term "kingdom of God" is almost never used in Jewish Scriptures. It is found a few times in Wisdom literature, the Qumran documents, and Philo,[47] but it is doubtful that these examples would represent a common knowledge background for Jesus and his audience. In New Testament scholarship the most common way to get around this problem is to say that although the term "kingdom of God" was not common, the notion of God as king was well known. The expectation that God would establish himself as king was in some circles part of an apocalyptic worldview. But it is significant that Jesus does not speak of God as king. This seems to be something he almost studiously avoids. The frequent use of the term "kingdom of God" seems to have been initiated by Jesus. It was central to his proclamation, but it did not play a prominent role in other early Christian literature. Thus, it seems to have been a term that was easily understandable, but not easily identified with any specific, given historic or cultural meaning.

Therefore, I suggest that in the Beelzebul controversy the term "kingdom of God" receives its meaning primarily from that context. Moreover, it is exactly this context and the logic of the argument that necessitate the use of "kingdom of God." So let us try to follow the logic of the accusation and of Jesus' response:

1. Jesus was accused that his exorcisms were by the power of Beelzebul, the leader of the demons (11:15). This was an accusation that placed Jesus outside the boundaries of Jewish society, together with Beelzebul, but it did not imply a separate realm or a unified system of demons.
2. In contrast, in Jesus' response the spatial images of *basileia* and *oikos* became metaphors for the *basileia* of Satan (11:17–18a), and the demons unified under his rule were placed in a realm.
3. Thus, the power that became visible in exorcisms, either belonging to Beelzebul (ironically in 11:19a) or to God, was already associated with the idea of a spatial realm, a *basileia*, that this power controlled.
4. These ideas were brought together and expressed in 11:20ab: "But if it is by the finger of God that I cast out demons, then there has come upon you God's kingdom." The saying in 11:20a effectively responded to that which had been the question all along (v. 15, 19a, b): by whom did Jesus (and the Jewish exorcists[48]) cast out the demons? Thus, with 11:20a the accusation from Jesus' critics in 11:15 was refuted not only by *reductio ad absurdum* as in 11:17–19,[49] but also with a positive statement, attributing Jesus' powers to God.

Why, then, follows the rejoinder about the kingdom of God in v. 20b? From the analysis above, it appears that it was the image of *basileia* in 11:17, and its application to Satan in v. 18, that required this addition.[50] The idea of Satan's power required a realm, a *basileia*. Therefore, the kingdom saying in v. 20b was necessary to respond to the idea of *basileia* that was already implied in the notion of power. Thus, the power of God's finger or spirit[51] was associated with God's realm, contra the realm of Satan. The two parts of 11:20 form a tautology: implied in the image of the power of God (his finger or Spirit) was the very notion that God had a kingdom over which he ruled.

Thus, it seems to be the logic of the argument, not a preconceived notion of an apocalyptic kingdom, that can best explain the use of "kingdom of God" in 11:20. It is difficult to attach as much importance to this Jesus saying in Q 11:20

as is often done. If we accept that it does not stand alone, but is part of the context, it does not stick out as such an original and central passage. Instead, it is part of the rhetoric of challenge and riposte between the opponents and Jesus, and receives its meaning from that context. Read within the full context, it is the spatial character of the exchange that dominates, not the time aspect that has been so prevalent in almost all discussions of the saying.[52] It was the use of the images *basileia* and *oikos* as spatial categories that led to these same spatial categories being used of Satan and God. Thus, it followed that when exorcisms were not brought about by Satan, and by his power and realm, it was by God's power, and it meant the presence of his realm.

There seem to be two types of spatial logic operating in Q 11:14–20. The Jews who accused Jesus of being a sorcerer thereby expelled him outside the boundaries of their community and made him, physically or mentally, like the pagans. Jesus' answer moves by a different logic, that of two realms that stand in opposition to each other. The picture of Satan not just as "outsider," but as lord of another realm, creates an image of two territories, or realms, each under a ruler, Satan or God. The picture that is created is that of a fight here and now, between two realms, being fought out on the same territory. The image of a battle at the periphery, at the boundaries, has shifted to that of a battle at the core of the map, between the kingdom of God and the kingdom of Satan, where the very issue of power becomes central. This corresponds to other "maps" in the discourses of Jesus, for instance, that there is less concern for purity at the borders and margins than at the center (Mark 7:1–23). And just as the power and realm of Satan must be challenged, so also the political power of Herod Antipas (Luke 13:31–32).[53]

It seems that the Beelzebul passage deals with three spatial realms: there is the realm of household and politics, then there is the realm of Satan, and finally that of God. The realms of Satan and of God are, so to speak, laid on the world that Jesus and his hearers inhabit. They are figures of speech or "spaces of representation" that give to experiences of being possessed and to exorcisms a spatial dimension. Against the attempt by the community leaders to marginalize Jesus, to make him one with the possessed that he healed, Jesus brings the issue of possessions and exorcisms to center stage with spatial imagery. He does not just say that he did the exorcisms by the power of God, but that God was establishing his kingdom. The images of the realm ruled by Herod Antipas and the Romans would easily come to mind. And in this context, *basileia* clearly has a connotation that identified kingdom with power over a place, a territory.

POSSESSIONS AND EXORCISMS IN JESUS' GALILEE

Following this discussion of exorcisms and kingdom of God in Q 11:20, we should look briefly at other narratives of exorcisms in the gospels to find whether they confirm the function of exorcisms as power over place. The gospels provide culturally representative ideas about places where one could expect to find possessed persons and where exorcisms would take place. Mark places the first possessed person in the setting of a village gathering, in a synagogue (1:23–28; Luke 4:31–37). This setting is described as confusing in terms of authority, with Jesus being favorably compared with the scribes (Mark 1:22; Matt. 7:28–29). The most famous narrative of a possessed person is that of the Gerasene demoniac (Mark 5:1–20 par.), who was expelled from his village community and lived outside the village in the impure area of the tombs (Mark 5:3). He gave the name of his demons, and thus possibly their source, as "Legion" (Mark 5:9, 15). That is, he identified the Roman legions with demons and, as someone who was possessed, he could express his opposition to Roman domination.[54] In two other examples, the setting is that of the house and household, and the possessed are children: a father with his son in Mark 9:15–27, and the Syro-Phoenician woman and her daughter in Mark 7:24–30.

In light of modern analyses it is possible to see demon possession as one of the coping mechanisms against pressures, where there are no good ways out or no possible solutions. The pressures might be caused not only by family situations, but also by situations of social and economic conflicts that peasants experienced in this period. They were not necessarily results of direct Roman intervention, but more often of the Hellenistic economy introduced by Herod and his elite.

If becoming possessed could be a coping mechanism, a way to internalize a situation that could not be fixed, *exorcisms* were a way to interact with the broader situation. It is remarkable how the gospel narratives place the exorcisms of Jesus in a larger area. We may speak of a political space with conflict and controversy. Mark places the first exorcism among a crowd of villagers and in conflict with the scribes (1:23–28). The teaching and exorcisms of Jesus are given as proofs that his power (*exousia*, 1:22) exceeded that of the scribes. And in the most-known controversy over exorcism, the Beelzebul episode, Jesus' opponents are identified in various ways—as local crowds (Luke 11:14), as Pharisees (Matt. 12:24), or as scribes from Jerusalem (Mark 3:22). Reports of his other exorcisms, for instance, in the form of summary statements, also place Jesus in the public arena (Mark 1:39; Luke 6:18). His exorcisms take place in the public center of the village or before crowds that are gathered from larger areas. The catchment areas are variously given,[55] and may reflect ideological considerations or the geographical knowledge of the authors. But the overall effect that the gospels present is one of public attention and gatherings of crowds, so Jesus' exorcisms are public events.

This public and potentially political function of Jesus' exorcisms is emphasized in the redactional activity of the gospel writers, in the way that narratives of Jesus' proclamation of the kingdom and his exorcisms are combined with reports of contacts or potential conflicts with Herod Antipas, the tetrarch of Galilee. Since political issues play little explicit role in the gospels, this link between the exorcisms of Jesus and the ruler of Galilee is remarkable. Mark 6 combines the rejection of Jesus in Nazareth (6:1–6) with the commissioning of the Twelve (6:7–13) to proclaim repentance with power over spirits and casting out demons. Some said to Herod that the powers that were at work in Jesus showed that he was John the Baptist raised from the dead (6:14). After this potential conflict with Antipas, Jesus wanders around primarily outside Galilee, avoiding Antipas's territory, and he ceases to proclaim the kingdom of God in Galilee.[56]

Luke has preserved and strengthened this relationship between exorcisms, the proclamation of the kingdom, and confrontation with Herod Antipas. The commissioning of the Twelve with power over demons and the right to preach the kingdom of God, Luke 9:1–6, is combined with Herod's perplexity and his desire to see Jesus (Luke 9:7–9).[57] A parallel narrative, the sending of the seventy, Q 10:1–12, is combined with criticism of towns in Galilee for not repenting (Luke 10:13–15), and the return of the disciples, rejoicing that the demons obeyed them (Luke 10:17–20), while Jesus saw Satan fall. Luke 13:31–33 reports that Herod will kill Jesus; Jesus calls Herod a "fox" and will continue his work to "cast out demons and perform cures."

CONFLICT OVER POWER:
JESUS' POWER FROM BELOW

With their redaction of the exorcism narratives, the gospel authors indicate that the healings and exorcisms of Jesus were linked to the political situation, that they were viewed as a threat to Herod. Thus, they were more than expressions of concern for the sick; they were obviously related to the power structures of society, to the questions of domination and control of social and political space. The exorcisms should not be classified as directly political acts, but their effects in terms of gathering crowds and of catching attention may well be called political.[58]

Herod Antipas was a symbol of the changes that took place in Galilee with the new type of economy, represented by the cities of Sepphoris and Tiberias, and the pressures that were put on the peasant population. Moreover, Antipas also represented the Roman influence over Galilee. Thus, he represented a type of rule, a "domination and control of space" against which Jesus protested with his proclamations of the kingdom of God. The socioeconomic pressures on the peasant population, and the social consequences that Antipas's economic policy represented, were of a type that might result in a passive response in the form of demon possession. Thus, demon possession could also be presented as a result of the domination and control of space by the elite. Persons under domination might respond to the pressure by means of passive resistance and unfocused aggression. Jesus' exorcisms represented a form of protest against this oppression, the empowering of persons who were possessed. And since he and his followers combined exorcisms with the proclamation of the kingdom, Jesus presented a different form of domination and control of space.

In what ways was it different, and how could it still be recognized as power? I think that the solution to that question lies in the way the discourse of possessions and exorcisms was combined with attacks on Jesus and accusations against

him for sorcery. In a study of the Roman Empire in late antiquity, Peter Brown
has sketched how the political and social situation may have caused a marked
increase of accusations of sorcery in the fourth century.[59] He describes the situation as one of conflict between change and stability in a traditional society, and
a clash between two systems of power. One is the articulate, defined, and accepted
power, the other is the inarticulate power, for instance, in the form of skills of
certain persons that succeed in ways that are difficult to understand. Among these
skills was rhetoric. It is, says Brown, where these two systems of power overlap
that one may expect to find the sorcerer.[60]

A similar analysis may be made of Palestine and Galilee in the first century
and the role of Jesus. He obviously had some sort of power, but one that was difficult to define by the usual system, and therefore suspect. It has been suggested
that Galilee had a tradition of Hasidic charismatics and that Jesus showed similarities to them.[61] He had been a disciple of John the Baptist, who with his criticism confronted Herod Antipas. It is therefore quite likely that Antipas and his
group watched Jesus with some apprehension when he became known in
Galilee.[62] Jesus' preaching was also a source of power. He attracted listeners and
took sons away from households and made them follow him. And his exorcisms
and healings were recognized as power by his audiences and compared with those
of other leaders.[63]

It is not difficult to understand that Jesus was an irritant to the systems of
power in Galilee, based on Antipas's administration, on the temple and Torah, as
well as traditions and structures of authority in village and household. These systems are what Brown calls "the single image," that is, a power based on visible
and recognized structures. From this perspective a sorcerer or a person accused
of sorcery presents a "double image": there is more than meets the eye. The exorcisms may be admired, but there is something underneath and behind them, possibly an illegitimate power. It is this concern that is reflected in a gospel narrative
where Jesus was challenged to reveal the source of his powers (Mark 11:27–33
par)—or, as in the Beelzebul controversy, he was accused of having his powers
from an illegitimate source. Challenges from local leaders took the form of verbal challenges and criticism, but Herod Antipas represented a more direct and
dangerous power, which might have forced Jesus to withdraw out of Galilee and
into the territory of Philip.

In contrast, Jesus' power through exorcisms and proclamation was of a different sort, but still effective. He represented a power that was not political, but
that brought to attention the presence of spiritual forces over space and the ultimate meaning of space.[64] For Jesus, exorcisms appeared to be a way to speak of
control and domination of space. In exorcisms it became visible that control over
the world was contested. The world was an area of competition and conflicts
between God and Satan. The type of hyperbolic language used, as in Q 11:15–20,
undercut political terminology. Political powers might also be subsumed under
the spiritual forces. An example of this type of criticism is the Q logion in 16:13,
which speaks of the two powers, and how people must choose their loyalty. It is

noteworthy that in this context the contrast is not one between God and Satan, but between God and mammon. Mammon here represents a demonic force that is not just "spiritual"—it affects the social and economic structures of communities and households.[65]

A study of the discourse of being possessed and exorcisms has brought us into conflict situations between Jesus and his followers on the one hand, and local leaders in Galilee on the other. The matter was not the modern question—whether exorcisms (or healings) are at all possible—but conflicts over what type of power was involved. Jesus' exorcisms challenged the ordinary system of power, and we saw the results in various challenge and riposte exchanges. These exchanges were both implicitly and explicitly located within a spatial worldview, or cosmology. Accusations against Jesus that he was possessed functioned to locate him outside the boundaries of society, with the demons.[66] In response, Jesus challenged their attempt and claimed to be centrally located in society, actually fighting for the very power over this center. He presented his challenge in locative categories, with the image of the realm of Satan in opposition to the realm of God, that is, the kingdom of God. Jesus identified himself through his exorcisms with the kingdom of God. His claim that the kingdom was present must be understood as a claim that the power of God was present in Galilee. When the kingdom of God was identified with the exorcisms of demons from the possessed in Galilee, the realm of Satan and the realm of God were presented as fighting over that territory. Thus, Jesus' language of the kingdom participated in a discourse that included both the spiritual and the political sides of control over Galilee.

CONCLUSION

In the previous chapter, chapter 6, we saw that with his sayings about the kingdom as "imagined places" Jesus entered a contested area of paternal authority over household and village life, and placed his followers in imagined households with God as their father. Jesus' sayings about the kingdom as household established a new home for his followers, who had left or experienced conflicts with their own household of origin. In that way his sayings entered directly into the space of daily life in Galilee, into the experience of being displaced from the most fundamental location of identity.

With his exorcisms, Jesus entered into another contested area of authority in Galilee. The exorcisms represented a form of power "from below" that was a challenge to established authorities. The state of being possessed and exorcisms were at the intersection of many areas of social life: health and illness, power and lack of power, being inside and outside of social boundaries. Therefore, exorcisms could take on many different meanings. Jesus' exorcisms could be interpreted primarily in terms of personal power. This is the way in which Mark tells the Beelzebul story: Jesus, who is filled with the Holy Spirit, stands powerful over against

Satan (Mark 3:28–29).[67] But this is not the way in which Q, probably the oldest version of the story, has told it. There the world is viewed as a battleground between God and Satan, and those who are possessed and exorcisms are placed in a spatial context of life in house and kingdom (*basileia*). Exorcisms as expressions of God's power thus signal that God establishes his kingdom over the land. In this way the kingdom was not just an "imagined place," but an experienced place.

Jesus' kingdom sayings and exorcisms presented a countercultural picture to the practice and ideology of houses and politics in Galilee. This conclusion puts question marks around the popular notion that Jesus was accepted in Galilee, that he expressed Galilean aspirations, and that it was his confrontation with Torah obedience represented by Jerusalem that led to his execution. Consequently, our discussion in chapter 6 and in this chapter raises the question of the relationship between Jesus and Galilee and of how to place Jesus there. It is to this task that we will turn in the next chapter.

Chapter 8

JESUS, HOUSEHOLD, AND KINGDOM IN GALILEE

In this chapter we will try to locate the discussions in the previous chapters more specifically in first-century Galilee. These discussions focused on Jesus and his relations to household and to what I have called *kingdom* (*basileia*), that is, politics.[1] We shall ask what "leaving home place" meant when we see Jesus within the context of Galilee, and in what way his teaching and actions regarding the kingdom were related to and affected Galilee.

We mentioned earlier the importance of recent studies of Galilee for the discussion of the historical Jesus. There has been an enormous growth of material on Galilee,[2] especially in archaeology, and as a result of that also in historical studies that have tried to draw consequences for the picture of Jesus.[3] It is impossible to even try to give a summary of "what Galilee was like" at the time of Jesus. Even an attempt to do that would contribute to the impression that it is possible to give an objective picture of Galilee, what it was *really* like. Such an idea is based on a presupposition that once was common—not only among geographers— that it is possible, through observation and gathering of information, to gain an objective picture and to re-create that through writing.[4] But this idea overlooks the effect of the human subject in observing and in organizing information— what we may call "the power of seeing."

To make a picture of an area like Galilee is always an interpretation; it is a hermeneutical task. This places the emphasis first on the interpreter: How do we today create an image of Galilee? But second, it emphasizes also the role of the first-century subject, Jesus, in shaping Galilee. This perspective on the construction of place represents a break with the traditional view of the relation between place and person. According to that view place determines person, and the person is more or less a result of the place from which he or she came. Instead, the discussion of Galilee in this chapter will take its starting point in the thesis of Jonathan Z. Smith: "Human beings are not placed, they bring place into being."[5] This means that we will see Jesus not as a passive result of influence from Galilee, but as an active agent. Galilee was not just a given background for Jesus, and the influence did not go in a one-way direction from Galilee to Jesus. Rather, I suggest that we should see this as a complex and two-way relationship between Jesus and Galilee. Therefore, this chapter will follow the same pattern as the previous chapters: a discussion of the role of Jesus in relation to place is combined with a discussion of the role and presuppositions of the modern interpreter. This time we shall start with the role of the modern interpreter in creating an image of Galilee.

IN THE SHADOW OF THE GALILEAN: SEARCHING FOR JESUS IN GALILEE[6]

I will use my own visit to Galilee in the summer of 2000 to illustrate my point about the role of the interpreter. This highly personal, impressionistic sketch inscribes itself in a long tradition of visitors' sketches of Galilee.[7] I hope it will provide a good starting point for a critical discussion of how places are conceptualized and how an eyewitness report opens for many different interpretations of a place.

"What was Galilee like as a place for Jesus?" I wondered as I traveled by bus from Tel Aviv to Tiberias. I was on my way to Galilee, first going north on a big modern highway along the Mediterranean coast. It followed the path of the ancient Via Maris, the Roman road from Egypt to Syria, before it turned inland toward the southern part of the Sea of Galilee. Later on my trip I picked up the Via Maris again, in Capernaum, which it passed on its way to Damascus in Syria. I was struck by how quickly it was possible to travel to Galilee and within Galilee itself. The short bus ride, less than two hours, made me aware of how small the area was. This caught me by surprise. In the classroom of my childhood there was a map of biblical Palestine. It was the same size as the map of Norway; so somehow I believed the two countries were the same size, about the size of Great Britain or Italy. But all of ancient Palestine was actually only the size of my home county, and Galilee was just a part of that again. In most places you could drive across Galilee, or from south to north, in less than two hours. Within that area, towns and villages known from the gospel narratives, like Nazareth, Cana, or, cities from the time of Jesus but not mentioned in the gospels, like Tiberias and Sepphoris, were only half an hour apart.

Modern roads crisscrossed the countryside and put their mark on the land-scape. An excellent system of buses with frequent departures brought locals, students, large numbers of young soldiers, and some tourists quickly from one point to another. A few days of travel, therefore, gave me a good feel of Galilee as a geographical region. Coming from the southwest, from the broad valley of Jezreel, it was very noticeable how the highland, with hill country, started as the bus made its way up to Nazareth, situated in the hills in the southern part of lower Galilee. This was the most populous and cultivated part of Galilee in the first century. This is the hill country, with valleys that run west to east. Upper Galilee, on the other hand, has higher mountain ranges, with valleys running north and south. In antiquity it had fewer people and lesser settlements than lower Galilee, there were fewer larger roads, and communications were not so easy. Another trip took me to Dan, one of the sources of the River Jordan, way north, close to Mount Hermon. There I was at the beginning of the Great Rift Valley, which the Jordan River follows until it feeds into the Sea of Galilee. The lake and the fruitful area around is part of that rift, well below sea level. It forms a third distinct area within Galilee, the Valley-Lake region. Below the lake, the Rift Valley continues south to the Dead Sea, and further to the Red Sea.

But what type of place was Galilee? I got conflicting and diverse pictures that were not easy to combine into one single pattern. Because I had primarily envisaged Galilee as a place for Jesus, I was disappointed that there was so little left that told about him. There were the churches in Nazareth, and a few along the northern shore of the Sea of Galilee, as at Capernaum and Tabgha. The large tourist map of Galilee showed how relatively insignificant the Christian sites were within the narrative of Galilee that this map provided. Other voices spoke louder. I visited a religious kibbutz that had a hall with large photos of excavations of ancient synagogues in Galilee, together with a map of Galilee showing synagogues in Roman and Byzantine times. The purpose was obviously to show the link between ancient Galilee as a place with many Jews and today's Jewish population. The map showed only the ancient synagogues, not the ancient churches that were likewise spread over Galilee in this period. Thus, it presented a hegemonic picture of ancient Galilee, a picture that hid the Christian presence in the region in that same period.

The pluralism of Galilee today could not be hidden on the ground, and it was included in the tourist map as well: it indicated Muslim, Christian, and Druze villages in Galilee. Sometimes Muslim, Christian, and Jewish settlements were very close to each other. In Nazareth, the Muslim and Christian town in the valley has a new Jewish town, Nazerat 'Illit (Upper Nazareth), right next to it. The neighboring locations and the identical names tell of a controversy over the right to Nazareth, as a physical location but also as a memory, tradition, and identity. And the contest over the right to the place became visible in little things—the direct bus from Tel Aviv to Nazerat 'Illit passed within three minutes from the city center of Arab Nazareth, but did not enter it, and instead wound its way through the residential areas of Nazerat 'Illit. The atmosphere of conflict and contest over the right to a place and its history and identity also became visible in

Nazareth itself, in a conflict between Muslims and Christians. Some Muslims wanted to build a large mosque on a market square next to the most holy Christian shrine in Nazareth, the large Church of the Annunciation. These Muslims had occupied the square and put up a tent roof that served as a makeshift mosque. At one point Nazareth was a town with a Christian majority, but now Christians make up only a minority among mostly Muslim Arabs, and thus the historic identity of the town, characterized by its Christian shrines, is contested.

The Golan Heights, the Syrian territory to the west and north of the Sea of Galilee, showed a similar picture of contested and constructed identities. Traveling in the Golan, we were in Syrian territory occupied by Israel in 1967, now visibly incorporated into Israel by means of kibbutzim as well as by historical excavations, museums, and parks. A museum showed a film about the ancient Jewish town of Gamla and its resistance against the Romans in the first century. It was clearly intended to draw an immediate connection between Jewish settlements in the Golan in antiquity and in the present, and to make it into a Jewish place, bypassing many hundred years of Arab settlements in the area. But there could be no unified picture, no single identity to the place. Ruins of Crusader and Muslim fortifications from the Middle Ages, as well as Druze villages, added new layers and new dimensions to the history and the identity of the area.

I was reminded that a place does not have only one identity; it may have several. The present attempt to create a unified Israeli identity in the Galilee and the Golan is related to the effort to put up strong borders. I was again struck by how small the area was and how close the borders were. The distances between the borders toward Jordan, Syria, and Lebanon could all be covered within a couple of hours' drive. The present borders are political divisions, not based on physical borders; in many instances rolling hills or broad plains continued on the other side of a borderline. Nor are they natural borders for different population groups. Each establishment of new borders has been followed by expulsions or flight of groups of the population. Thus, places can be given a specific identity and character by the use of power and force. Contact across borders is now either difficult or impossible. Those without power have little possibility of contesting these borders and the new political identities of ancient places. I saw one example of that on a bus from the Jordanian border crossing coming into Israel. The Israeli security guards spotted a young man from the Jordanian side, maybe a Palestinian, who was among the passengers. He was removed from the bus before it entered the immigration office and taken away, and the bus continued without him. However, I encountered one small example of how those without power contest forced occupation of places. I learned that from a peasant in Jordan. From a hilltop close to the Sea of Galilee and the Golan, he pointed to the broad view in front of us. He explained that we could see both Syria and Lebanon, completely negating that the Golan was now occupied by Israel, and even overlooking Galilee on the other side of the Sea of Galilee.

After these experiences of contested places, I put my hope in the landscape itself. Maybe the area around the lake was most unchanged, since that was "pure nature," I thought, as the bus wound its way down the hillside to Tiberias at the Sea of Galilee. But is there such a thing as "pure nature"? There are changes in cultivation and vegetation; for instance, large herds of sheep will eat away on small bushes before they can grow. When you take away the sheep, in a few years' time the bushes will start to grow. And was there a different type of farming in the first century than in the twentieth, so that the land was used in a different way? What looks natural might not be that after all, but simply a culturally formed landscape, shaped within the last generations. It is now possible to document some of these changes that have taken place within, at least, the last eighty years. Some areas of Galilee were photographed by aerial photography during World War I and with intervals afterward until today.[8] Probably the last century was a period with more physical changes than all of the preceding eighteen hundred years. The first pictures of Galilee around the lake south of Tiberias show a much more barren landscape, with a smaller population, mostly in little villages or scattered dwellings. But before we think that this must be more what Galilee was like in ancient times, it is necessary to study descriptions of Galilee in antiquity, as well as the results of archaeological surveys. They indicate a Galilee that was fruitful and productive and densely populated. So we seem to encounter not one Galilee, but different landscapes with different configurations of vegetation, cultivation, human developments, and social structures.

It was a hot summer day when I arrived in Tiberias, and in the extreme summer heat the lake was glimmering in the sun, while the shore and hills on the other side were partly hidden in the haze. This was obviously a day for a boat trip, in the hope of catching a little cool wind on the crossing to the other side. Was it a day like this that Jesus walked with his disciples along the seashore? The loudspeaker aboard the boat that blasted out popular Oriental music shattered the illusion of being close to the original experience, however. Or was it my own illusions of what was appropriate that were shattered? Had I imagined that a boat plowing the waters that Jesus had walked should play "sacred music" by Bach or Handel or another European tradition? Unconsciously my expectations were formed by my own cultural and religious presuppositions, so that I was reading the landscape from my particular place. And the episode with the Oriental music made me suddenly aware that Jesus, after all, was not European. If he had been a local person in Tiberias today, Oriental music would have been much more a part of his environment than Bach's organ concerts, which belonged to my own Northern European place.

At the end of my journey I realized that the question that I started out with— "What was Galilee like as a place for Jesus?"—had become much more complicated. Any expectations that coming to Galilee I could have an unmediated access to the original place of Jesus turned out to be false. There were not only too many changes, too much history between Jesus and me, but I realized that there was no such thing as an unmediated access. My experience was always mediated through my own expectations and images. And also the idea of "the original place" faded. There could be no expectation of an "original place" in terms of a place with a settled, undisputed meaning that was waiting to be deciphered.

My experiences in Galilee also disproved my expectations that the nature of Galilee would provide a direct access to Jesus. Not only does nature change with time, but in addition nature is always read within a cultural framework. An idea that made nature the key to understand the personality and character of Jesus, based on the presupposition that "place determines person," was an oversimplification. It was similar to a perspective that painted the picture of Galilee only in terms of Jewish religious observance. It was represented by the map of ancient synagogues in Galilee that I saw in a kibbutz. To a modern viewer unaware that most synagogues dated from the third century and later, the map supported a traditional view of Jesus in conflict with the synagogues. Therefore, it created a picture of Galilee identified as "Judaism," common to many studies of the historical Jesus, in particular in the Second Quest.[9] This was also an oversimplified picture.

What struck me most, and what I was least prepared to meet, was the complexity of Galilee in terms of different communities, and its location at the crossroads of so many political, ethnic, and religious divisions. Thus, both the internal divisions and the external neighbors indicated that this was an area with contested and complementary identities. Due to the political situation, the competition for power was strong, and there were conflicts between various forms of power. In some ways this was an unsettling experience; it destroyed my power of seeing, that is, the all-powerful eye that can observe and describe its object. On the other hand, it made the constructed character of the place extremely visible— it was easy to see how people bring places into being.

It was this insight I wanted to bring to bear on an interpretation of Galilee at the time of Jesus. Galilee at that time showed some of the same complexities, as a border area under changing rulers, surrounded by Decapolis cities. Therefore it was a relevant question to ask in what ways Jesus participated in shaping the Galilee of his time, when his words and actions interacted with others in this crossroad setting. It is this question that we shall explore in what follows.

CREATING PLACES, CONTROLLING SPACES IN GALILEE: HEROD ANTIPAS VS. JESUS

It may seem strange to put up Jesus over against Herod Antipas. To say about Jesus, who said of himself that "the son of man has nowhere to lay his head" (Q 9:58), that he shaped Galilee may seem extravagant. Herod Antipas was at the center of power in Galilee, while Jesus came from the lower part of the power pyramid. However, the Jesus tradition suggests that there was some connection between them, and that Herod was aware of Jesus and his activities. He could hardly be called a competitor to Antipas, but maybe an irritant. Jesus addressed "ordinary" people in Galilee, those who worked on the fishing boats, in the fields, or in the courtyards of peasant houses. These were the people who were affected by the changes that Antipas's rule introduced. And Jesus' activities and proclamations of the kingdom of God were in some sense reactions to the way Antipas ruled his "kingdom" in Galilee.[10] Therefore, we may be justified in looking at both Herod Antipas and Jesus in light of the quote from Jonathan Z. Smith that "human beings . . . bring place into being." This statement emphasizes the human element in shaping the meaning of a place. Another way to put it is to say that "a 'place' is formed out of the particular set of social relations which interact at a particular location."[11] Therefore, the relevant question is to ask what were the set of social relations that interacted in Galilee?

There obviously were great differences in power between the elite and ordinary peasants, and therefore great differences in the way they could influence Galilee as a place. Here we should also remember the different aspects of relations and locations. First there is the material practice, then the representation of place, that is, the ideology of place. These aspects of place are usually dominated by the elite, for instance, through the political power supported by ideological power in the form of Torah and temple. But there is a third aspect involved in interaction about place, what Lefebvre called "spaces of representation," and that we have spoken of as the "imagination of place." This is also a creative impulse, often from the "underside" of society, one that represents a subversive form of power. It was this sort of power that Jesus represented.

HEROD ANTIPAS AND THE URBANIZATION OF GALILEE

The perspective in this section is summed up in a quotation from David Harvey: "Command over space is a fundamental and all pervasive source of social power in and over everyday life."[12] We shall start with the changes in these forms of domination and control of space that Herod Antipas introduced. The city foundations of Herod Antipas can be viewed against the background of the large-scale building programs of his father, Herod the Great. Of Herod it has been said that he "shaped the world in which early Christianity began."[13] He founded cities, such as Caesarea Maritima, built roads, harbors, aqueducts, and a series of fortifications and palaces. In Jerusalem his most important and significant project was the new temple. The temple in particular signified the importance of his building programs, which can be summed up by a headline: "Controlling Spaces: Creating Places."[14] By creating new places, Herod clearly showed that he controlled space in Palestine; he put up visible markers of power, benevolence, and planning. Building roads, harbors, aqueducts, and other forms of infrastructure created possibilities of travel, commerce, and social interaction, and served as a constant reminder of whose power lay behind their establishment. At the same time, these structures facilitated exploitation of resources on a larger scale, and moved control and ownership from small-scale farming and fishing to the wealthy elite. By the goodwill of the Romans, Herod ruled as a king over a large area, with a large tax base and huge personal income.

Herod Antipas had to resign himself to work on a much smaller scale, with only Galilee as his territory, and with a small income base. But within these confinements, he followed the example of his father. The best-documented example of how Antipas created places, and thereby expanded control over spaces, is the way in which he developed Sepphoris and made it into his capital.[15] This town was not an example of organic growth; it became a planned city. It was modeled after a typical Roman city in terms of structure and important buildings. It was obvious that these structures were not just practical matters, but that they conveyed meaning: they represented the idea of a Roman city.[16]

If we try to read the city plan and structures of Sepphoris as a text, what do they say? First of all, they speak a Roman language of order and control. The city plan itself, with the *cardo* and the *decumanus* intersecting, included the inhabitants in a structure that was identified as Roman. The common source of water, brought to Sepphoris at great cost in labor and construction, was one of the most important factors of city life that set it apart from rural areas.[17] Administrative buildings signaled that here was a seat of power that was beyond the city itself. And a large number of shops were signs of a commercialization of space, of a marketization of the economy. The beneficiaries of that economy lived in the city; many large houses showed that there was here an accumulation of wealth. One aspect of that was that while peasants in villages had a common pool for ritual purifications, many of the inhabitants in Sepphoris had private *miqva'ot* in their houses. These also indicated that the inhabitants were observant Jews.

Sepphoris was planned as an administrative center for Galilee, so what we could read about power and control from the text of the city itself had repercussions in a larger area of Galilee.[18] The establishment of Sepphoris as an administrative center was an attempt by Herod Antipas to introduce an economic model that built on Hellenistic presuppositions. In this system a social elite dominated in economic affairs and justified their activities by means of an extension of patron-client relations. Urban centers were perceived as mediators of distant power and control over a region. In the case of Sepphoris, it represented an economic structure that brought changes in the lives of Galilean peasants, and represented a different mentality and ethos. Moreover, this practice was legitimated through an ideology based on Hellenistic ideals.

The establishing of Sepphoris and later the foundation of Tiberias were visual representations of this control of local space. They also represented an ideological representation of space that would justify this form of change. With its name, Tiberias signaled the Roman authority over Galilee. The old kinship-oriented family economy of subsistence farming, which was a traditional part of life on the land, was challenged by a political economy.[19] Herod Antipas introduced a market economy that furthered the domination and control of space by the elite. It represented a pressure on the types of use of space by the households and kinship groups that were based on internal solidarity. This is not to say that nobody in the villages could benefit from this new economic system. It has been proved, for instance, that much of the production of pottery in Galilee took place in villages not far from Sepphoris. Thus, there must have been a great deal of trade between these villages and Sepphoris.[20] However, this does not take away the unequal power structure between the city as the base for Herod Antipas and the local elite, on the one hand, and the villages on the other.[21] Moreover, it is not unusual that some individuals or some groups may benefit from socioeconomic changes, but most important are the overall effects on the larger part of the population.

So what was the effect on the households and villages, and their "appropriation and use of space" on a local level? Galilee had a traditional peasant population that worked hard for a living under many differing rules over the centuries before Jesus. They had been under Persian, Seleucid, than Hasmonean, and finally Herod's rule, followed by his son, Herod Antipas. New rulers in themselves did not basically change the life of the peasants; it was based on kinship structure and their work on the land. The household working the land, or on a fishing boat on the Sea of Galilee, was the basic social unit. Theirs was a subsistence economy; the margins between a balance or a small surplus and a loss with a lack of resources were small.[22] At least one fifth of the crop had to be saved for next year's seed. Then there were taxes, land taxes on the harvest, poll tax on house members, and in all likelihood also tithes to the temple.[23] It is also difficult to estimate the type of land ownership that existed in Galilee, whether most was large estate land, partly run by tenant farmers, or whether there were also a substantial number of landholders. But the difference in living might not be so great one way or the other, with most peasant households working hard for their upkeep. The landless day laborer had an even more difficult situation.

During the reigns of Herod the Great and Herod Antipas the situation for the peasant household deteriorated. Herod the Great caused protests with his taxation, while the period of Herod Antipas appears to have been quieter. But the changes he introduced were far-reaching, working to establish a Greco-Roman-style economy, which favored cities and the elite. Many peasants became landless through the expansion of great estates and through the marketization of the economy. The area around Tiberias provides an example of this type of economic change that we have described, and it happened before the time of Antipas. It is possible that the development of a "fishing industry" in the area was part of Hasmonaean or Herod the Great's initiatives. The result of this was a modernization process in fishing, with the establishment of a fishing industry and marketization.[24] This industry, including fishing by boat, was regulated and taxed, and controlled by the elite. It is likely that this development had the same effect as in agriculture, namely, that more people worked without any ownership or security.

The economic changes in this period described above affected the viability of peasant households as social groups. As the household lost control over the space it needed to support itself, the social cohesion of the group itself was threatened. Moreover, the old solidarity network of the larger kinship group was not able to function any longer, due to a lack of resources all around. Thus, the ability to keep the household and family united was put in doubt. Probably the first thing to happen was that younger sons left the household. The result of this social contraction of the household group was also that the father of the household was losing authority, since he could no longer protect the livelihood of his family. The values of the traditional society were disintegrating, the authority structures of the household and village could not be sustained, and the ancient norms of support and solidarity could not be maintained.

JESUS AND CONFLICTS IN HOUSEHOLDS AND VILLAGES

It is against this background that we must try to place Jesus and his movement. Richard Horsley, especially, has argued that Jesus' primary purpose was the renewal of village life according to the traditional values that were threatened by outside forces.[25] It is valuable that Horsley sees Jesus in the context of Galilean village society, and not just engaged in conflicts over religious issues, but I think his thesis is questionable. A break with the household represented also a break with local authority and customs. Jesus' conflicts in the villages should be seen in terms of conflict over localized identity and read in light of studies of local communities as places of identity.[26] Households and villages typically had a localized identity that was bound to a place, which was defined vis-à-vis other places. Jesus provoked by breaking with boundaries, and thereby establishing *a different relationship between identity and place.*

Breaks with Household and Family

Since house and household was the central locality for the identity of Galilean peasants, Jesus' break with his own family and his call to followers to do the same take on a much more significant role than leaving home does in a modern, individualistic society. It represented a dislocation at the single most important point for identity and relocation in a liminal situation. The gospel narratives give an indication of how significant this break on the part of Jesus was. The primary challenge from Jesus was directed explicitly at the household and family institution itself.[27] With his call to abandon everything, Jesus challenged kinship values. With his ideal of a community based on love and forgiveness, he criticized the patriarchal family structure. He was disruptive of existing family practice while he applied family imagery and values to the new social group that gathered around him. This might be a message that resonated with the really destitute, but his words were addressed not to those, but to people who owned land and had possessions.[28]

In a situation in which the values and social viability of the traditional household were threatened by the new economy of Herod Antipas, Jesus must have appeared to join forces with those who put the household at risk. Most calls to leave household were to leave the paternal household, and the primary reason for conflicts with households was this break with tradition, obligations, and loyalties to family and in particular the father. At stake was, therefore, the social organization of home space, and Jesus signaled a new spatial practice. The asceticism of

Jesus was first of all a rejection of the household and the authority of the father, and was not based primarily on a discussion of the dangers of sexuality. Both from his own sayings and from criticism directed against him, we must draw the conclusion that Jesus placed himself outside the household structure: he had no place, that is, not only no house, but he also rejected his original household as a social structure. In consequence, he had no honor, or recognition, in his own home place—that is, in household as well as village community. He went beyond boundaries of acceptable behavior and role expectations; note the accusations that he was a eunuch and a glutton and drunkard. Thus, he established an identity that was no longer identified with these particular places.

The same appears to be true of at least some of his followers. The praxis of Jesus appears to have been to gather young men, called out from their households, and marginal women, around him. With its diversity of members this group represented a "queering," so to speak, of the traditional family, even more so in its ideological representations. It is possible that he spoke of this group as his "brothers and sisters," that is, in terms of a fictive kinship group. It is worth noticing that he did not speak of himself as "father" for this group, he was a "brother" among them. The authority of the father was not applied to anybody in the group, so in terms of household it was an incomplete group.

But even if the group was formed on the basis of leaving the primary place of identity, it appears that Jesus gave it a new, localized identity. He spoke of God as Father, that is, as father of a household, in which the followers of Jesus were the children. When Jesus spoke of God as Father, and thereby created an image of a household with his followers as children, this was an "imagined place." But it was also a way to interpret their experiences of being supported by sympathizers, sedentary "followers" of Jesus. In this way the experiences of social relations in specific locations were located in the imagined place of the household of God. As a symbolic place this household was unique in that Jesus spoke of the father-son relationship primarily in terms of the father relationship to his sons (and daughters), and not of their obligations toward the father. Jesus emphasized the responsibilities of the father for providing and caring for his sons and daughters. We may say that Jesus presented an invisible but real household as substitution for the old ones that his followers had left.

Break with the Village Community

Another set of conflicts was with the larger group, the village community. In many studies Jesus' conflicts in local communities have been viewed in terms of conflicts over the law, exemplified by controversies in synagogues. The synagogues were regarded as specifically religious institutions. But this view has come up for revision. The important role of the village community throws light on the narratives about Jesus' conflicts with the local synagogues. Recent studies have shown that most synagogue buildings excavated in Galilee are much later than first century C.E.,[29] and that the influence of Pharisees and rabbis was also a later phenomenon.[30] Our perceptions of the synagogues mentioned in the gospel narratives have been colored by later traditions. In Galilee at the time of Jesus, synagogues most likely were gathering places for the village, covering a broad range of communal affairs and dominated by local community leaders.[31] At least some of the narratives about Jesus in synagogues reflect their position as localities for village identity, and the center of the conflicts seems to be that Jesus was perceived as a challenge to fundamental values in the community. And these values were not an abstract law—they were embedded in the role of tradition, in the authority of the elders, and in the honor of the community. This is highlighted in the narrative of the conflict in the synagogue in Nazareth (Mark 3:1–6; Matt. 13:53–58; Luke 4:22–30): Jesus was perceived as going beyond the boundaries of proper behavior, as overextending himself and not keeping his place as the son of Joseph, and whose brothers and sisters were still part of the local village. As a result, Jesus' identity was no longer located in his home village.

Entering into Liminal Spaces

There seem to be traces of this break with local village communities in the gospel narratives. Midway in all the synoptic gospels the synagogue assembly disappears from sight as location for the activities of Jesus.[32] There is a change in place; Jesus moves his activities to other, less formalized and structured, places: the agora in towns, the seashore, the lake, the open road, mountains, and the wilderness. In comparison with the synagogue as the organized structure of the community, most of these other places are liminal, outside the structures. This change in place is followed also by a change in the constitution of the group. Instead of the local community based in the village, with its formal and informal leadership structures, we read about a small, more or less stable group of disciples and changing groups of followers. If the gospel narratives are to be trusted in terms of types of followers, some appear to have been already in a marginal position: sick, "sinners," tax collectors; others were people who had chosen a liminal position to follow Jesus. It appears to be a combination of people in marginal and liminal positions, typical of groups at the *communitas* stage of group formation.[33] Jesus' activities here were not so much dislocation from households as relocating people in new social bodies, maybe more in terms of sporadic group formations than into permanent bodies. Thus, these groups may have been more liminal, lasting for a while before people returned to their previous life in the villages.

Beyond the Boundaries of Galilee

This pattern of breaking with social and spatial boundaries inside Galilee appears to correspond with a crossing of boundaries to other regions. It is reported in several instances that Jesus traveled across boundaries from the lake region. This was, for example, to the Decapolis cities, Tyre and Sidon and their hinterlands, and the area toward Caesarea Philippi.[34] There may be a correspondence between the liminality of some of these areas in contrast to the Jewish areas in Galilee,[35] and the social liminality of the people attracted to Jesus.

JESUS' GALILEE: GOD'S HOUSEHOLD AS KINGDOM

In relation to the pressures that peasant households and villages in Galilee experienced, Jesus seems to have represented a strategy that created conflict and resistance from the local village communities. Jesus took followers away from their households, and therefore he must have seemed to side with forces that disrupted household and village life. But his role must have been ambiguous, because he also engaged in conflicts with the elite and its command over space and people's lives. That is, he entered into the political realm. It is obvious that Jesus did not represent the same type of power as Herod Antipas over Galilee. He did not control material practices, nor did he represent an ideology that legitimated these practices.

The differences in power between him and the elite meant that what was left to Jesus was mostly "imagined places." This perspective of "imagined places" is significant for the study of a nonelite relation to and shaping of space—it gives the nonelite an active role in shaping its own place.[36] These "imagined places" were created through Jesus' exorcisms, healings, and common meals,[37] but also through his speeches and teaching and parables. Their content could be construed as imaginations about the kingdom and ways to organize the world under God that were critical of the present power. By contrasting the present "kingdom" under Herod Antipas with "the kingdom of God," he defined Galilee differently.

Exorcisms and the Land

Material from the gospel tradition indicates that the exorcisms of Jesus played a role in the politics of Galilee. Exorcisms represented an expression of power from outside the established form of political and ideological power. Moreover, exorcisms identified forces of domination over the land, for instance, in the claim that Jesus' exorcisms showed that the land belonged to God, and not to Satan (Q 11:20). But this form of power apparently was unsettling to "ordered" society. Thus, the early Jesus tradition has it that his exorcisms were the reason for Herod Antipas's interest in Jesus, and that Jesus was regarded as a potential danger for Antipas (Mark 6:13–14). The example of John the Baptist showed that a popular preacher, who was regarded by many people as speaking with a voice from God, could be a dangerous force and somebody with whom the ruler had to reckon. So it seems that Herod Antipas was sufficiently interested in Jesus to want to detain him, and this reaction was threatening enough for Jesus to leave Galilee and to withdraw into Philip's territory.[38] Thus, it may be that the major conflict with leaders of Galilean society was with Herod Antipas; not with "religious" leaders, and that the reason was Jesus' exorcisms and powers that attracted crowds. Apparently, Jesus did not seek this confrontation, but rather moved away, although Luke 13:32–33 shows a defiant attitude. Therefore, it seems most appropriate to characterize Jesus' movement as "prepolitical," in that it did not challenge Antipas directly.

Direct Protest against Antipas—and His Cities?

But did he challenge Antipas indirectly, in more subtle ways of resistance to his politics? One reason to ask this question is that scholars have for a long time discussed why the two towns that Antipas rebuilt or founded, Sepphoris and Tiberias, are not mentioned in the gospel.[39] Since distances in Galilee were small, and since Jesus journeyed in the area, it is hard to imagine that he did not visit them.[40] Jesus grew up in Nazareth, an hour's walk from Sepphoris, and Tiberias was just a short distance from Capernaum. But in the narratives of Jesus' public activities none of the gospels mention these two towns, or any visit by Jesus there. This could, of course, be a result of sparse information, that reports of Jesus' visits there have not been preserved, and that nothing of importance happened that made these visits memorable. But it could also be that the lack of reports means that Jesus avoided these towns. Again, such avoidance could have several reasons—it might be as a protest against Herod Antipas and his economic rule, and a deliberate choice of villages as a basis of operation. Silence about them in the Jesus narratives is strange. It may be part of the same resistance toward towns by the village population that is also reflected in Josephus's writings. For instance, as a reaction to roads that opened for commerce and exploitation, an example of resistive adaptation from villagers would be to avoid cities.[41] This cannot be documented, of course, but it is plausible enough so that is has been suggested that Jesus chose this strategy vis-à-vis Sepphoris and Tiberias.

Parables as Protest

There is no evidence that can decide beyond doubt whether Jesus actually visited these cities or not. I suggest, therefore, that we should look elsewhere for a response to the underlying issue—his relations to the policies of Herod Antipas—and that Jesus' sayings, in particular his parables, are the best sources. The power of rhetoric was an important form of power among a nonliterary population. And from contemporary reports it appears that Jesus was a master of words. Many of his sayings were of a wisdom type, some similar to those found among Cynic wandering philosophers, but many more explicitly radical and countercultural. His parables seem to have represented an innovation in terms of vivid imagery compared to Jewish parables.[42]

Many of the parables of Jesus reflect the way in which life was localized: they start with the relation to house and household, with the father at the center, and move toward the village and finally to the city and that which is far away.[43] The parables of the kingdom do not give names of villages or towns, and they speak in general terms. Therefore, we shall not expect to find direct references to specific towns or persons. But we may ask about the way in which village life is presented, whether Jesus understood the space of the village population as a space under domination and control.[44] Although Sepphoris and Tiberias are not mentioned in Jesus' sayings, the effects of the economic policy that they represented are made visible, in particular in Jesus' parables.

We can surmise this criticism in many of Jesus' parables, for instance, in the contrast between "rich" and "poor" (Luke 16:19–31) or the relations between patron and clients (Luke 16:1–9; Matt. 20:1–15). A number of parables in the context of a peasant society stand within an aristocratic domination system.[45] The function of the parables is to start a reflection over the domination and exploitation that are found in these parables. But their point of view is different from that of the elite perspective that justified control and domination. Instead the parables subvert this discourse, as in the parable of the dishonest steward (Luke 16:1–9).[46] Although this parable is difficult to interpret, and the servant is a morally ambiguous character, the outcome is hopeful for the peasants. Other parables of the kingdom are more straightforward in the way in which they break with the "old" organization of space (see, e.g., Luke 14:7–24). They are imagined places; they draw up localities with new social structures, freed from domination. They show how people are liberated to act in space in a new way, for instance, as honored guests inside the house instead of being beggars at the outside.

A New Spatial Ordering—an Economy of the Kingdom

We may speak of these parables as examples of the "economy of the kingdom," with the term economy in the old meaning of "householding" (*oikonomia*), in contrast to the peasants' experiences of the political economy of Galilee. The relations between the elite and the peasant population can be understood in terms of the system of reciprocities, which take different forms: negative, balanced, and generalized.[47] Negative reciprocity is characterized by taking away without giving anything in return; that was typical of unequal relationships with a great distance between the powerful and the peasants and the poor. Balanced reciprocity, that of expecting a return quickly, characterizes relationships between groups or persons on an equal level (Luke 14:12–14). Generalized reciprocity, on the other hand, is typical of the exchange between persons in a close relationship, especially within the household. The experiences that the Galilean peasants had of negative reciprocity, based on the ideology of Hellenistic kingdoms, were confronted with a different ideal: the generalized reciprocity ("pure gift") of the household relations. Therefore, in Jesus' criticism of the relations within Galilee as kingdom, his alternative was based on the ideal exchanges from a different place, from the *household.*

The parables have parallels in other parts of the Jesus material, in certain sayings that also encourage a change in economic and social relations. For instance, in Q 6:32–36, Jesus urges a transformation from reciprocal relationship to the pure gift, and the ultimate example of this pure gift is the mercy of "your Father"

(Q 6:36). Again, Jesus' argumentation ends in the image of household relations between God as father and children. Behind the exhortation to change social and economic behavior, therefore, lies a model of spatial relations: from distant or "balanced" relations, to relations that are very close and characterized by sharing without expecting a return.

Like everybody else among the peasants in Palestine and Galilee of his time, Jesus lived within the two axes of human and social life made up of household and politics, in shorthand, *kingdom*. The central importance of household and kingdom as the two foci and institutions of human life is confirmed through Jesus' sayings and activities, in a way that at the same time questions their authority and sets up alternatives. There can be no doubt that the kingdom of God was the driving force in Jesus' life, and that this spatial metaphor was, so to speak, the central code for Jesus in his activity. I use the term code, because it is rarely explained, but instead used to interpret the rule of God in spatial dimensions. Jesus speaks of the kingdom of God not in imperial pictures, but with images from households, with God as a housefather. But this is not a way to "scale down" the ambitions of Jesus' proclamations of the kingdom. It is to make the place of the household, with generalized reciprocity as the form of householding, to be the model for politics. It represents a turning away from domination and control of place, as typical of politics over a place, into appropriation and use of place.

Again it is God's household as kingdom that is Jesus' ideal, not just for the households in Galilee, but also for politics, for kingdom. "Kingdom" in Jesus' parables is not a fourth spatial category, in addition to house, village, and city, but an imagined place that relates to and challenges the spatial structure of these other places by establishing an alternative structure. The image of the household of God remains the central picture that Jesus employs as alternative to the households that he and his followers had left. In Jesus' vision of "imagined place" in Galilee, the two spatial structures, the household and the kingdom, meet in the image of the household of God.

Abbreviations

AB	Anchor Bible
ABD	*Anchor Bible Dictionary.* Edited by D. N. Freedman. 6 vols. New York 1992.
ALGHJ	Arbeiten zur Literatur und Geschichte des hellenistischen Judentums
ANRW	*Aufstieg und Niedergang der römischen Welt.: Geschichte und Kultur Roms im Spiegel der neueren Forschung.* Edited by H. Temporini and W. Haase. Berlin, 1972–
ATANT	Abhandlungen zur Theologie des alten und Neuen Testaments
BA	*Biblical Archaeologist*
BASOR	*Bulletin of the American Schools of Oriental Research*
BETL	Bibliotheca Ephemeridum Theologicarum Lovaniensium
BTB	*Biblical Theological Bulletin*
CBQ	*Catholic Biblical Quarterly*
CCSL	Corpus Christianorum: Series latina. Turnhout, 1953
EKKNT	Evangelish-katholischer Kommentar zum Neuen Testament
FRLANT	Forschungen zur Religion und Literatur des Alten und Neuen Testaments
GCS	Die griechische christliche Schriftsteller der ersten Jahrhunderte
HTR	*Harvard Theological Review*
JAAR	*Journal of the American Academy of Religion*
JECS	*Journal of Early Christian Studies*
JBL	*Journal of Biblical Literature*
JSJ	*Journal for the Study of Judaism*
JSNT	*Journal for the Study of the New Testament*
JSNTSup	Journal for the Study of the New Testament Supplement Series
JSOTSup	Journal for the Study of the Old Testament Supplement Series
JTS	*Journal of Theological Studies*
NovTSup	Novum Testamentum Supplements
NTS	*New Testament Studies*
NTTS	New Testament Tools and Studies

P.Oxy.	*The Oxyrhynchus Papyri.* Published by the Egypt Exploration Society in Graeco-Roman Memoirs. London.
RAC	*Reallexikon für Antike und Christentum.* Edited by T. Kluser et al. Stuttgart, 1950–
RB	*Révue Biblique*
SBLMS	Society of Biblical Literature Monograph Series
SBS	Stuttgarter Bibelstudien
SC	Sources chrétiennes. Paris: Cerf. 1943–
SNTSMS	Society for New Testament Studies Monograph Series
ST	*Studia Theologica*
TDNT	*Theological Dictionary of the New Testament.* Edited by G. Kittel and G. Friedrich. Translated by G. W. Bromiley. 10 vols. Grand Rapids, 1964–1976.
TJT	*Toronto Journal of Theology*
WMANT	Wissenschaftliche Monographien zum Alten und Neuen Testament
WUNT	Wissenschaftliche Untersuchungen zum Neuen Testament
ZNW	*Zeitschrift für die neutestamentliche Wissenschaft*

Notes

Chapter 1

1. See E. P. Sanders (*Jesus and Judaism* [Philadelphia: Fortress, 1985], 61–76), who starts with placing Jesus in the temple and uses the temple episode, Mark 11:15–18, as a key to explain Jesus' death.
2. See several studies on the relation between Galilee and Jerusalem, a major topic as it is presented in the gospels.
3. In recent scholarship, see especially Sanders, *Jesus and Judaism*, as well as many Jewish studies of Jesus; H. Moxnes, "Jesus the Jew: Dilemmas of Interpretation," in *Fair Play: Diversity and Conflicts in Early Christianity; Essays in Honour of Heikki Räisänen* (ed. I. Dunderberg, C. Tuckett, and K. Syreeni; NovTSup 103; Leiden: Brill, 2002), 83–103.
4. See, e.g., *Readings from This Place*, vol. 1, *Social Location and Biblical Interpretation in the United States*; vol. 2, *Social Location and Biblical Interpretation in Global Perspective* (ed. Fernando F. Segovia and Mary Ann Tolbert; Minneapolis: Fortress, 1995).
5. See S. Freyne, "Town and Country Once More: The Case of Roman Galilee," in his *Galilee and Gospel* (WUNT 125; Tübingen: Mohr Siebeck, 2000), 60–62. Freyne relates how his experiences from the rural West Ireland of his youth informed his understanding of the situation of Galilee under Roman domination in the first century.
6. See as an example of poignant criticism of Western historical Jesus studies, Pui-Lan Kwok, "On Color-Coding Jesus: An Interview with Pui-Lan Kwok," in *The Post-Colonial Bible* (ed. R. S. Sugirtharajah; Sheffield: Sheffield Academic Press, 1998), 161–80.
7. See especially Elisabeth Schüssler Fiorenza, *Jesus and the Politics of Interpretation* (New York: Continuum, 2000).
8. See D. Georgi,"The Interest in Life of Jesus Theology as a Paradigm for the Social History of Biblical Criticism," *HTR* 85 (1992): 51–83; another sign is the Consultation on "Social History of Biblical Scholarship" in the Society of Biblical Literature.
9. H. Moxnes, "Jesus from Galilee in an Age of Nationalism," in *Discovering Jesus in Our Place: Contextual Christologies in a Globalised Age* (ed. S. Stålsett; Madras: ISPCK, forthcoming).
10. See L. W. Hurtado, "A Taxonomy of Recent Historical-Jesus Work," in *Whose Historical Jesus* (ed. W. E. Arnal and M. Desjardins; Studies in Christianity and Judaism 7; Waterloo, Ont.: Wilfred Laurier University Press, 1997), 272–95.
11. An example of such titles is John D. Crossan's book, *The Historical Jesus: The Life of a Mediterranean Jewish Peasant* (San Francisco: Harper, 1991). The sub-

title suggests that Crossan uses models from peasant studies and the subcategory of anthropology that is concerned with the Mediterranean as a distinct cultural area. The title of John P. Meier, *A Marginal Jew: Rethinking the Historical Jesus*, vols. 1 and 2 (New York: Doubleday, 1991–94), suggests that he uses a model from sociological studies of social groups and marginality; but as a matter of fact, Meier is explicitly critical of the social sciences, so the title seems more designed to catch attention than to tell anything about the content of the book.

12. See David M. Halperin, *Saint=Foucault: Towards a Gay Hagiography* (New York: Oxford University Press, 1995), 62–66.

13. Lee Edelman, *Homographesis: Essays in Gay Literature and Cultural Theory* (New York: Routledge, 1994), 114.

14. See, e.g., Rom. 6:17–22; 7:5–6; 11:30; Gal. 4:8–9.

15. Edward S. Casey, *The Fate of Place* (Berkeley: University of California Press, 1998), x.

16. David Harvey, *The Condition of Postmodernity* (Oxford: Blackwell, 1989).

17. J. Appleby, L. Hunt, and M. Jacob, *Telling the Truth about History* (New York: Norton, 1994), 52–90.

18. Edward S. Casey, *Getting Back into Place: Toward a Renewed Understanding of the Place-world* (Bloomington: Indiana University Press, 1993); and Casey, *Fate of Place.*

19. Casey, *Fate of Place*, 77.

20. Ibid., xii.

21. Ibid., 201.

22. Appleby, Hunt, and Jacob, *Telling the Truth*, 55.

23. Harvey, *Condition of Postmodernity*, 205.

24. Doreen Massey, *Space, Place and Gender* (Cambridge: Polity Press, 1994), 6–7.

25. Appleby, Hunt, and Jacob, *Telling the Truth.*

26. Marc Auge, *Non-places: Introduction to an Anthropology of Supermodernity* (London: Verso, 1995), 77–78.

27. Harvey, *Condition of Postmodernity*, 302.

28. Massey, *Space, Place and Gender*, 4–5.

29. Ibid., 5.

30. Halvor Moxnes, "The Historical Jesus: From Master Narrative to Cultural Context," *BTB* 28 (1999): 135–49.

31. Ernest Renan, *Vie de Jésus* (Paris: Michel Levy Frères, 1863).

32. F. Schleiermacher, *The Life of Jesus* (ed. and with introd. by J. C. Verheyden; Philadelphia: Fortress, 1975), 170–75.

33. William David Davies, *The Gospel and the Land: Early Christianity and Jewish Territorial Doctrine* (Berkeley: University of California Press, 1974). See also his *The Territorial Dimension of Judaism* (Minneapolis: Fortress, 1991), which contains responses to his book from a symposium in which Jewish scholars participated.

34. Günther Bornkamm, *Jesus of Nazareth* (New York: Harper & Row, 1960). Eng. trans. from German original, 1956.

35. Ibid., 55.

36. Ibid.

37. Ibid., 57.

38. One typical example, although from a later period, is a collection of essays edited by James H. Charlesworth, *Jesus' Jewishness: Exploring the Place of Jesus within Early Judaism* (New York: Crossroad, 1991). The subtitle of the book starts with *Exploring the Place of Jesus*, but it turns out that it was not *place* in terms of a specific, local place that was in the mind of the contributors, but abstract categories like "Judaism" and "Jewishness," in contrast to other abstract categories like "Christianity" and "Christian."

39. See, for instance, Jon Sobrino, *Jesus the Liberator: A Historical-Theological Reading of Jesus of Nazareth* (Maryknoll: Orbis, 1993).
40. Massey, *Space, Place and Gender*, 5.
41. Ibid., 168–69.
42. Harvey, *Condition of Postmodernity*, 226.
43. Still a different distinction is made by Linda McDowell in "Spatializing Feminism," in *Body Space: Destabilizing Geographies of Gender and Sexuality* (ed. Nancy Duncan; London and New York: Routledge, 1996), 31–32. She distinguishes between "space as relational and place as a location," that is, place has more of a permanence and solidity, and space consists of a set of places.
44. Henri Lefebvre, *The Production of Space* (Oxford: Blackwell, 1991).
45. In order to apply Harvey's model to Palestine in first century C.E., we need to know the structures and systems of that particular society. I will draw on K. C. Hanson and Douglas E. Oakman (*Palestine in the Time of Jesus: Social Structures and Social Conflicts* [Minneapolis: Fortress, 1998]), who explain in an exemplary fashion the social forms and the sources of power in Palestine at the time of Jesus, based on kinship, political patronage, and political economy and religion.
46. Harvey, *Condition of Postmodernity*, 219.
47. Ibid., 222.
48. Lefebvre, *Production of Space*, 32–33.
49. Harvey, *Condition of Postmodernity*, 218–19.
50. Lefebvre, *Production of Space*, 33.
51. Pamela Shurmer-Smith and Kevin Hannam, *Worlds of Desire, Realms of Power: A Cultural Geography* (London: Edward Arnold, 1994), 125–39.
52. Sanders, *Jesus and Judaism*; Geza Vermes, *Jesus the Jew* (London: Collins, 1973).
53. Tim Cresswell, *In Place, out of Place: Geography, Ideology, and Transgression* (Minneapolis: University of Minnesota Press, 1996).
54. Ibid., 14.
55. Ibid., 18.
56. Ibid., 8.
57. Massey, *Space, Place and Gender*, 5.
58. Ibid., 6–10.
59. Ibid., 120–22.
60. In his classic article on "The Problem of the Historical Jesus," from 1953 (now reprinted in N. A. Dahl, *Jesus the Christ* [ed. D. H. Juel; Minneapolis: Fortress, 1991], 97), N. A. Dahl claimed that the best method for the historical Jesus research was to combine the critically assured minimum with the maximum of tradition.
61. John S. Kloppenborg Verbin, "Discursive Practices in the Sayings Gospel Q and the Quest of the Historical Jesus," in *The Sayings Source Q and the Historical Jesus* (ed. A. Lindemann, BETL 158; Leuven: Leuven University Press, 2001), 155: "Thus our 'canon' of documents now expands to include Q, Mark, Matthew, Luke and Thomas, with Q, Mark, and Thomas occupying position of privilege. Of course not *all* of Q, Mark, and Thomas, but those portions which are not obviously the product of redaction and, in the case of Thomas, which are apparently independent of the Synoptics."
62. See the suggestion by John S. Kloppenborg ("City and Wasteland: Narrative World and the Beginning of the Sayings Gospel [Q]," *Semeia* 52 [1990]: 145–60) that the beginning of the Q gospel establishes a sacred map built around the contrast between the periphery and the city as the center.
63. Peter Richardson, "First Century Houses and Q's Setting," in *Christology, Controversy and Community: New Testament Essays in Honour of David R. Catchpole* (ed. D. Horrell and Chr. M. Tuckett; Leiden: Brill, 2000), 70.

64. Bernard Brandon Scott, *Hear Then the Parable: A Commentary on the Parables of Jesus* (Minneapolis: Fortress, 1989).
65. There is a large overlap between the sayings material in Q, the *Gospel of Thomas* and Mark; e.g., are there 46 sayings parallels between the *Gospel of Thomas* and Q, and 27 parallels in sayings and parables between the *Gospel of Thomas* and Mark (see Helmut Köster, *Ancient Christian Gospels* [Philadelphia: Trinity Press, 1990], 87–88, 107–8). And many of these sayings belong to the earliest tradition material, ibid., 95, 112. Stephen J. Patterson, in *The Gospel of Thomas and Jesus* (Sonoma, Calif.: Polebridge, 1993), 231–41, finds a common ground between the sayings tradition in the synoptic gospels and in the *Gospel of Thomas* in three areas: wisdom sayings, sayings that are unconventional and express social radicalism, and parables. He holds that "it is this common ground that stands the best chance of holding a more or less direct connection to the preaching of Jesus himself" (231). B.T. Viviano, in "The Historical Jesus in the Doubly Attested Sayings: An Experiment," *RB* 103 (1996): 367–410, argues that the overlap between Mark and Q provides the securest basis for a knowledge of the historical Jesus.
66. See Kloppenborg Verbin, *Discursive Practices*; and for Q and Mark, see Gerd Theissen and A. Merz, *The Historical Jesus: A Comprehensive Guide* (London: SCM, 1998), 27, 29; on Q1, Dale C. Allison, *The Jesus Tradition in Q* (Harrisburg, Pa.: Trinity Press International, 1997), 60–62.
67. E.g., Köster, *Ancient Christian Gospels,* 287–88; the opposite position, that Mark is dependent on Q, is argued, e.g., by H. T. Fleddermann, *Mark and Q: A Study of the Overlap Texts* (BETL 122, Leuven: Leuven University Press, 1995).
68. The view that the core material in the *Gospel of Thomas* is very old, with many similarities to Q and independent of the synoptic tradition, was first argued by J. T. Robinson and H. Köster in *Trajectories through Early Christianity* (Philadelphia: Fortress, 1971) and has been accepted by many, mostly American scholars. For recent presentations of this position, see Köster, *Ancient Christian Gospels,* 75–128; Patterson, *Gospel of Thomas and Jesus,* 17–93. For the contrary position, that the *Gospel of Thomas* is wholly dependent on the synoptic tradition and therefore late, see Meier, *Marginal Jew* 1:124–39; and James H. Charlesworth and Craig A. Evans, "Jesus in the Agrapha and Apocryphal Gospels," in *Studying the Historical Jesus* (ed. B. Chilton and C. A. Evans; NTTS 19; Leiden: Brill, 1994), 496–503. See the careful evaluation of the various positions in the discussion of the relationship between *Gospel of Thomas* and the synoptic gospels in Jens Schröter, *Erinnerung an Jesu Worte: Studien zur Rezeption der Logionüberlieferung in Markus, Q und Thomas* (WMANT 76, Neukirchen-Vluyn: Neukirchener, 1997), 122–40. Schröter is not convinced that the core of the *Gospel of Thomas* is as old as Köster and Robinson, for example, argue; he finds, however, that it cannot be explained as dependent on the synoptic tradition, but holds its own place within the development of early Christianity.
69. Allison, *The Jesus Tradition in Q,* 61: "Q1 remains such a good source for the historical Jesus not only because it remembered his words, adding little to them, but because it preserved something of its original context. Most of the sayings in Q were no doubt spoken by Jesus not to the public at large but to the small circle that shared his missionary task. But Q 1 was addressed to a very similar group, that is, itinerant Christian missionaries."
70. For Q, I follow the text of J. M.Robinson, P. Hoffmann, and J. S. Kloppenborg, *The Critical Edition of Q* (Hermeneia; Minneapolis: Fortress, 2000). However, I do not follow their translations "son of humanity," but prefer "son of man" or "reign of God," but prefer "kingdom of God," to retain the spatial dimension. For the *Gospel of Thomas* I follow the text and translation of J. M. Robinson, *The Nag Hammadi Library in English* 3, revised (Leiden: Brill, 1988).

71. R. H. Lightfoot, *Locality and Doctrine in the Gospels* (New York and London: Harper, 1938).

72. Elisabeth Struthers Malbon, *Narrative Space and Mythic Meaning in Mark* (Sheffield: Sheffield Academic Press, 1991).

73. See R. Kieffer, *Le monde symbolique de Saint Jean* (Paris: Cerf, 1989), 11–32.

74. See H. Moxnes, "The Construction of Galilee as a Place for the Historical Jesus," *Biblical Theology Bulletin* 31 (2001): 26–37, 64–77.

75. The literature is enormous; see some examples: S. Freyne, *Galilee, Jesus and the Gospels* (Dublin: Gill and MacMillan, 1988); Freyne, *Galilee and Gospel*. Especially on the use of archaeology of Galilee and Jesus studies, see Eric M. Meyers, "Jesus and His Galilean Context," *Archaeology and the Galilee* (ed. Douglas R. Edwards and C. Thomas McCollough; South Florida Studies in the History of Judaism 143; Atlanta: Scholars Press, 1997), 57–66; Jonathan L. Reed, *Archaeology and the Galilean Jesus* (Harrisburg, Pa.: Trinity Press International, 2000). E. P. Sanders is skeptical of the notion that Galilee provides a specific context for Jesus, distinct from the rest of a Jewish environment in Palestine, see, e.g., his "Jesus in Historical Context," *Theology Today* 50 (1993): 429–48; and "Jesus' Galilee," in *Fair Play: Diversity and Conflicts in Early Christianity: Essays in Honour of Heikki Räisänen* (ed. I. Dunderberg, C. Tuckett, and K. Syreeni; NovTSup 103; Leiden: Brill, 2002), 3–41.

76. Sean Freyne, *Galilee from Alexander the Great to Hadrian, 323 B.C E. to 135 C.E.* (Wilmington, Del.: M. Glazier, 1980).

77. See R. M. Nagy, C. L. Meyers, E. M. Meyers, Z. Weiss, eds., *Sepphoris in Galilee: Crosscurrents of Culture* (Winona Lake, Ind.: Eisenbrauns, 1996); this was the catalog for the large exhibition on Sepphoris in the North Carolina Museum of Art, Raleigh, N.C.

78. Especially Eric M. Meyers has argued for the necessity of a dialogue between archaeology, literary, and historical studies in Galilee—see, e.g., his "The Bible and Archaeology," *BA* 47 (1984): 36–40—and has initiated much of the work in this area. The large activity in Galilean studies has sparked an interest among many scholars in different fields as well—in art history, rabbinic studies, early Christian studies, history of the Greco-Roman period. Among the results of this activity are international conferences on Galilee and large exhibitions of art and archaeology, and publications on Galilee. See the following conference volumes, Lee I. Levine, ed., *The Galilee in Late Antiquity* (New York: Jewish Theological Seminary of America, 1992); and Eric M. Meyers, ed., *Galilee through the Centuries: Confluence of Cultures* (Duke Judaic Studies Series 1; Winona Lake. Ind.: Eisenbrauns, 1999); Douglas R. Edwards and C. Thomas McCollough, eds., *Archaeology and the Galilee* (South Florida Studies in the History of Judaism 143; Atlanta: Scholars Press, 1997).

79. See D. Oakman, "Models and Archaeology in the Social Interpretation of Jesus," in *Social Scientific Models for Interpreting the Bible: Essays by the Context Group in Honor of Bruce J. Malina* (ed. J. J. Pilch; Biblical Interpretation Series 53; Leiden: Brill, 2001), 102–9; and Hanson and Oakman, *Palestine in the Time of Jesus*.

Chapter 2

1. "When space feels thoroughly familiar to us, it has become place," Tuan, in J. Z. Smith, *To Take Place* (Chicago: University of Chicago Press, 1992), 28. This is a statement that sums up much of the implicit, taken-for-granted notions about place and how place is associated with *identity.*

2. Ibid., 30.

3. There is a "uniquely complex significance of home in the English language," D. Sopher, in ibid., 30. Some Anglo-Saxon languages have an equivalent to the English "home," e.g., German and the Scandinavian languages, but Latin languages do not. Italian, for instance, has just one word, *casa*, for the two English words "house" and "home."

4. See, e.g., L. G. Perdue et al., *Families in Ancient Israel* (Louisville, Ky.: Westminster John Knox, 1997); S. J. D. Cohen, ed., *The Jewish Family in Antiquity* (Brown Jewish Studies 289; Atlanta: Scholars Press, 1993); C. Osiek and D. L. Balch, *Families in the New Testament World* (Louisville, Ky.: Westminster John Knox, 1997); H. Moxnes, ed., *Constructing Early Christian Families* (London: Routledge, 1997); J. W. van Henten and A. Brenner, *Families and Family Relations as Represented in Early Judaism and Early Christianities* (Studies in Theology and Religion 2; Leiden: Deo, 2000).

5. Often the issue gets dogmatic overtones. For instance, the discussion whether his "brothers" were in fact only half brothers or cousins may be colored by an interest to protect the idea of the continuing virginity of Mary after the birth of Jesus, a belief that is important in Roman Catholic and Orthodox churches. A review of the historical evidence is given by John P. Meier, *A Marginal Jew: Rethinking the Historical Jesus*, vol. 1 (1991), 317–71.

6. A few examples will have to suffice. In Günther Bornkamm's *Jesus of Nazareth*, an important book from the Second Quest, neither Jesus' family and household nor his village play any role. Similarly, in E. P. Sanders's influential *Jesus and Judaism,* family and household are barely mentioned, and they are not listed in the topical index. Finally, in the massive survey of recent scholarship *Studying the Historical Jesus,* ed. B. Chilton and C. A. Evans, none of the essays discuss Jesus' origin or the relationship to his family.

7. This is true, for instance, of Joseph Klausner, *Jesus of Nazareth: His Life, Times and Teaching* (1925 ed.; reprint, New York: Bloch, 1989), 229–38; Geza Vermes, *Jesus the Jew: A Historian's Reading of the Gospels,* 33–34. David Flusser with R. Steven Notley, *Jesus* (2d ed.; Jerusalem: Magnes Press, 1998), 24–36, treats Jesus' relation to his family as a matter of Jesus' psychology. Recently, this type of approach has been followed up by John W. Miller in a study of Jesus' break with his family in light of Freud and developmental psychology, in *Jesus at Thirty: A Psychological and Historical Portrait* (Minneapolis: Fortress, 1997).

8. Meier, *Marginal Jew,* 1:317–71.

9. D. Georgi, "The Interest in Life of Jesus Theology as a Paradigm to the Social History of Biblical Criticism," *HTR* 85 (1992): 51–83.

10. John S. Kloppenborg, *Excavating Q: The History and Setting of the Sayings Gospel* (Edinburgh: T. & T. Clark, 2000), 419–20.

11. But see now G. Theissen and A. Merz, *The Historical Jesus: A Comprehensive Guide* (London: SCM, 1998), 185–239. This chapter, which is titled "Jesus as Charismatic: Jesus and His Social Relationships," combines discussions of Jesus' relations to his family, to John the Baptist, to the disciples and other followers, to women, and finally, to his opponents. Theissen and Merz attribute great importance to Jesus' social relationships, saying that "they are a key to understand Jesus" (185).

12. John R. Gillis, *A World of Their Own Making: Myth, Ritual, and the Quest for Family Values* (Cambridge, Mass.: Harvard University Press, 1996), 109–32.

13. F. Moretti, *Atlas of the European Novel: 1800–1900* (London: Verso, 1999), 17–18.

14. A. Giddens, *Modernity and Self Identity* (Cambridge: Polity Press, 1991), 88–97.

15. For this development in American families, see *Religion, Feminism, and the Family* (ed. A. Carr and M. Stewart Van Leeuwen; Louisville, Ky.: Westminster John Knox, 1996).
16. Starting in Denmark in 1991, many European countries have legalized same-sex partnerships with rights similar to those of (heterosexual) marriages.
17. In the U.S.A., comprehensive studies of families in historical and contemporary perspectives have been undertaken by the project "Religion, Culture and Family," at the Institute for Advanced Study in the University of Chicago Divinity School, chaired by Professor Don S. Browning, and funded by the Lilly Endowment. A number of the studies undertaken by this project were published in the series The Family, Religion, and Culture (ed. Don S. Browning and Ian S. Evison) by Westminster John Knox Press.
18. H. Moxnes, "What Is Family?" in *Constructing Early Christian Families* (ed. H. Moxnes; London: Routledge, 1997), 16–18.
19. K. C. Hanson, "Kinship," in *The Social Sciences and New Testament Interpretation* (ed. R. L. Rohrbaugh; Peabody, Mass.: Hendrickson, 1996), 62–79.
20. See a similar combination in the Tenth Commandment, not to covet one's neighbor's *oikia* and *agros,* together with his wife, servants, and livelihood stock (Exod. 20:17 LXX; Deut. 5:21 LXX).
21. The structure of the list seems to be an unresolved problem. It breaks with the common system of listing couplets, in that the list of household members divides the house from the fields; see e.g., in Deut. 5:21: "your neighbor's house, his field, or his manservant, or his maidservant, his ox, or his ass." "House" and "field" are commonly joined also in other Near Eastern texts, e.g., in many legal documents from Ugarit, W. R. Moran, "The Conclusion of the Decalogue (Ex 20,17=Dt 5,21)," *CBQ* 29 (1967): 548–51.
22. See Ivan Illich, *Gender* (New York: Pantheon, 1982), 117–18, based on material from medieval peasant cultures in E. Le Roy Durie, *Montaillou : village occitan de 1294 à 1324* (Paris: Gallimard, 1976). This is an instance in which the translation "home" of *oikia* in the *Good News Bible* does not capture this aspect, missing the perspective of "house" as subject and history.
23. Luke 18:29 includes *gynaika* in the list after *oikia*. Both Mark 10:29 and Matt. 19:29 have variant readings that include *gynaika* in the list, mostly just before *tekna*.
24. Luke 4:22 gives a very abbreviated version: "Is not this Joseph's son?"
25. See the discussion in J. Meier, *Marginal Jew,* 1:318–32.
26. Parallels in Matt. 13:57; Luke 4:24; John 4:44; *Gos. Thom.*, 31; pOxy. 1; see J. W. Pryor, "John 4:44 and the *Patris* of Jesus," *CBQ* 49 (1987): 254–63. I translate *patris* with "home town" instead of "country" in RSV, to emphasize the local community; see W. Bauer, *A Greek-English Lexicon on the New Testament and Other Early Christian Literature.* Transl. and adaptation of 4th rev. ed. by W. F. Arndt and F. W. Gingrich, 2d rev. ed. by Gingrich and F. W. Danker (Chicago: University of Chicago Press, 1979), 637.
27. S. C. Barton, *Discipleship and Family Ties in Mark and Matthew* (*SNTSMS* 80, Cambridge: Cambridge University Press, 1994), 86–87.
28. Cf. the use of *gē* and *syngeneia* in Acts 7:3.
29. For *The Proto-Gospel of James, The Infancy Gospel of Thomas, the Arabic Infancy Gospels,* the *Gospel of Pseudo-Matthew,* see Ron Hock, *The Infancy Gospels of James and Thomas* (The Scholars Bible 2; Santa Rosa, Calif.: Polebridge, 1995); and *The Apocryphal Jesus* (ed. J. K. Elliott; Oxford: Oxford University Press, 1996), 19–30.
30. R. E. Brown, *The Birth of the Messiah: A Commentary on the Infancy Narratives in Matthew and Luke* (Garden City, N.Y.: Doubleday, 1977), 37–38.

31. T. Karlsen Seim, *The Double Message: Patterns of Gender in Luke and Acts* (Nashville: Abingdon, 1994), 112–18.
32. Ibid., 249–56.
33. J. Schaberg, *The Illegitimacy of Jesus: A Feminist Theological Interpretation of the Infancy Narratives* (San Francisco: Harper and Row, 1987), 74–75; and E. Wainewright, "The Gospel of Matthew," in *Searching the Scriptures*, vol. 2 *A Feminist Commentary* (ed. E. Schüssler Fiorenza; New York: Crossroad, 1994), 641–44.
34. H. Moxnes, "Honor and Shame," *BTB* 23 (1993): 167–76; but see the criticism by Elisabeth Schüssler Fiorenza (*Jesus and the Politics of Interpretation*, 98–100) that the concepts honor and shame are unduly objectified.
35. The accusation that Jesus really was illegitimate, borne by Mary as a result of sexual contact with a man other than Joseph, was an important part of this polemic. The most complete form of this accusation is found in Celsus, ca. 180 C.E., and it can be reconstructed from the response by Origen. According to Celsus it was Jesus himself who invented the story that he was born by a virgin. In fact, his mother was a poor woman who was turned out of the house by her husband, a carpenter, when she was convicted of adultery with a Roman soldier by the name of Panthera. Such accusations were widely spread in Jewish circles, and in the Middle Ages these accusations were developed in legends about Jesus, especially the *Toledot Yeshu*; see Brown, *Birth of the Messiah,* 534–42; Schaberg, *Illegitimacy of Jesus,* 165–78.
36. Schaberg, *Illegitimacy of Jesus,* 20–77.
37. It was the normal procedure that the father gave the newborn child its name. In Luke 1:31 it is Mary who receives the command from the angel about the name of Jesus.
38. Cf. how Simon Schama (*Landscape and Memory* [London: HarperCollins, 1995]) traces myths and stories that have shaped landscapes and given them meaning.
39. Brown, *Birth of the Messiah,* 223–25.
40. D. D. Gilmore, "Introduction: The Shame of Dishonour," in *Honour and Shame and the Unity of the Mediterranean* (American Anthropological Association Special Publication 22; ed. D. D. Gilmore; Washington: American Anthropological Association, 1987), 14–15; M. Bettini, *Anthropology and Roman Culture: Kinship, Time, Images of the Soul* (Baltimore: Johns Hopkins University Press, 1991), 5–114.
41. B. Malina, *The Social World of Jesus and the Gospels* (London and New York: Routledge, 1996), 97–120.
42. Ibid., 110.
43. More critical is J. M. Lieu, "The Mother of the Son in the Fourth Gospel," *JBL* 117 (1998): 61–67. But we can recognize this culturally shaped expectation of a relationship of suffering between mother and son in later Byzantine portrayals of the crucifixion. It is John's version, with Mary at the cross, that is represented. It seems that an expectation of this special relationship is still alive and strong in the Mediterranean world. Pasolini's film about Jesus is built on the Gospel of Matthew. But in the last scene, of the crucifixion, he "imports" the setting from John's Gospel, with Jesus' mother explicitly present. Is that because it was impossible to imagine that scene without his mother being present? (Jesus' mother was actually played by Pasolini's own mother!)
44. This is a topic in the *Infancy Gospel of Thomas*; see R. Hock, *The Infancy Gospels of James and Thomas.*
45. Miller (*Jesus at Thirty,* 31–45) attempts to combine the cultural and the psychological in Jesus' relationship to his father (Joseph).

46. L. G. Perdue, "The Household, Old Testament Theology, and Contemporary Hermeneutics," in L. G. Perdue et al., *Families in Ancient Israel*, 225–26.
47. S. J. D. Cohen, "Introduction," in *Jewish Family in Antiquity*, 1–8.
48. Massey, *Space, Place and Gender*, 169.
49. See Ruth Vale, "Literary Sources in Archaeological Description: The Case of Galilee, Galilees and Galileans," *JSJ* 18 (1987): 209–26.
50. See the comments by the historian Andrew Wallace-Hadrill on the meaning of the Roman house: "Anthropology has helped the historian see the social significance of the way different societies shape domestic space," in "The Social Structure of the Roman House," *Papers of the British School at Rome* 56 (1988): 50.
51. J. L. Reed, *Archaeology and the Galilean Jesus*, 131–32.
52. S. Guijarro, "The Family in First-Century Galilee," in *Constructing Early Christian Families*, 42–65.
53. Especially significant is a study by Y. Hirschfeld, *The Palestinian Dwelling in the Roman-Byzantine Period* (Jerusalem: Franciscan Printing Press, 1995). Hirschfeld documents how the construction of houses in Palestine shows a large degree of continuity from antiquity until the present time. Hirschfeld studied buildings from the Roman-Byzantine period and supplemented archaeological material with studies of buildings and construction techniques used by Bedouins in this century. This study was undertaken at the very last minute for the use of such comparative material, because with the use of cement, introduced in the last decades, the old building techniques have gone out of use. However, we now know that there was in this area a continuity in building style and construction that lasted from antiquity for many centuries. Apart from the insight it provides in the specific area of housing, it also gives support to the hypothesis that studies of "traditional" societies in the Mediterranean of today can illuminate investigations into ancient communities, cultures, and customs in the same area. Hirschfeld points out one major difference, however, between houses from antiquity and those of Bedouins from more recent periods. Whereas most houses in antiquity were divided into several rooms, Bedouin houses mostly had one large room. The review by M. Fischer, O. Potchter, and Y. Jacob ("Dwelling Houses in Ancient Israel: Methodological Considerations" [*Journal of Roman Archaeology* 11 (1998): 671–78]) is critical to Hirschfeld's use of the comparison between twentieth-century Arab evidence and ancient houses, and suggests drawing more on the environment and climate to explain the development of domestic architecture in various parts of Palestine.
54. L. E. Stager, "The Archaeology of the Family in Ancient Israel," *BASOR* 260 (1985): 1–36.
55. Hirschfeld, *Palestinian Dwelling*, 29–34.
56. Ibid., 50–57, 82–97.
57. Reed, *Archaeology and the Galilean Jesus*, 125–26.
58. Hirschfeld, *Palestinian Dwelling*, 98–99.
59. James C. Anderson, *Roman Architecture and Society* (Baltimore: Johns Hopkins Press, 1987), 304–16; John E. Staumbaugh, *The Ancient Roman City* (Baltimore: Johns Hopkins Press, 1988), 174–82.
60. For instance, in Meiron, see Hirschfeld, *Palestinian Dwelling*, 30–31.
61. Guijarro, *The Family in First-Century Galilee*, 57–61. See also his *Fidelidades en conflicto: la ruptura con la familia por causa del discipulado y de la misón en la tradición sinóptica*. Plenitudo Temporis 4 (Salamanca: Universidad Pontifica, 1998), 75–96. M. Sawicki (*Crossing Galilee: Architectures of Contact in the Occupied Land of Jesus* [Harrisburg, Pa.: Trinity Press, 2000], 20) is critical of this attempt; she argues that houses are permanent fixtures, while the household structure and size may change much over time.

62. Reed, *Archaeology and the Galilean Jesus*, 157.
63. Richardson, "Q's Setting," 70.
64. M. Peskowitz, "Family/ies in Antiquity: Evidence from Tannaitic Literature and Roman Galilean Architecture," in *Jewish Family in Antiquity*, 28–31.
65. M. Jameson, "Private Space and the Greek City," in *The Greek City from Homer to Alexander* (ed. O. Murray and S. Price; Oxford: Clarendon House, 1990), 171–95.
66. Wallace-Hadrill, "Roman House."
67. For instance, Capernaum (Reed, *Archaeology and the Galilean Jesus,* 152–57) and Yodefat (Richardson, "Q's Setting," 68).
68. D. Fiensy, *The Social History of Palestine in the Herodian Period* (Studies in the Bible and Early Christianity 20; Lewiston, N.Y.: Mellen Press, 1991), 126–32.
69. Peskowitz, "Family/ies in Antiquity," 33.
70. This Lukan version gives the word as a warning. Q 12:3, reconstructed in Robinson et al. *Critical edition of Q* follows Matt. 10:27 and *Gos. Thom.* 33:1, and rendered it as an exhortation to the disciples: "What you hear whispered in the ear, proclaim on the housetops."
71. Reed, *Archaeology and the Galilean Jesus*, 159.
72. Ibid., 43–49.
73. Ibid., 47–49.
74. M. Goodman, *The Ruling Class of Judea: The Origins of the Jewish Revolt against Rome AD 66–70* (Cambridge: Cambridge University Press, 1987), 68–70.
75. G. Theissen, *Social Reality and the Early Christians* (Minneapolis: Fortress, 1992), 90–92.
76. The designation *Nazōraios* is used mostly by Matthew (e.g., 2:23; 26:71) and Luke (e.g., Luke 18:37; Acts 2:22; 3:6), whereas Mark prefers *Nazarēnos* (e.g., 1:24; 10:47).
77. The most common meanings of *tekton* are mason, carpenter, woodworker; W. D. Davies and Dale C. Allison, *A Critical and Exegetical Commentary on the Gospel According to Saint Matthew*, vol. 2 (Edinburgh: T. & T. Clark, 1991), 456.
78. B. B. Scott, *Hear Then the Parable,* 79–202.
79. Ibid., 79.
80. Ibid., 65.
81. Richardson, "Q's Setting."
82. Ibid., 78.
83. In his discussion of the Jesus tradition, J. D. Crossan, *Historical Jesus,* 434–42, locates many of the same passages that Richardson mentions in early layers of the Jesus material.

Chapter 3

1. For instance, it is not on the list of the generally accepted "facts" about the life of Jesus, which include his upbringing and early life in Nazareth, his baptism by John, his activity as preacher and healer in Galilee; see E. P. Sanders, *Jesus and Judaism,* 11; idem, *The Historical Figure of Jesus* (London: Penguin, 1993), 10–11; J. D. G. Dunn, in *Authenticating the Words of Jesus* (ed. B. Chilton and C. A. Evans; NTTS 28:1; Leiden: Brill, 1999), 46–47.
2. Edelman, *Homographesis,* 114 speaks of "dislocations of 'identity'."
3. Cf. the short story "The Displaced Person," by Flannery O'Connor, in her *The Complete Stories* (New York: Farrar, Straus and Giroux, 1971), 194–235. I am grateful to Leif Vaage, who pointed out this story to me.
4. See a similar list and similar evaluations of the material in S. Guijarro Oporto, "Kingdom and Family in Conflict: A Contribution to the Study of the

Historical Jesus," in *Social Scientific Models for Interpreting the Bible: Essays by the Context Group in Honor of Bruce J. Malina* (Biblical Interpretation Series 53; ed. J. J. Pilch; Leiden: Brill, 2001), 210–38.

5. This way to divide the material may be illuminated by the three sections of Edelman's phrase about (1) "dislocation of identity," (2) "that create a zone of possibilities" (but presently only possibilities), (3) "in which the embodiments of the subject may be experienced otherwise." This gives the following list:

1. Dislocating identities into no-places: Mark 6:4; Q 9:58, *Gos. Thom.* 86 (Q 7:33–34).
2. "Creating a zone of possibilities" (not-yet places): Mark 1:16–20; 2:13–14; Q 9:59–60; Q 14:26, *Gos. Thom.* 55, 101; Q 12:51–53, *Gos. Thom.* 16.
3. Embodiment in new households: Mark 3:31–35 par; Mark 10:29–30.

6. The title of a master's thesis in sociology at the University of Oslo, 1987, by Arnfinn J. Andersen: "Coming Out, Coming Home," illustrates this. It is a study of gay men's coming-out process: how they leave home and move to larger cities and establish a new identity through a network of friends who become their new "home."
7. Casey, *Getting Back into Place,* xii.
8. Ibid., ix–x.
9. *The Critical Edition of Q* has "son of humanity" (see discussion of translation p. lxx) instead of the literal "son of man," which I have chosen to retain, here and in other instances, since for the purpose of a scholarly discussion a more literal translation seems desirable. But this does not imply that I hold that "son of man" is necessarily used as a christological title in these instances.
10. Patterson (*Gospel of Thomas,* 133) argues that "rest" here should be understood in line with "lay his head," and not in a gnosticizing sense of "final repose."
11. Leif E. Vaage, "Q 1 and the Historical Jesus: Some Peculiar Sayings (7:33–34; 9:57–58, 59–60; 14:26–27)," *Forum* 5:2 (1989): 159–76.
12. Hans Dieter Betz, The *Sermon on the Mount* (Hermeneia; Minneapolis: Fortress, 1995), 472–75.
13. Mahlon H. Smith, "No Place for a Son of Man," *Forum* 4:2 (1988), 99.
14. Cresswell, *In Place, out of Place,* 153.
15. Robert Doran, "The Divinization of Disorder: The Trajectory of Matt 8:20// Luke 9:58// *Gos. Thom.* 86," in *The Future of Early Christianity: Essays in Honor of Helmut Koester* (ed. Birger A. Pearson; Minneapolis: Fortress, 1991), 210–19.
16. M. H. Smith, "No Place for a Son of Man," 87–91.
17. Ibid., 94–95: the Hebrew *ben adam* is translated *bar nasha*, which gives the translation "son of man," while the LXX has the generic term *anthrōpos.*
18. Leif E. Vaage, "The Son of Man Saying in Q: Stratigraphical Location and Significance," *Semeia* 55 (1991): 125.
19. For the translations of "patris" with "home town," and for parallels, see ch. 2, n.26.
20. Arland D. Jacobson, "Jesus against the Family: The Dissolution of Family Ties in the Gospel Tradition," in *From Quest to Q: Festschrift James M. Robinson* (BETL 146; ed. J. Ma. Asgeirsson, K. de Troyer, and M. W. Meyer; Leuven: Leuven University Press, 2000), 205; Patterson, *Gospel of Thomas,* 135–36.
21. Cf. that Mark may have expanded the list in 6:4 to correspond to its context.
22. R. Redfield, *The Little Community: Viewpoints for the Study of Human Whole* (Chicago: University of Chicago Press, 1955).

23. J. Pitt-Rivers, "Honour and Social Status," in *Honour and Shame: The Values of Mediterranean Society* (ed. J. G. Peristiany; London: Weidenfeld and Nicholson, 1966), 19–77.

24. Jacobson, "Jesus against the Family," 205.

25. This term "to know one's place" is one that P. Bourdieu uses often as expression of classification of places, together with "a sense of limit." To classify place in this way by means of spatial categories shows how important place and space are as categories of experience. Cresswell, *In Place,* 152.

26. J. Z. Smith, *To Take Place,* 46.

27. See the discussion in Schaberg, *The Illegitimacy of Jesus,* 60–64; Brown et al. (*Mary in the New Testament* [Philadelphia: Fortress, 1978], 61–64), and H. K. McArthur ("Son of Mary" [*NovT* 15 (1973]: 38–58), cannot find any solution to the puzzle, and suggest that the term "son of Mary" is just a description, without a formal genealogical function, i.e., by all records a nonsolution.

28. Matthew emphasizes this contrast between the Jesus whose place they know and the unknown source of his prophetic speech by stating it first in 13:54 and then repeating it in 13:56: "And are not all his sisters with us? Where then [*oun*] did this man get all this?"

29. Challenge and riposte are parts of the hostile exchanges in a society based on competition for honor. The elements are (1) claim to honor, (2) a challenge to that claim, (3) a riposte to the challenge, and (4) public verdict by onlookers; Jerome H. Neyrey, *Honor and Shame in the Gospel of Matthew* (Louisville, Ky.: Westminster John Knox, 1998), 44–50. For the anthropological model, see P. Bourdieu, "The Sentiment of Honour in Kabyle Society," in Peristiany, *Honour and Shame,* 191–241.

30. See note 26 above.

31. Cresswell, *In Place,* 153.

32. *Opus maius* 1.1.5, quoted in J. Z. Smith, *To Take Place,* 24.

33. Scott, *Hear Then the Parable,* 79.

34. Byron R. McCane, "'Let the Dead Bury Their Own Dead': Secondary Burials and Matt 8:21–22," *HTR* 83 (1990): 31–43.

35. In Luke's version, leaving the house is the central issue also in the last dialogue of the group of three, Luke 9:61–62.

36. Arland A. Jacobson, "Divided Families and Christian Origins," in *The Gospel behind the Gospels: Current Studies on Q* (SupNT 75; ed. Ronald A. Piper; Leiden: Brill, 1995), 361–63; "Jesus against the Family," 191–92; Vaage, "Q 1 and the Historical Jesus," 167–71.

37. Q 9:60b to "proclaim the kingdom of God" is most likely added by Luke; see Harry T. Fleddermann, "The Demands of Discipleship: Matt 8:19–22 par. Luke 9:57–62," in *The Four Gospels: Festschrift Frans Neirynck,* vol. 1 (ed. F. Van Segbroeck et al; Leuven: Leuven University Press, 1992), 547.

38. Casey, *Getting Back into Place,* 306.

39. Jack Dean Kingsbury, "The Verb *akakolouthein* ('to follow') as an Index of Matthew's View of His Community," *JBL* 97 (1978): 56–73.

40. James R. Butts, "The Voyage of Discipleship: Narrative, Chreia, and Call Story," in *Early Jewish and Christian Exegesis: Studies in Memory of William Hugh Brownlee* (ed. C. A. Evans and W. F. Stinespring; Atlanta: Scholars Press, 1987), 212–13. This complex of stories in Luke 9:57–62 and Matthew 8:19–22 has a parallel in another combination of narratives that shares the same structure: an unsuccessful call story with a radical demand is followed by stories about disciples that illustrate the fulfillment of the demand. That is the story of the call to the rich young man who refuses to leave everything, followed by the

dialogue with the disciples who have left everything: house, household, etc. (Mark 10:17–22, 23–31; Matt. 19:16–22, 23–30; Luke 18:18–23, 24–30).

41. Markus Bockmuehl ("'Let the Dead Bury Their Dead' [Matt 8:22/Luke 9:60]," *JTS* 49 [1998]: 553) points particularly to Martin Hengel, who with his book *The Charismatic Leader and His Followers* (Edinburgh: T. & T. Clark, 1981; trans. from the German original of 1968) framed the discussion in this way. He builds on the emphasis in Judaism on the obligation to bury one's dead, and argues that Jesus showed a drastic departure from Jewish law and tradition, showing his "sovereign freedom in respect of the law of Moses." Bockmuehl holds that Hengel interpreted the saying along "familiar supersessionist lines of a law-gospel polarity" (555). E. P. Sanders (*Jesus and Judaism,* 254–55), who interprets Jesus very much within the context of Judaism, at this point follows Hengel. For an earlier criticism of Hengel along similar lines, see Vaage, "Q 1 and the Historical Jesus," 167–71.

42. Parallels in Matt. 4:18–22; Luke 5:1–11; John 1:35–51.

43. Malbon, *Narrative Space,* 76.

44. See K. C. Hanson, "The Galilean Fishing Economy and the Jesus Tradition," *BTB* 27 (1997): 99–111.

45. Jacobson, "Jesus against the Family," 202–3.

46. See the discussion of this question in C. Breytenbach, "Mark and Galilee: Text World and Historical World," in Meyers, *Galilee through the Centuries,* 75–85.

47. As in the NRSV trans. But see E. Struthers Malbon ("*The Oikia autou:* Mark 2:15 in Context" [*NTS* 31 (1985): 282–92]), who argues that it is Jesus' house.

48. For the form of the Q saying, which probably included Luke 17:33, as it is part of Matt. 10:37–39, see Arland D. Jacobson, *The First Gospel: An Introduction to Q* (Sonoma, Calif.: Polebridge, 1992), 221–22. In this saying, the household is described by its members in terms of social relations. In Luke there is a three-generation household: it is the son who is addressed, who has a father and mother, wife and children, brothers and sister, and finally "his own life." Matthew is probably closer to the original Q; he has a smaller three-generation household, and the addressees, who have son(s) and daughter(s), may be both men and women. *Gos. Thom.* 55 speaks of a two-generation household, with father and mother and brothers and sisters; the parallel 101 speaks only of father and mother. "Hate" (so Luke and *Gos. Thom.* 55) is probably the original, modified by Matthew into "love more."

49. Jacobson, "Divided Families," 222.

50. Malina, *Social World of Jesus,* 81.

51. Ibid.

52. Cf. the use of "hate" together with "divorce" in some Jewish texts, e.g., the Elephantine Papyri, and in Mal. 2:15, so that "to hate" can become a synonym for divorce; John J. Collins, "Marriage, Divorce and Family in Second Temple Judaism," in L. G. Perdue, J. Blenkinsopp, J. J. Collins, and C. Meyers, *Families in Ancient Israel* (Louisville, Ky.: Westminster John Knox, 1997), 125–26.

53. Jacobson, "Divided Families," 223.

54. This saying is consistent with other sayings of Jesus on family; it has a double attestation, Q and *Gos. Thom.* (Crossan, *Historical Jesus,* 439), but many Q scholars and the Jesus Seminar do not think that it goes back to Jesus (Jacobson, "Jesus against the Family," 193; R. W. Funk and Roy W. Hoover, eds., *The Five Gospels: The Search for the Authentic Words of Jesus* [New York: Macmillan, 1993], 342–43).

55. *The Critical Edition of Q* (Hermeneia; ed. J. M. Robinson, P. Hoffmann, J. S. Kloppenborg; [Minneapolis: Fortress, 2000], 380–87) does not accept 12:52 as part of Q: "For henceforth in one house there will be five divided, three

against two and two against three." This section is lacking in Matt. 10:34–36, but is included in *Gos. Thom.* 16: "Men think, perhaps that it is peace which I have come to cast upon the world. 2. They do not know that it is dissension which I have come to cast conflicts upon the earth: fire, sword, and war. 3. For there will be five in a house: three will be against two and two against three, the father against the son and the son against the father, 4. And they will stand solitary."

56. Luke's terminology for "divide," *diamerizō*, is the same as in the Beelzebul pericope, about a kingdom divided (11:17; cf. Mark 3:25–26 about a house divided that cannot remain standing). Matthew reaches the same result by quoting in full from Mic. 7:6, including the last phrase "and a man's foes will be those of his own household," Matt. 10:35–36.
57. Q probably had *machairan*, "sword," Matt. 10:34, and not *diamerismon*, Luke 12:51.
58. Jacobson, "Jesus against the Family," 193.
59. Risto Uro, "Asceticism and Anti-Familial Language in the *Gospel of Thomas*," in *Constructing Early Christian Families*, 220.
60. Patterson, *Gospel of Thomas*, 153; Uro, "Asceticism," 225.
61. Cf. *Gos. Thom.* 30, reconstructed by H. Attridge, quoted in Patterson, *Gospel of Thomas*, 153: "Where there are [three], they are [without God], and where there is but [a single one], I say that I am with [him]."
62. Malina, *Social World of Jesus*, 56–57.
63. Breytenbach, "Mark and Galilee."
64. The "house" of Jesus does not play such an important role in Matthew and Luke. Also, Matthew 12:46–50 and Luke 8:19–21 have softened the criticism of Jesus' family; Luke, especially, is eager to describe Mary as an example of the true disciple who hears and does the word of God (see 2:19, 51; 11:27–28).
65. Malbon, "*Oikia autou.*"
66. Malbon, *Narrative Space*, 131–36.
67. Patterson (*Gospel of Thomas*, 135) on *Gos. Thom.* 99 suggests that it is a question of social formations. *Thomas*'s Christians saw themselves as familial in their relations to one another.
68. Parallels in Matt. 19:27–30; Luke 18:28–30.
69. *panta*, Mark 10:28; *ta idia*, Luke 18:28.
70. Jacobson, "Jesus against the Family," 208.
71. Against Mary Ann Tolbert ("Asceticism and Mark's Gospel," in *Asceticism and the New Testament* [ed. Leif E. Vaage and V. Wimbush; London and New York: Routledge, 1999], 41–42), who interprets the persecution in light of the cross and the suffering of Jesus.
72. Ibid., 41.
73. Werner H. Kelber, *The Kingdom in Mark: A New Place and a New Time* (Philadelphia: Fortress, 1974), 87–92.
74. In the transmission of this text, the mention of groups in plural (*oikias*) apparently was seen as a problem, so that many manuscripts have changed it to singular.
75. One may argue that it was their wish to postpone fulfillment to an eschatological future that lies behind these changes. But see how Luke in another instance turns an eschatological saying into a present possibility, when he translates non-marriage in the resurrection (Mark 12:25) into a present possibility for "those who are accounted worthy to attain to that age and to the resurrection from the dead" (Luke 20:34–35); see Turid Karlsen Seim, "Children of the Resurrection: Perspectives on Angelic Asceticism in Luke-Acts," in *Asceticism and the New Testament*, 115–25.

76. Jerome H. Neyrey, "Loss of Wealth, Loss of Family and Loss of Honour: The Cultural Context of the Original Macarisms in Q," in *Modelling Early Christianity* (ed. Philip F. Esler; London: Routledge, 1995), 139–58.
77. Neyrey discusses the four macarisms in their present redaction in Q, where they form a unit, not their history of origin as separate macarisms (see *Gos. Thom.* 54, 68, 69; Patterson, *Gospel of Thomas,* 42–43, 51–53; John S. Kloppenborg, *The Formation of Q* [Harrisburg, Pa.: Trinity Press], 172–73). At the level of the redaction of Q that includes the fourth macarism, all four are understood as directed to the community (Neyrey, "Loss of Wealth," 144–45; Jacobson, "Jesus against the Family," 100). It is commonly argued that originally the three first were addressed to "the general human conditions of poverty and suffering" (Kloppenborg, *The Formation of Q,* 173). However, in the macarisms in *Gos. Thom.*, which most likely builds on a separate tradition from Q, the second (hunger) and fourth (persecution) macarism are combined in *Gos. Thom.* 69, in the reverse order, with no apparent change in addressees. H. D. Betz (*Sermon on the Mount,* 147–50, 578–82) agrees that the slander, persecution, etc., in Luke 6:22 and Matt. 5:11 do not refer to expulsion from synagogues, but to social expulsion from members of the community.
78. Neyrey uses the Lukan text for Q 6:22; *The Critical Edition of Q* follows Matt. 5:11: "Blessed are you when they insult and [persecute] you, and [say every kind of] evil [against] you because of the son of man." This is a bit surprising, since the terminology in Matthew is less specific and more general; instead of *aforizō* (separate) it has *diōkō* (persecute); Ulrich Luz, *Das Evangelium nach Matthäus,* vol. 1 (Neukirchen-Vlyn: Neukirchener, 1985), 214. But the use of *oneidizō* (insult) and "say every kind of evil against you" indicates a setting of social conflict, not of official persecution. Cf. also a version of the logion in 1 Pet. 4:14: "If you are reproached [*oneidizesthe*] for the name of Christ, you are blessed." The term *oneidizō* "is a standard term for verbal abuse and public shaming," so the situation is informal, not one of official incrimination or persecution; John H. Elliott, *1 Peter* (AB 37B; New York: Doubleday, 2000), 778–79.
79. Neyrey, "Loss of Wealth," 145–47.
80. Richard L. Rohrbaugh, "A Dysfunctional Family and Its Neighbours (Luke 15:11–32)," in *Jesus and His Parables: Interpreting the Parables of Jesus Today* (ed. V. G. Shillington; Edinburgh: T. & T. Clark, 1997), 141–64.
81. Here we leave aside that also the father acted against the rules of honor in the village society, see below, and Rohrbaugh, "A Dysfunctional Family," 155–60.
82. Martin Goodman, *The Ruling Class of Judea,* 69–70; Gerd Theissen, "'We have left everything . . .' (Mark 10:28): Discipleship and Social Uprooting in the Jewish-Palestinian Society of the First Century," in his *Social Reality and the Early Christians,* 90–92.
83. John W. Pryor, "Jesus and Family—a Test Case," *Australian Biblical Review* 45 (1997): 56–69.
84. Notice especially S. C. Barton, *Discipleship and Family Ties.*
85. Pryor, "Jesus and Family," 66.
86. The distinction between ii and iii is small, and depends on one's view of what passion Jesus is consumed by.
87. This is a terminology that is also used by Barton, *Discipleship and Family Ties* e.g., 123, together with "natural kinship per se," etc. Much of the criticism directed against Pryor can also be directed against Barton; cf. Jacobson, "Jesus against the Family," 200.
88. Pryor, "Jesus and Family," 67.
89. Ibid., 65.
90. Ibid., 67.

91. I suppose that Pryor means "Jewish." It is strange that he uses the term "Eastern," as it seems to be a typical example of Orientalism, which, one should think contrary to Pryor's intention, makes the designated position appear more foreign, an expression of "the Other."

92. Cf. Jacobson ("Jesus against the Family," 200) who makes a similar point against Barton.

93. Carolyn Osiek ("The Family in Early Christianity: Family Values Revisited," *CBQ* 58 [1996]: 1–24) makes a similar point.

94. Pryor, "Jesus and Family," 64.

95. Crossan, *Historical Jesus*, 300.

96. Malbon, "*Oikia autou.*"

97. The saying in Mark 6:4, *Gos. Thom.* 31, John 4:44 becomes the basis for the narrative in Mark 6:1–6; Mark 3:34–35, *Gos. Thom.* 99 for Mark 3:31–35. W. Arnal ("Major Episodes in the Biography of Jesus: An Assessment of the Historicity of the Narrative Tradition," *Toronto Journal of Theology* 13 [1997]: 209) has made the same observation for a number of other stories in Mark: the baptism of Jesus, the temple scene, and the passion narrative. He describes the outcome as: "a singly attested narrative which has thematic links with multiply attested sayings and serves to illustrate those sayings with an activity of Jesus himself." See also R. J. Miller, "Historical Method and the Deeds of Jesus," *Forum* 8 (1992): 27–28.

98. Against André Myre, "Jesus avait-il une maison?" in *"Où demeures-tu" (Jn 1, 38): La maison depuis le monde biblique* (ed. Jean-Claude Petit; Quebec: Fides, 1994), 305–19.

99. Victor W. Turner, *Dramas, Fields and Metaphors: Symbolic Action in Human Society* (Ithaca, N.Y.: Cornell University Press, 1974), 231–71.

100. See, e.g., Amy-Jill Levine, "Who's Catering the Q Affair? Feminist Observations on Q Paraenesis," *Semeia* 50 (1990): 145–61; Alan Kirk, "Crossing the Boundaries: Liminality and Transformative Wisdom in Q," *NTS* 45 (1999): 1–18. But see also the criticism against Turner, below, chap. 5, especially C. W. Bynum, "Women's Stories, Women's Symbols: A Critique of Victor Turner's Theory of Liminality, " in *Anthropology and the Study of Religion* (eds. R. L. Moore and F. L. Reynolds; Chicago: Center for the Scientific Study of Religion, 1984), 105–25.

Chapter 4

1. See the previous chapter. In sayings where the gender of the persons called to follow Jesus could be identified, they appear to be young men.

2. M. Kuefler, *The Manly Eunuch: Masculinity, Gender Ambiguity, and Christian Ideology in Late Antiquity* (Chicago: University of Chicago Press, 2001), 274.

3. E. Schüssler Fiorenza, last in *Jesus and the Politics of Interpretation* (New York: Continuum, 2000).

4. For this discussion, see V. Wimbush and R. Valantasis, eds., *Asceticism* (New York: Oxford University Press, 1995); L. E. Vaage and V. Wimbush, eds., *Asceticism and the New Testament* (New York: Routledge, 1999). Especially for the use of Scripture in asceticism, see now the magisterial study by Elizabeth A. Clark, *Reading Renunciation: Asceticism and Scripture in Early Christianity* (Princeton, N.J.: Princeton University Press, 1999).

5. Richard Valantasis, "Constructions of Power in Asceticism," *JAAR* 63 (1995): 775–821; idem, "A Theory of the Social Function of Asceticism," in *Asceticism* (ed. V. Wimbush and R. Valantasis; New York: Oxford University Press, 1995), 544–52.

6. Valantasis, "Power in Asceticism," 797, my italics.
7. This definition corresponds to the theoretical perspectives in Edelman and Harvey and Lefevbre (chap. 1) about the possibility of creating a new embodiment of the subject, and of new ways to structure the world.
8. For a general overview of the history of interpretation, see Ulrich Luz, *Das Evangelium nach Matthäus,* vol. 3 (1997), 104–6; for patristic exegesis, see Walter Bauer, "Matt 19,12 und die alten Christen," in *Aufsätze und kleine Schriften* (ed. G. Strecker; Tübingen: Mohr, 1967; publ. orig. 1914), 253–62; Clark, *Reading Renunciation: Asceticism and Scripture,* 90–92.
9. For illuminating examples, see David J. A. Clines, "*Ecce Vir,* or, Gendering the Son of Man," in *Biblical Studies/Cultural Studies* (JSOT Sup 266; ed. J. Cheryl Exum and S. D. Moore; Sheffield: Sheffield University Press, 1998), 352–75; David Morgan, "The Masculinity of Jesus in Popular Religious Art," in *Men's Bodies, Men's Gods* (ed. Björn Krondorfer; New York: New York University Press, 1996), 251–66; Stephen D. Moore, "Ugly Thoughts: On the Face and Physique of the Historical Jesus," in *Biblical Studies/Cultural Studies,* 376–99.
10. For an excellent and illuminating discussion, see M. Kuefler, *Manly Eunuch.*
11. J. Blinzler, "*Eisin eunouchoi,*" *ZNW* 48 (1957): 254–70; Luz, *Matthäus* 3:107; K. Niederwimmer, *Askese und Mysterium* (FRLANT 113; Göttingen: Vandenhoeck & Ruprecht, 1975), 55.
12. This is the evaluation by Meier (*Marginal Jew,* 1:344–45) which, applying by the criteria of embarrassment, discontinuity with early Christianity and coherence with Jesus' other teachings, may be typical; see also Dale C. Allison, *Jesus of Nazareth: Millenarian Prophet* (Minneapolis: Fortress, 1998), 183–84; Luz, *Matthäus,* 3:109; Heinrich Baltensweiler, *Die Ehe im Neuen Testament* (ATANT 52; Zürich: Zwingli Verlag, 1967), 103.
13. It has a different wording; the list starts with those who have been made eunuchs by men; see Josef Blinzler, "Justinus *Apol.* I 15,4 und Matthäus 19:11–12," in *Mélanges Bibliques: En homage au R.P. Beda Rigaux* (ed. A. Descamps and A. de Halleux; Gembloux: Duculot, 1970), 45–55.
14. Blinzler, "*Eisin eunouchoi,*" 268–70; Luz, *Matthäus,* 3:110–11; Francis Moloney, "Matthew 19:3–12 and Celibacy: A Redactional and Form Critical Study," *JSNT* 2 (1979): 42–60; Allison, *Jesus of Nazareth,* 183.
15. Arthur J. Dewey ("The Unkindest Cut of All? Matt 19:11–12," *Forum* 8:1–2 [1992]: 113–22) is an exception in that he notices the ambiguities of the term "eunuch" and the challenges it poses for understandings of masculinity.
16. Allison, *Jesus of Nazareth,* 183–84.
17. Ibid., 202.
18. In a discussion of how fieldwork among anthropologists is also constructed by "heroic masculinism," Matthew Sparke asks: "What is the spatiality not represented yet implied (unseen) by the masculinist fielding of the field?" in "Displacing the Field in Fieldwork: Masculinity, Metaphor and Space," in *Bodyspace: Destabilizing Geographies of Gender and Sexuality* (ed. N. Duncan; London: Routledge), 220.
19. I use the category "antiquity" to include both Greco-Roman and Jewish cultures in the period under discussion, the centuries around the time of Jesus.
20. Eph. 5:22–6:9; Col. 3:18–4:1; 1 Pet. 2:13–3:7.
21. Studies of families as well as of masculinities have shown that there are many similarities that cut across ethnic and cultural boundaries, and that many of the differences are found within the various cultures, rather than between them. We should also notice that "male" means the free male, as a member of the society under discussion; slaves and "others" are not included. See S. J. D. Cohen, ed., *The Jewish Family in Antiquity* (Atlanta: Scholars Press, 1993); Stephen D.

Moore and Janice C. Anderson, "Taking It Like a Man: Masculinities in 4 Maccabees," *JBL* 117 (1998): 249–73; Halvor Moxnes, "Conventional Values in the Hellenistic World: Masculinity," in *Conventional Values in the Hellenistic World* (ed. P. Bilde et al.; Aarhus: Aarhus University Press, 1997), 263–84; Michael L. Satlow, "'Try to Be a Man': The Rabbinic Construction of Masculinity," *HTR* 89 (1996): 19–40; Steve Young, "Being a Man: The Pursuit of Manliness in the Shepherd of Hermas," *JECS* 2 (1994): 237–55.

22. E.g., Stephen Barton, *Discipleship and Family Ties.* Barton finds parallel to passages about leaving family in Mark and Matthew in Jewish sources: "There is no lack of material from the biblical and Jewish sources which provides further evidence for what we found in the analysis of Philo, Josephus and the Qumran documents: that, fundamentally speaking, allegiance to God and devotion to the will of God transcends family ties and legitimate their subordination" (55–56). Barton does not seem to notice the misogynistic tendencies in this material.

23. Satlow, "Masculinity," 21–26.

24. Richard A. Baer, *Philo's Use of the Categories Male and Female* (ALGHJ 3; Leiden: Brill, 1970), 38–44.

25. T. Engberg-Pedersen, "Philo's *De Vita Contemplativa* as a Philosopher's Dream," *JSJ* 30 (1999): 40–64.

26. Apuleius, *Golden Ass* VII.28.

27. Gilmore, "Introduction: The Shame of Dishonour."

28. Peter Guyot, *Eunuchen als Sklaven und Freigelassene in der griechisch-römische Antike* (Stuttgarter Beiträge zur Geschichte und Politik 14; Stuttgart: Klett-Cotta, 1980); Johannes Schneider, "Eunochos, eunochizo," TDNT 2: 765–68; Piotr O. Scholz, *Der ermannte Eros* (Düsseldorf: Artemis & Winkler, 1997).

29. Kathryn M. Ringrose, "Living in the Shadows: Eunuchs and Gender in Byzantium," in *Third Sex, Third Gender* (ed. G. Herdt; New York: Zone, 1994), 85–109; Shaun F. Tougher, "Byzantine Eunuchs: An Overview, with Special Reference to Their Creation and Origin," in *Women, Men and Eunuchs: Gender in Byzantium* (ed. L. James; London: Routledge, 1997), 168–84.

30. Scholz, *Eros,* 116–62; Shaun Marmon, *Eunuchs and Sacred Boundaries in Islamic Society* (Oxford: Oxford University Press, 1995).

31. *The Book of the Risings of the Full Moon of the Dwellings of Joy,* by Ala al-Din al Ghuzuli, discussed in Marmon, *Eunuchs and Sacred Boundaries,* 3–15.

32. Jaqueline Long, *Claudian's In Eutropium: Or, How, When and Why to Slander a Eunuch* (Chapel Hill: University of North Carolina Press, 1996).

33. Garth Thomas, "Magna Mater and Attis," *ANRW* II.17.3 (1984): 1500–1535.

34. Monika Hörig, "Dea Syria—Atargatis," *ANRW* II.17.3 (1984): 1537–81.

35. G. Sanders, "Gallos," *RAC* 8: 984–1034.

36. Ibid., 990.

37. Ibid., 996.

38. Louis Richard, "Juvenal et les galles de Cybèle," *Revue de l'Histoire des Religions* 169 (1966): 51–67.

39. G. Sanders, "Gallos," 1024.

40. G. Sanders, "Kybele und Attis," in *Die Orientalischen Religionen im Römerreich* (ed. M. J. Vermaseren; Leiden: Brill, 1981), 283–84.

41. Kuefler, *Manly Eunuch,* passim.

42. G. Sanders, "Kybele and Attis," 268.

43. G. Sanders, "Gallos," 1026–27.

44. "If any one in sickness has been subjected by physicians to a surgical operation, or if he has been castrated by barbarians, let him remain among the clergy; but if any one in sound health has castrated himself, it behoves that such an one, if (already) enrolled among the clergy, should cease (from his ministry), and that

from henceforth no such person should be promoted. But as it is evident that this is said of those who wilfully do the thing and presume to castrate themselves, so if any has been made eunuchs by barbarians, or by their masters, and should otherwise be found worthy, such men the Canon admits to the clergy," *The Seven Ecumenical Councils*, Nicene and Post-Nicene Fathers Ser. 2, 14 (ed. H. R. Percival; Edinburgh: T. & T. Clark, 1991), 8. See also *Apost. Const.* 21–22 (ibid., 595): "21. An eunuch, if he has been made so by the violence of men, or (if his *virilia* have been amputated) in times of persecution, or if he has been born so, if in other respects he is worthy, may be made a bishop. 22. He who has mutilated himself cannot become a clergyman, for he is a self-murderer, and an enemy to the workmanship of God."

45. Bauer, "Matt 19:12"; Clark, *Reading Renunciation,* 90–92.
46. L. W. Barnard (Justin Martyr, *The First and Second Apologies* [Introd. by L. W. Barnard; New York: Paulist Press, 1997], 32) translates *sōphrosyne* with "chastity." For the tendency among early Christian Latin fathers to translate *sōphrosyne* with terms for chastity, see Clark, *Reading Renunciation,* 103–5.
47. Guyot, *Eunuchen,* 45–51.
48. Justin contrasts this young man as an example of the heroic virtue of chastity with Antinous, Hadrian's young Greek favorite. The latter had drowned (himself?) in the Nile some years earlier, and was now venerated as a god, although "they knew both who he was and what was his origin." This was a not-so-veiled criticism of Antinous, whom Justin with Christian eyes would regard as both sexually licentious and effeminate.
49. For the term "figurative reading," which encompasses both allergorical and typological reading, see Clark, *Reading Renunciation,* 76–78.
50. Origen, *Comm. Matt.* 15.1; Clark, *Reading Renunciation,* 91–92.
51. Eusebius, *Hist. Eccl.* 6.8, 1.2.
52. Brown (*The Body and Society: Men, Women and Sexual Renunciation in Early Christianity* [New York: Columbia University Press, 1988], 168) thinks that the sources are reliable.
53. Clark, *Reading Renunciation,* 173.
54. The phrase is from Clark, *Reading Renunciation,* 91.
55. Jerome, "necessitas non voluntas est," *Commentaire sur S. Matthieu,* vol. 2 (introd. E. Bonnard; SC 259; Paris: Éditions du Cerf, 1979), 72. Similarly, in his letter to Eustochium, *Epist.* 22.19, Jerome makes a contrast between *necessitas* and *voluntas*: "Some people may be eunuchs from necessity; I am one of free will." In *Hom. Matt.* 62.2 to Matt. 19:12, John Chrysostom makes a similar distinction between *nature* and *choice*. He offers many arguments against an understanding of "made themselves eunuchs" as castration: it would be murder, it would give reason to slander God's creation, it would give the Manichaeans an argument, and it would be as unlawful as similar acts among the Greeks (probably the galli). But his strongest argument is the contrast between human choice and freedom on the one hand and nature on the other, or between mind and nature.
56. For Jerome's hierarchy of ascetic over nonascetic, and of various levels of asceticism, see Clark, *Reading Renunciation,* 167–69.
57. "*Cum possint esse viri, propter Christum eunuchi fiunt.*"
58. Kuefler, *Manly Eunuch,* 275–78.
59. Tertullian, *Apol.* 12, 4; *Marc.* 1,13,4; on castration, *Apol.* 15, 4–5; *Nat.* 1, 10, 46–47; 2, 7, 16; G. Sanders, "L'opinion chrétienne," 1064–69.
60. Kuefler, *Manly Eunuch,* 265–67. For the following, and for a much broader discussion of Tertullian and his view of Christian ascetics and of the galli of the Cybele cult, see G. Sanders, "L'opinion chrétienne."

61. For instance, Tertullian, *Ux.* 1.6.5, where it is applied to a married couple who decide to practice continence while they remain married; likewise *Mon.* 8.7, where he does not use the term *spado,* but seems to refer to Matt. 19:12 with "*alios post nuptias pueros.*"
62. G. Sanders, "L'opinion chrétienne," 1079–80.
63. "*Ipso Domino spadonibus aperiente regna caelorum, ut et ipso spadone, ad quem spectans et apostolus propterea et ipse castratus continentiam mauult.*"
64. *Mon.* 7.3, "*Tertio quoniam spadones et steriles ignominiosi habebantur.*"
65. *Mon.* 7.4, "*Et spadones non tantum ignominia caruerunt, uerum et gratiam meruereunt inuitati in regna caelorum.*"
66. G. Sanders, "L'opinion chrétienne," 1079–80.
67. Tertullian's statement, in n. 63 above, *Mon.* 3.1, is in support of the Montanist position, yes, an even more strict position, says Tertullian—that of absolute chastity and continence.
68. Isa. 56:4–5; Wis. 3:13–14; Deut. 23:1.
69. But see *Jeb.* 8.4–6, which provides a parallel to Matt. 19:12ab: the distinction between a eunuch, *saris,* emasculated by men, and one by nature; Schneider, "Eunochos," 767.
70. Schneider, "Eunochos," 766.
71. Esth. 1:10–12; 2 Esd. 11:11; 3 Kgdms 22:9; R. North, "Postexilic Judean Officials," *ABD* 5:87.
72. Hörig, "Dea Syria," 1550–64.
73. M. J. Vermaseren, *Corpus Cultus Cybelae Attidisque (CCCA),* vol. 1, *Asia Minor* (Leiden: Brill, 1987), 264–65.
74. Meier, *Marginal Jew,* 1:344; Luz, *Matthäus,* 3:110.
75. Paul made a similar "bloody joke" when he compared circumcision to castration in his ironic letter to the Galatians, Gal. 5:12. He sends a warning to the Christians in Galatia not to let themselves be convinced by his opponents, who argue that they must be circumcised to become true Christians. *The New English Bible* tries to catch the gist of Paul's remark, with "as for these agitators, they had better go the whole way and make eunuchs [*apokoptein*] of themselves!" (Gal. 5:12). "This reference does not imply that some Galatians were under the influence of the galli, but it does suggest that the Galatians had knowledge of the galli, as well as of the stock ridicule that was leveled against them by diatribe preachers; Hans Dieter Betz, *Galatians: A Commentary on Paul's Letter to the Churches in Galatia* (Philadelphia: Fortress, 1979), 270.
76. Allison, *Jesus of Nazareth,* 202; Luz, *Matthäus,* 3:110–11.
77. Luz, *Matthäus,* 3:103–11.
78. Luz, *Matthäus,* 3:108 n.118. Athenagoras (*Suppl.* 33.3) combines *parthenia* and *eunouchia,* in such a way that they clearly have a similar meaning, "virginity" and "continence."
79. Niederwimmer, *Askese,* 55.
80. See, e.g., Matt. 4:1–11; 6:1–18; 10:26, 28, 31; Alexander Sand, *Reich Gottes und Eheverzicht im Evangelium nach Matthäus* (SBS 109; Stuttgart: Katholisches Bibelwerk, 1983), 57–58. Origen has a similar discussion in *Comm. Matt.* 15.1; see above.
81. Origen, and among modern interpreters Sand, *Reich Gottes,* 67. Sand suggests that the term "eunuch" in all three instances means "unmarried," but especially for the first group it seems forced to speak of a special group who were "unmarried from birth on."
82. Niederwimmer, *Askese,* 56–57; P. Bonnard, *L'Évangile selon Saint Matthieu* (Commentaire du Nouveau Testament 2. ser. vol. 1; Geneva: Labor et Fides, 1982), 284.

83. Stephenson H. Brooks, *Matthew's Community: The Evidence of His Special Sayings Material* (JSNTSup 16. Sheffield: Sheffield University Press, 1987), 109; Meier, *Marginal Jew,* 1:342-44.
84. This is the way the Vulgate has understood it: "*Et sunt eunuchi qui se ipsos castraverunt propter regnum caelorum.*" However, there are variant readings that only transcribe the Greek word, and thus may seem to weaken the idea of castration: *eunuchizauerunt,* and *eunuchaverunt.*
85. We may find a possible parallel usage of a similar term when Paul in Gal. 2:14 speaks about forcing Gentiles to "judaize" (*ioudaizein*). It is in a context where Paul criticizes Peter—that although he is a Jew, he lives like a Gentile and not as a Jew. *Ioudaizein* here refers to adopting a (total?) lifestyle as a Jew, but the focusing point is of course circumcision, Gal. 2:3. Paul uses the same terminology: to force (*anankazein*) to Judaize, 2:14, or to force to be circumcised, 2:3.
86. According to Josephus (*A.J.* 16. 230; *B.J.* 1. 488), Herod the Great had eunuchs at his court; Guyot, *Eunuchen,* 100, 231–34.
87. It is not certain that all references to eunuchs at the courts of Babylon or Jerusalem are to castrated men, but sufficiently many are for the ambiguity to remain. Many court eunuchs experienced slander and plotting where accusations of feminine traits were common; see Long, *Claudian's In Eutropium*; Ringrose, "Byzantium"; Tougher, "Byzantine Eunuchs."
88. Sand, *Reich Gottes,* 56–57.
89. Davies and Allison, *Matthew* 3, 25 n. 131.
90. William B. Turner, *A Genealogy of Queer Theory* (Philadelphia: Temple University Press, 2000), 1–35.
91. Herdt, *Third Sex, Third Gender.*

Chapter 5

1. There is a shift in method in this chapter: from the in-depth study of the eunuch saying in chap. 4, we move to more sweeping overviews of a larger group of texts.
2. Arthur Darby Nock, "Eunuchs in Ancient Literature," in Nock, *Essays on Religion and the Ancient World* (*ARW* 23 [1925]; reprint, Oxford: Clarendon, 1972), 7–15. For a similar comparison between eunuchs and children in a modern society, see Marmon, *Eunuchs and Sacred Boundaries in Islamic Society,* 90.
3. The Jesus Seminar gives Matt. 19:14 par. a pink vote; see Funk and Hoover, eds., *The Five Gospels,* 221.
4. Crossan, *Historical Jesus,* 267.
5. Also in Greek in *P.Oxy* 654.21–27.
6. See also Tertullian, *Mon.* 8.7, in an example of how Jesus taught chastity, both by his example and teachings: "He tells [them] that 'the kingdom of heaven's' is 'children's,' while he associates with these [children] others who, after marriage, remained [or became] virgins" (*cum consortes illis facit alias post nuptias pueros*). This is most likely a reference to Matt. 19:14 and 12.
7. Marvin W. Meyer, "Making Mary Male: The Categories 'Male' and 'Female' in the Gospel of Thomas," *NTS* 31 (1985): 558–59; Jonathan Z. Smith, *Map Is Not Territory* (1978 ed; reprint, Chicago: University of Chicago Press, 1993), 18–23.
8. This is also suggested by B. J. Pitre, "Blessing the Barren and Warning the Fecund: Jesus' Message for Women Concerning Pregnancy and Childbirth," *JSNT* 81 (2001): 59–80.
9. Mark 13:17–19; Matt. 24:19–21; Luke 21:23–24; Luke 23:28, 30–31.
10. Gen. 17:16–19; 25:21–26; 29:31; 30:22–24; Judg. 13:2–5; 1 Sam. 1:2–20; Luke 1:5–25; Rom. 4:19–21.

11. That parallel was also drawn by some rabbis, *Yeb.* 8.3.4, and Tertullian, *Mon.* 7.3. For the description of the law-abiding eunuch, see a similar passage in Isa. 56:3b–5.
12. Patterson, *Gospel of Thomas,* 154–55.
13. Turid Karlsen Seim, *The Double Message: Patterns of Gender in Luke-Acts,* 208–29; Allison, *Jesus of Nazareth,* 208–9.
14. Wayne A. Meeks, "The Image of the Androgyne: Some Uses of a Symbol in Earliest Christianity," *History of Religion* 13 (1974): 165–208.
15. Antti Marjanen, "Women Disciples in the *Gospel of Thomas,*" in *Thomas at the Crossroads: Essays on the Gospel of Thomas* (ed. Risto Uro; Edinburgh: T. & T. Clark, 1998), 102–3.
16. Patterson, *Gospel of Thomas,* 154; see also Meyer, "Making Mary Male," 563–67.
17. See Lone Fatum, "Image of God and Glory of Man: Women in the Pauline Congregations," in *The Image of God: Gender Models in Judeo-Christian Tradition* (ed. Kari E. Børresen; Minneapolis: Fortress, 1995), 50–133.
18. Eph. 5:21–6:9; Col. 3:18–4:1; 1 Tim. 3:1–7; 1 Pet. 2:18–3:7; see David L. Balch, *Let Wives Be Submissive: The Domestic Code in 1 Peter* (SBLMS 26; Chico, Calif.: Scholars Press, 1981); J. H. Elliott, *A Home for the Homeless: A Social-Scientific Criticism of 1 Peter, Its Situation and Strategy* (2d ed.; Minneapolis: Augsburg Fortress, 1990), 208–20; J. H. Elliott, *I Peter,* 503–11.
19. Steve Young, "Being a Man," 244.
20. R. A. Horsley and J. S. Hanson, *Bandits, Prophets and Messiahs: Popular Movements in the Time of Jesus* (Minneapolis: Winston, 1985), 69–76; E. W. Stegemann and W. Stegemann, *The Jesus Movement: A Social History of Its First Century* (Edinburgh: T. & T. Clark, 1999), 173–78.
21. T. Nonn, "Hitting Bottom: Homelessness, Poverty and Masculinities," *Theology & Sexuality* 3 (1995): 11–26.
22. E. Hobsbawm (*Primitive Rebels: Studies of Archaic Forms of Social Movements in the 19th and 20th Centuries* [New York: Norton, 1959], 17–18) suggests that young men are most likely to join such movements.
23. See above, ch. 2, and Theissen, *Social Reality and the Early Christians,* 90–92.
24. As in all naming of groups in the gospels, the names of those singled out for particular mention vary. Only Mary from Magdala appears to be a permanent feature; also Mary the mother of the disciples James and Joses is frequently mentioned (Luke 8:1–3; Mark 15:40; Luke 24:10; Matt. 27:55–56: John 19:25). Some appear by name or other identification only once, as Joanna, the wife of Chuza (Luke 8:1–3), or the mother of the sons of Zebedee (Matt. 20:20).
25. Seim, *Double Message,* 81–88.
26. See especially Mary Magdala in John's Gospel, 19:25; 20:1–18. Cf. Antti Marjanen, *The Woman Jesus Loved: Mary Magdalene in the Nag Hammadi Library and Related Documents* (Nag Hammadi and Manichaean Studies 40; Leiden: Brill, 1996).
27. Valantasis ("Power in Asceticism," 805) develops this type on the basis of the *Acts of Peter and the Twelve Apostles,* an apparently non-Gnostic text from the Nag Hammadi Library.
28. Valantasis, "Power in Asceticism," 809.
29. See C. W. Bynum, "Women's Stories, Women's Symbols: A Critique of Victor Turner's Theory of Liminality," in *Anthropology and the Study of Religion* (ed. R. L. Moore and F. L. Reynolds; Chicago: Center for the Scientific Study of Religion, 1984), 105–25. Bynum's criticism and alternative readings are relevant also regarding Valantasis's ideal types.

30. Valantasis, "Power in Asceticism," 803. Valantasis did not use texts specifically about women as his source for this type, he built this part of his hypothesis on the Nag Hammadi document *On the Eighth and the Ninth.*
31. Victor W. Turner, *Dramas, Fields and Metaphors: Symbolic Action in Human Society* (Ithaca, N.Y.: Cornell University Press 1974), 231–71.
32. See Bynum, "Women's Stories, Women's Symbols."
33. Ross Kraemer, *Her Share of the Blessings: Women's Religions among Pagans, Jews and Christians in the Greco-Roman World* (New York: Oxford University Press, 1992), 133.
34. Mothers of disciples as followers of Jesus are mentioned in Mark 15:40; Matt. 20:20–21; 27:55–56. The fathers of disciples are mentioned only to identify their sons, as, for example, Mark 2:14; 3:17–18; Luke 6:16; John 1:42; see A. Destro and M. Pesce, "Kinship, Discipleship, and Movement: An Anthropological Study of John's Gospel, " *BibInt* 3 (1995): 270.
35. For instance, 1 Cor. 11:1–16 and 1 Tim. 5:3–16; see the influential study by J. M. Bassler, "The Widows' Tale: A Fresh Look at 1 Tim. 5:3–16," *JBL* 103:23–41.
36. This saying probably does not go back to Jesus, but to an early Jesus tradition; Luz, *Matthäus,* 3:298.
37. Gail P. Corrington, "The Defense of the Body and the Discourse of Appetite: Continence and Control in the Greco-Roman World," *Semeia* 57 (1992): 65–74.
38. This was also an ideal for women, for instance, early Christian women ascetics. But it is significant that the regulation of women's appetites became a preoccupation of early Christian male authors. Moreover, women's avoidance of food could be understood as a means to redefine gender, "to become male" (Corrington, "Defense of the Body," 70).
39. Bruce J. Malina, *Christian Origins and Cultural Anthropology* (Atlanta: John Knox Press, 1986), 185–204.
40. See Mary Douglas, *Natural Symbols: Explorations in Cosmology* (with new introduction; New York: Pantheon, 1982), 65–81.
41. For an interpretation mainly along the lines of a combination of fasting and accusations of demon possession, see Wendy J. Cotter, "Children Sitting in the Agora," *Forum* 5:2 (1989): 70–75.
42. Cotter, "Children," 78–79.
43. Leif E. Vaage, *Galilean Upstarts: Jesus' First Followers according to Q* (Valley Forge, Pa.: Trinity Press International, 1994), 87–89.
44. Jerome H. Neyrey, "Meals, Food, and Table Fellowship," in *The Social Sciences and New Testament Interpretation* (ed. R. L. Rohrbaugh; Peabody, Mass.: Hendrickson, 1996), 159–82.
45. Marshall Sahlins, *Stone Age Economics* (Chicago: Alderdine-Atherton, 1972), 215.
46. Davies and Allison, *Matthew,* 3:25 n. 118.
47. Mark 2:18–20 has a parallel in *Gos. Thom.* 104, and therefore a double source attestation. Although not parallel to Q 7:33–34, they deal with the same theme, and this makes Crossan (*Historical Jesus,* 259–60) treat them as sources for the historical Jesus.
48. Cf. Valantasis's definition of asceticism, in "Power in Asceticism," 797: "Asceticism may be defined as performances within a dominant social environment intended to inaugurate a new subjectivity, different social relations, and an alternative symbolic universe."
49. Creswell, *In Place, out of Place,* 166.
50. "Queer" does not indicate a positive or clearly defined identity; rather, it "demarcates not a positivity but a *positionality* vis-à-vis the normative," David

M. Halperin, *Saint-Foucault: Towards a Gay Hagiography* (New York: Oxford University Press, 1995), 62.

51. To reach this conclusion, I have been challenged and inspired by a number of feminist studies; besides, of course, the many works by Elisabeth Schüssler Fiorenza, also Diane Jacobs-Malina, *Beyond Patriarchy: The Images of Family in Jesus* (New York: Paulist Press, 1993), and Elizabeth Green, "More Musings on Maleness: The Maleness of Jesus Revisited," *Feminist Theology* 20 (1999): 9–27. Rosemary Ruether ("What Do the Synoptics Say? The Sexuality of Jesus," *Christianity and Crisis* 38 [1978]: 134–37) has the intriguing notion of Jesus in an "intermediate space" between marriage and celibacy, hetero- and homosexuality. Likewise, R. Goss (*Jesus Acted Up: A Gay and Lesbian Manifesto* [San Fransisco: Harper, 1993]) has destabilized the heterosexuality of Jesus, which I surmise is a presupposition underneath much of the discussion of Jesus and the family.

52. Cf. the term "asceticism of transgression" to characterize Cynic asceticism, Leif E. Vaage, "Like Dogs Barking: Cynic *parrēsia* and Shameless Action," *Semeia* 57 (1992): 25–39.

53. Ibid.

Chapter 6

1. Alberto Manguel and Gianni Guadalupi, *The Dictionary of Imaginary Places* (rev. ed., Toronto: Knopf, 1999 [orig. ed. 1980]).

2. Ibid., xi.

3. See W. Willis, ed., *The Kingdom of God in 20th-Century Interpretation* (Peabody, Mass.: Hendrickson, 1987); D. Duling, "Kingdom of God, Kingdom of Heaven: New Testament and Early Christian Interpretation," *ABD* 4 (1992): 62–65.

4. See the strong criticism of this combination by Jean Carmignac, "Les dangers de l'eschatologie," *JBL* 17 (1971): 365–90; further developed in *Le Mirage de l'eschatologie: Royauté, règne et royaume de Dieu . . . sans eschatologie* (Paris: Letouzey et Ané, 1979).

5. Carmignac, "Les dangers de l'eschatologie," 365–70.

6. Bruce J. Malina, "Christ and Time: Swiss or Mediterranean?" in his *The Social World of Jesus,* 179–214.

7. Johannes Weiss, *Jesus' Proclamation of the Kingdom of God* (trans., ed., and with introd. by R. H. Hiers and D. L. Holland; Philadelphia: Fortress, 1971); trans. of *Die Predigt Jesu vom Reiche Gottes* (Göttingen: Vandenhoeck & Ruprecht, 1892).

8. Albert Schweitzer, *The Quest of the Historical Jesus* (1st complete ed.; ed. J. Bowden [Minneapolis: Fortress, 2001]), 198–201, 315–54; trans. of *Geschichte der Leben-Jesu-Forschung* (Tübingen: Mohr, 1906, 1913, 1950).

9. C. H. Dodd, *The Parables of the Kingdom* (1935; rev. ed., New York: Scribner's, 1961).

10. Marcus J. Borg, *Jesus in Contemporary Scholarship* (Valley Forge, Pa.: Trinity Press International, 1994), 47–96.

11. Sometimes, as in liberal Protestantism in the end of the nineteenth century, kingdom was internalized and made into an ethical category. Another form of internalization happened again in the twentieth century, especially with the interpretation of the parables. It was argued that the parables functioned to shatter the worldview of their listeners and, by implication, the internalized and existential worldview of modern readers as well. See especially J. D. Crossan, *In Parables: The Challenge of the Historical Jesus* (New York: Harper & Row, 1973).

12. Edward W. Soja, *Postmodern Geographies: The Reassertion of Space in Critical Social Theory* (London: Verso, 1989), 10–42.
13. The classic article is N. A. Dahl, "Parables of Growth," *ST* 5 (1951): 132–66; but see a criticism of his (time-oriented) eschatological model of interpretation by B. B. Scott, *Hear Then the Parable*, 305–6. Scott argues that the eschatological model derives from outside the parables themselves, and that they should be interpreted in light of the metaphorical networks they employ, especially that of the kingdom as a farm or a house.
14. Joachim Jeremias, *The Parables of the Kingdom* (trans. S. H. Hooke; New York: Scribner's, 1965), 149.
15. Scott, *Hear Then the Parable*, 305–6.
16. The versions in Mark and the *Gospel of Thomas* (and partly, Matthew) share a common outline in four parts: (a) the mustard seed is a referent of the kingdom; (b) the seed is introduced into the soil; (c) the seed produces a much larger growth; (d) this final growth provides shelter for the birds. See W. Cotter, "The Parable of the Mustard Seed and the Leaven: Their Function in the Earliest Stratum of Q," *Toronto Journal of Theology* 8 (1992): 39. Cotter does not mention how different the Q version is.
17. See Stephen J. Patterson, "Wisdom in Q and Thomas," in *In Search of Wisdom* (ed. Leo G. Perdue et al.; Louisville, Ky.: Westminster/John Knox, 1993), 201–5.
18. Scott, *Hear Then the Parable*, 381–83.
19. *Gos. Thom.* 20 has the simplest statement; Mark and Q have a version that is more closely modeled to biblical texts: "the birds of the sky nest in its branches" (Q 13:19).
20. Robert W. Funk, *Jesus as Precursor* (Semeia Suppl. 2; Philadelphia: Fortress, 1975), 19–28.
21. Soja (*Postmodern Geographies*, 268–69) speaks of a "third space," which does not follow from the binary opposition or contradiction, but "seeks instead to disorder, deconstruct and tentatively reconstitute in a different form the entire dialectical sequence and logic." Soja says of this "third space" that it is not a dialectical synthesis, but represents something "other" that disrupts the dialectical opposites: "It shifts the 'rhythm' of dialectical thinking from a temporal to a more spatial mode, from a linear or diachronic sequencing to the configurative simultaneities and synchronies," 269.
22. See the following parable, on the woman and the leaven, Q 13:20–21, and the parable of the good Samaritan, Luke 10:29–37.
23. See above, "Entering a New Household."
24. Ibid.
25. For a discussion of various views of the relations between itinerant followers and sedentary sympathizers, see Kloppenborg, *Excavating Q*, 179–84.
26. David R. Catchpole, *The Quest for Q* (Edinburgh: T. & T. Clark, 1993), 201–28. Kloppenborg (*Excavating Q*, 144–47) sees these passages belonging to clusters of sayings in the first stratum of Q, which are united by paraenetic concerns and a radical social practice: Q 6:20b–49; 9:57–10:24; 11:2–4, 9–13; 12:2–7, 11–12, 22b–31, 33–34.
27. Kloppenborg, *Formation of Q*, 320–21. Kloppenborg speaks of the role of the wisdom in the earliest strata of Q, that it both "disorients the hearer with respect to ordinary existence," with reference to some of the texts that we discussed in chap. 3, for example, Q 9:57–60; 14:26, and "reorients towards the new reality of the kingdom (6:20b) and God (6:35, 36; 11:9–13; 12:4–7, 22–31, 33–34)."
28. See the discussion of these texts with respect to the Q community in Kloppenborg, *Excavating Q*, 169.

29. It is commonly held that this petition is eschatological, and that it secures an eschatological interpretation of the prayer as a whole. An eschatological interpretation is in analogy with Jewish prayers, but they are mostly later than this prayer; Vaage, *Galilean Upstarts,* 58–59. However, just because prayer language is so conservative, it is significant that the petition "Your kingdom come" is so terse, without any of the explanatory additions that are common in Jewish prayers; Meier, *Marginal Jew,* 2:298–300. It is therefore difficult to draw a clear conclusion about a meaning in terms of *time* for this petition.

30. See especially J. Jeremias, *Prayers of Jesus* (London: SCM, 1967). It was accepted by many scholars; see the overview of the discussion in Marianne Meyer Thompson, *The Promise of the Father: Jesus and God in the New Testament* (Louisville, Ky.: Westminster John Knox, 2000), 21–34.

31. The first serious criticism was Mary Rose D'Angelo, "ABBA and 'Father': Imperial Theology and the Jesus Traditions," *JBL* 111 (1992): 612–13; see the discussion in Thompson, *Promise of the Father.*

32. Dio Chrysostom, *Or.* 1.39–40.

33. Epictetus, *Diatr.* 19.7.

34. Geza Vermes, *The Religion of Jesus the Jew* (London: SCM Press, 1993), 121–35, 173–80; Klaus W. Müller, "König und Vater," in *Königsherrschaft Gottes und himmlischer Kult* (ed. M. Hengel and A. M. Schwemer; WUNT 55; Tübingen: Mohr, 1991), 21–43.

35. Thompson, *Promise of the Father,* 34–55.

36. Matt. 5:34; 25:31–46.

37. Vermes, *Religion of Jesus the Jew,* 124.

38. Thompson, *Promise of the Father,* 35–40.

39. Vaage, *Galilean Upstarts,* 59. This is similar to sayings about the coming of the kingdom in Q 11:20 and 10:9, which can only give meaning when interpreted in light of their context, not from a preconceived notion about eschatology.

40. Luke 11:5–8, which also deals with prayer, most likely did not belong to the Q collection; Kloppenborg, *Formation of Q,* 203–4.

41. Kloppenborg (*Formation of Q,* 205–6) thinks that 11:9–10 very early was attached to 11:11–13; Catchpole (*Quest for Q,* 218–23) instead sees 11:5–9 and 11:11–13 as parallel units, with 11:10 as an addition. Both Kloppenborg and Catchpole see the main motifs as God's provisions for the needy, with links to Q 12:22–31.

42. *Gos. Thom.* 2, 92, and 94 present parallels only to Q 11:9, without the broader context of material needs in Q 11:2–13. Therefore the encouragement to "seek and find" becomes much more open-ended. The *Gospel of Thomas* is much more mysterious about what one shall seek; maybe it is part of an esoteric tendency in the *Gospel of Thomas*; see Patterson, *Gospel of Thomas and Jesus,* 202–4. That "seek and find" is the theme of saying 2 suggests how important the theme is for Thomas; S. L. Davies, *The Gospel of Thomas and Christian Wisdom* (New York: Seabury Press, 1983), 36–40.

43. H. Moxnes, *Economy of the Kingdom* (Philadelphia: Fortress, 1988), 34–35.

44. Ibid., 136–38.

45. *agatha,* "good things," from Matthew is preferred as the original reading of Q to Luke's "the Holy Spirit," Robinson et al., *Critical Edition of Q,* 220–21, also by Catchpole, *Quest for Q,* 212.

46. David Catchpole, "Q and the 'Friend at Midnight' (Luke xi.5–8/9)," *JTS* n.s. 34 (1983): 415–16. This corresponds also to the use of *agatha* in Jewish tradition, in many instances used of food (e.g., Ps. 34:10: 107:9), or as God's provisions for the needy (Sir. 11:12; 39:25–27).

47. Moxnes, *Economy of the Kingdom,* 83–93.

48. Betz (*The Sermon on the Mount*, 460–65) has argued for a setting within a context of the discussion of anxieties among writers, especially moral philosophers in the Greco-Roman (including Jewish) world. It follows from this setting that Betz finds that the collection addresses a general audience.
49. Luz, *Matthäus*, 1:371.
50. Catchpole (*Quest for Q*, 227–28) suggests that they might even have been in sequence in the Q tradition.
51. In Luke, the passage on anxieties is preceded by a warning against avarice (12:13–15) and the parable of the rich fool (12:16–21). Matthew places other sayings about anxiety in the immediate context of 6:25–34. In 6:19–21 and 24, it is an anxiety over possessions, and it comes to a conclusion with the conflict between serving God and mammon. A similar change in social context is reflected in the later allegorical interpretation of the parable of the sower. One of the great dangers that prevent the seed from producing a crop is anxieties over riches (Mark 4:19/Matt. 13:22/Luke 8:14). The real danger with anxieties is thus that they create divided attention and divided commitment; instead of an embodiment, persons become disembodied and scattered (cf. Luke 10: 38–42; 1 Cor. 7: 32–35).
52. Ronald A. Piper, "Wealth, Poverty and Subsistence in Q," in *From Quest to Q: FS James M. Robinson* (ed. J. Ma. Asgeirsson, K. de Troyer, and M. W. Meyer; BETL 146; Leuven: Leuven University Press, 2000), 245.
53. It is repeated a third time in the addition to the passage, Matt. 6:34; Luke 12:32.
54. Q 12:25–26 is generally accepted as a later addition.
55. I owe this observation to Reidar Aasgaard who has used the term "splinter" in his analysis of the family patterns in Paulus; see his "'My Beloved Brothers and Sisters!': Christian Siblingship in the Apostle Paul (London: Continuum [T. & T. Clark], forthcoming).
56. In other passages, other aspects of household relations are re-created, for instance, the duty to follow the example of one's father and thereby becoming sons/children of God, Q 6:35; Matt. 6:12–15; 18:35.
57. See, e.g., Chr. Tuckett (*Q and the History of Early Christianity* [Edinburgh: T. & T. Clark, 1996], 149–52), who without argument takes "kingdom" in and by itself to imply eschatology. His interpretation of the passage is on the level of Q, but it is very different from how I have tried to read the sayings as a reflection of Jesus' attitude. Cf. his summary: "The redactional elements seem to be trying to *redirect* Q Christians' energy *away* from concern for food (with a passing reference to the claim that God will provide) and to refocus their efforts in relation to the kingdom," 151 n. 40. This is a reading that places Q close to Matthew's position, but I find the downgrading of the importance of the motive that God will provide to "a passing reference" to be simply wrong.
58. Luz (*Mattäus*, 1:365) sees the dilemma of ascribing too much meaning to the term; he says that it "can be directed only to listeners who have already heard of Jesus' proclamation of the kingdom of God." Kloppenborg (*Formation of Q*, 219–20) also appears to accept the time orientation of the statement, and that it in and by itself introduces something new: "The mention of the kingdom indeed seems to introduce an eschatological aspect." But he sees a dilemma in that this eschatological (or apocalyptic) statement does not in substance say anything new: "While the introduction of the apocalyptic aspect is novel, the logic and the basic motif of 12:31 is quite in keeping with the sapiential teaching on divine provision and providence." Piper ("Wealth, Poverty and Subsistence in Q," 258–59) furthermore questions the importance that is attributed to the kingdom saying within the passage as a whole, and points out that it

appears in 12:22–31 only at the end. It is the needs of God's children, not the kingdom, that is the starting point of the argument.

59. Vaage, *Galilean Upstarts*, 62: "To 'seek his kingdom' means to seek the father, who, in 12:30b, knows what you need."

60. Ronald A. Piper, *Wisdom in the Q-Tradition: The Aphoristic Teaching of Jesus* (SNTSMS 61; Cambridge: Cambridge University Press, 1989), 31.

61. R. Valantasis, *The Gospel of Thomas* (London: Routledge, 1997), 193.

62. Robert Hamerton-Kelly, *God the Father: Theology and Patriarchy in the Teaching of Jesus* (Philadelphia: Fortress, 1979), 102–3.

63. Phillis Trible, "Review of R. Hamerton-Kelly, *God the Father*," *Theology Today* 37 (1980): 118.

64. See, e.g., Virginia Burrus, *"Begotten, Not Made": Conceiving Manhood in Late Antiquity* (Stanford, Calif.: Stanford University Press, 2000).

65. See, among others, E. Schüssler Fiorenza's *Jesus: Miriam's Child, Sophia's Prophet* (New York: Continuum, 1994), 12–24; *Jesus and the Politics of Interpretation* (New York: Continuum, 2000), 1–29 and passim.

66. "'Kyriarchy' means the domination of the lord, slave, master, husband, the elite freeborn educated and propertied man over all wo/men and subaltern men," Schüssler Fiorenza, *Jesus and the Politics of Interpretation,* 95.

67. I think that Elisabeth Schüssler Fiorenza has a point (*Jesus and the Politics of Interpretation,* 98–101) when she claims that I and other members of the Cultural Context Group reify "honor and shame" as "facts" of ancient Mediterranean society in contrast to modern (U.S.) societies, and overlook how this is a construction based on a general notion of domination that is at work in modern societies as well. But I still think that domination takes various forms in different societies, and that "honor and shame" may be useful analytical categories. I think, for instance, that in other societies physical or military power, or money, may be the main sources of domination.

68. Scott, *Hear Then the Parable,* 80–85.

69. Rohrbaugh, "A Dysfunctional Family," 141–64.

70. Christoph Burckhard, "Jesus of Nazareth," in *Christian Beginning* (ed. J. Becker; Louisville, Ky.: Westminster/John Knox, 1993), 42.

71. Vermes, *Religion of Jesus the Jew,* 146.

72. Kloppenborg, *Excavating Q,* 391–92.

73. Vermes (*Religion of Jesus the Jew,* 146) speaks of Jesus' teaching that "transforms into reality the 'unreal' ingredients of the inherited imagery of the Kingdom."

74. There is a similar argument in 1 Peter; see John H. Elliott, *A Home for the Homeless.*

75. This political perspective has been largely neglected in studies of the kingdom of God, but see now Richard A. Horsley, *Jesus and Empire: The Kingdom of God and the New World Disorder* (Minneapolis: Fortress, 2000) and Bruce J. Malina, *The Social Gospel of Jesus: The Kingdom of God in Mediterranean Perspective* (Minneapolis: Fortress, 2001).

Chapter 7

1. For a discussion of this function of discourse, based on Bourdieu, Lefebvre, and Foucault, see Rob Shields, *Places on the Margin: Alternative Geographies of Modernity* (London and New York: Routledge, 1991), 29–70.

2. Cf. Ibid., 54. Shields discusses Lefebvre and the way in which he sees that underground spatial practices provide alternatives to institutionalized discourses of space, and continues: "It is on this 'level' that 'space' operates as an

overcoding meta-concept which imbues other conceptual categories and symbolic systems with an often unrecognized 'spatial life.'"

3. Cf. Barry L. Blackburn, "The Miracles of Jesus," in *Studying the Historical Jesus* (ed. B. Chilton and C. A. Evans; NTTS 19; Leiden: Brill, 1994), 353–94.

4. Paul W. Hollenbach, "Jesus, Demoniacs and Public Authorities: A Socio-Historical Study," *JAAR* 49 (1981): 567–88.

5. Stevan L. Davies, *Jesus the Healer* (New York: Continuum, 1995), 9–15.

6. G. Vermes, *Jesus the Jew* (London: Collins, 1973; reprint, Philadelphia: Fortress, 1981), 58–82.

7. See Hector Avalos, *Health Care and the Rise of Christianity* (Peabody, Mass.: Hendrickson, 1999). John J. Pilch, *Healing in the New Testament: Insights from Medical and Mediterranean Anthropology* (Minneapolis: Fortress, 2000) has a broader cultural perspective, but little explicit discussion of exorcisms.

8. See A. Kleinmann, *Patients and Healers in the Context of Culture* (Berkeley: University of California Press, 1980).

9. I have learned much about healing in an African context through one of my students, Daniel Addae Owusu, in "Jesus the African Healer," his master's thesis, Faculty of Theology, University of Oslo, 2001.

10. Michael Taussig, *Shamanism, Colonialism, and the Wild Man: A Study in Terror and Healing* (Chicago: University of Chicago Press, 1986); quotation from 435.

11. Ibid., 335.

12. Jonathan Z. Smith, "Towards Interpreting Demonic Powers in Hellenistic and Roman Antiquity," *ANRW* II 16.1 (1978), 425–39; quotations are from 429, 430.

13. Hollenbach, "Jesus, Demoniacs and Public Authorities"; Crossan, *Historical Jesus,* 319.

14. Bruce J. Malina and J. H. Neyrey, *Calling Jesus Names: The Social Value of Labels in Matthew* (Sonoma, Calif., Polebridge, 1988).

15. Ibid., 20–32; Douglas, *Natural Symbols,* 107–24.

16. Malina and Neyrey, *Calling Jesus Names,* 40.

17. For an analysis of the different versions of the story in the gospels, see Vernon K. Robbins, "Rhetorical Composition and the Beelzebul Controversy," in *Patterns of Persuasion in the Gospels* (ed. Burton L. Mack and Vernon K. Robbins; Sonoma, Calif.: Polebridge, 1989), 161–93.

18. Q 11:14–20 was probably followed by the simile of the strong man, Q 11:21–22; Kloppenborg, *Formation of Q,* 125, but it was maybe not in the first stratum of Q; see Robinson et al., *Critical Edition of Q,* 234–35, and its original text form is uncertain; see n. 39. Q 11:23 was most likely originally an independent saying; Kloppenborg, *Formation of Q,* 125. As for the text of Q 11:14–20 itself, most scholars hold that vv. 16 and 18b did not belong to the core of Q tradition; Kloppenborg, *The Formation of Q,* 122–24.

19. Heikki Räisänen, "Exorcisms and the Kingdom: Is Q 11:20 a Saying of the Historical Jesus?" in *Symbols and Strata: Essays on the Sayings Gospel Q* (ed. Risto Uro; Publications of the Finnish Exegetical Society 65 [Göttingen: Vandenhoeck & Ruprecht, 1996]), 127–35; Kloppenborg, *Formation of Q,* 121–27.

20. Michael L. Humphries, *Christian Origins and the Language of the Kingdom of God* (Carbondale and Evansville: Southern Illinois University Press, 1999), 28; see G. Theissen, *The Miracle Stories of Early Christian Tradition* (Philadelphia: Fortress, 1983), 43–80.

21. See chap. 3 n. 29.

22. Mark's version in 3:22–27 does not have the saying about God's kingdom; it moves directly to the parable of the strong man (3:27), and adds a saying about sin against the Holy Spirit, 3:28–30.

23. For a thorough discussion and argument for this position, see Meier, *Marginal Jew,* 2:404–23.
24. Ibid., 2:407–11.
25. For a review of the discussion, see Sanders, *Jesus and Judaism,* 133–35; Jacobson, *The First Gospel,* 163; Räisänen, "Exorcisms and the Kingdom," 129; Humphries, *Christian Origins,* 33.
26. This illustrates the point made by Carmignac ("Les dangers de l'eschatologie"), that since the nineteenth century historical critical scholarship has understood the kingdom of God within the modern category of eschatology. For a history of interpretation, see Räisänen, "Exorcisms and the Kingdom," 119–27.
27. It has been understood either as future eschatological or as present eschatological; for an overview of various positions, see Sanders, *Jesus and Judaism,* 33–34; for a more thorough discussion of the term, see Robert F. Berkey, "*Engizein, phtanein,* and realized eschatology," *JBL* 82 (1963): 177–87.
28. Räisänen, "Exorcisms and the Kingdom," 133–42.
29. Ibid., 128–33; Humphries, *Christian Origins,* 33–34.
30. Crossan, *Historical Jesus,* 318–20.
31. Joseph A. Fitzmyer, *The Gospel According to Luke,* vol. 2, 2 ed. AB 28 A (Garden City, N.Y.: Doubleday, 1985), 918.
32. What is of interest in these versions is that the accusers are listed as people of authority, not the historical accuracy of the reports.
33. J. Z. Smith, "Interpreting Demonic Powers," 427.
34. In Q 11:18 it is replaced by Satan, a much more common figure in Jewish demonology; W. Foerster, "Beelzebul"; *TDNT* 1 (1964), 605–6.
35. Humphries, *Christian Origins,* 13–22.
36. Q 11:17 speaks of "being laid waste, depopulated" (*erēmoutai*) as the result of divisions, while Mark 3:24 speaks of it more in terms of rule, "it cannot stand" (*stathēnai*).
37. Mark 13:8 par. speak not of internal divisions, but of conflicts between kingdoms.
38. Above, chap. 2.
39. I follow the Lukan text in Q 11:21–22, since that is closer to Q 11:17–20, see n. 40. Robinson et al. (*Critical Edition of Q,* 234) follow the Matthean version, Matt. 12:29, that is closer to Mark 3:27. For a review of the inconclusive discussion of an "original" Q text, see Schröter, *Erinnerung an Jesu Worte,* 261–64.
40. Thus, the version of this Q simile in Luke paints a different picture than that of the "robbery of the strong man" in Matt. 12:29; Mark 3:27; and *Gos. Thom.* 35. This corresponds to the different approaches between Mark and Q that we noticed in regard to Q 11:17–20 and Mark 3:23–26. Q pictures two kingdoms in conflict with each other, whereas Mark describes the conflict more in personal terms; Kloppenborg, *Formation of Q,* 125; John P. Meier, *Marginal Jew* 2 (1994): 418–19.
41. Anton Fridrichsen, *The Problem of Miracle in Early Christianity* (Minneapolis: Augsburg, 1972), 104–5.
42. G. Foerster, "Daimon," *TDNT* 2 (1964), 10–16.
43. G. Foerster, " Satanas," *TDNT* 7 (1971), 154–56.
44. G. Foerster, "Satanas," 159; H. Kruse, "Das Reich Satans," *Biblica* 58 (1977); 29–64.
45. This is not an impossible thought. Consciously or unconsciously, that seems to be the case in Mark's version of the story of the Gerasene demoniac, where the possessed man gives his name as "Legion, for we are many." Thus, the demons are identified with the Roman military presence; see Hollenbach, "Jesus, Demoniacs and Public Authorities," 581.

46. Thus, Jesus and the early Christians more than the Jews seem to concur with Smith's evaluation when he asks ("Interpreting Demonic Powers," 437) "Why is it that the demonic, associated with the marginal, the liminal, the chaotic, the protean, the unstructured appear cross-culturally as so rigidly organized a realm?"

47. Wis. 6:4; *Pss.Sol.* 17:3; 1QM 6:6; 12:7; Philo, *Spec.* 4.164.

48. Humphries (*Christian Origins,* 33) reads Q 11:19b in light of 11:20b to indicate that also Jewish exorcists could bring the kingdom of God by their exorcisms. Exactly that conclusion has been the main reason why most scholars have objected to a reading that combines 11:19 and 20 and sees them as part of the same argument. Some of the objections are based on grammatical or stylistic reasons (Kloppenborg, *Formation of Q,* 124–25), but most are based on theological presuppositions; see n. 25. There is not anything in Q 11:19–20 that speaks against the implication that the works of Jewish exorcists might also reflect the presence of the kingdom, but it is not directly expressed.

49. Kloppenborg, *Excavating Q,* 391.

50. Leif E. Vaage, "Q and Cynicism: On Comparison and Social Identity," in *The Gospel Behind the Gospels,* 222–23.

51. "Finger" may be the original reading in Q (Meier, *Marginal Jew,* 2:410–11), and go back to a tradition of interpretation of God's finger in Ex. 8:15; see van der Horst, "'The Finger of God': Miscellaneous Notes on Luke 11:20 and Its *Umwelt*," in *Sayings of Jesus: Canonical and Non-Canonical: Essays in Honour of T. Baarda* (ed. W. L. Petersen, J. s. Vos, H. J. de Jone; NoviSup 89; Leiden: Brill, 1997), 89–103. It makes Jesus parallel to Moses, who was in conflict with Egyptian sorcerers; Dale C. Allison, *The Intertextuality of Jesus* (Harrisburg, Pa.: Trinity, 2000), 53–57.

52. Risto Uro ("Apocalyptic Symbolism and Social Identity in Q," in *Symbols and Strata* [ed. Risto Uro; Publications of the Finnish Exegetical Society 65 (Göttingen: Vandenhoeck & Ruprecht, 1996)], 80–88) argues against attributing too much importance to temporal aspects of *ephtasen* in Q 11:20.

53. This passage, although only singly attested by Luke, may contain historical material, especially in 13:31–32a; Rudolf Bultmann, *The History of the Synoptic Tradition* (Oxford: Blackwell, 1963), 35. For discussion, see B. L. Blackburn, "The Miracles of Jesus," 360–61; Allison (*Jesus of Nazareth,* 66–67) finds the picture consistent with secure aspects of Jesus as eschatological prophet and as healer and exorcist.

54. Hollenbach, "Jesus, Demoniacs and Public Authorities," 581.

55. All of Galilee, Mark 1:39; Syria, Decapolis, Jerusalem, beyond the Jordan, Matt. 4:24–25; Judea, Jerusalem, regions of Tyre and Sidon, Luke 6:17–19.

56. Harold W. Hoehner, *Herod Antipas* (SNTSMS 17; Cambridge: Cambridge University Press, 1972), 200–201.

57. Ibid., 196–97.

58. See Richard A. Horsley, *Jesus and the Spiral of Violence: Popular Jewish Resistance in Roman Palestine* (San Francisco: Harper & Row, 1987), 167–208.

59. Peter Brown, "Sorcery, Demons and the Rise of Christianity: From Late Antiquity into the Middle Ages," in *Religion and Society in the Age of St. Augustine* (New York: Harper & Row, 1972), 119–46.

60. Ibid., 124.

61. Vermes, *Jesus the Jew,* 58–81, on Galilean prophets as possible models for Jesus; but see the strong criticism of Vermes's hypothesis by Sean Freyne, "Hanina ben Dosa: A Galilean Charismatic," in his *Galilee and Gospel: Collected Essays* (WUNT 125; Tübingen: Mohr, 2000), 132–59.

62. J. Murphy-O'Connor, "John the Baptist and Jesus: History and Hypotheses," *NTS* 36 (1990): 371–72.

63. See Morton Smith, *Jesus the Magician* (New York: Harper & Row, 1978). Smith suggests that his opponents regarded Jesus as a magician, and lists parallel figures in antiquity.

64. Cf. Taussig, *Shamanism, Colonialism, and the Wild Man,* 335: "Indian medicine men . . . arouse the slumbering meaning of space long colonized by the white man and carry him through it to uncover the hidden presence not only of God but of the sorcerer."

65. See Moxnes, *Economy of the Kingdom,* 143–46.

66. This corresponds to J. Z. Smith's observation ("Interpreting Demonic Powers," 438): "In the locative cosmology, the demonic was the out-of-place on an essentially horizontal map of center and periphery, of domain and boundaries."

67. Mark presents the response to the accusation that Jesus was a deviant in strongly personal terms. Mark does not in his gospel combine healings or exorcisms directly with the kingdom of God. Instead, the emphasis is on the recognition by the unclean spirits of the power of Jesus and, in personal terms, that he is the son of God (3:11; 5:7). This is a personalized approach to the exorcisms of Jesus that corresponds to that of later apologists who also had to defend Jesus against accusations of sorcery; see G. W. H. Lampe, "Miracles and Early Christian Apologetics," in *Miracles: Cambridge Studies in Their Philosophy and History* (ed. C. F. D. Moule; London: Mowbray, 1965), 211–14. J. Z. Smith ("Interpreting Demonic Powers," 438–39) suggests that in late antiquity there were various cosmologies at work; one of them implied a shift from a locative (place-oriented) cosmology to an anthropological, utopian one. It was no longer a question of a holy place that gave access to the divine center, but the holy man, as a negotiator and power holder, also in and between social communities.

Chapter 8

1. The first chapters (2–5) studied the local place and the use and importance of that place: home place and the appropriation of place (house, household, village), and gendered place (male place). The next section (chaps. 6 and 7) focused on kingdom as alternative space, a space that was created from below, partly in contrast to household and village, but mostly in contrast to political place, that is, the aspect of control and domination of place/space.

2. The first recent study was Sean Freyne, *Galilee from Alexander the Great to Hadrian, 323 B.C.E. to 135 C.E.*; see also the collection of Freyne's later essays, *Galilee and Gospel.* See the conference volumes: Lee I. Levine, ed. *The Galilee in Late Antiquity*; and Meyers, ed., *Galilee through the Centuries: Confluence of Cultures*; Edwards and McCollough, eds., *Archaeology and the Galilee.* Other studies are listed in the notes below.

3. See above, chap. 1 n.75.

4. J. Duncan and D. Ley, eds., *Place, Culture, Representation* (London: Routledge, 1993), 2.

5. J. Z. Smith, *To Take Place,* 30. Or, to speak in the more modest terminology of Duncan and Ley (*Place, Culture, Representation,* 332): "the mutual construction of place and identity."

6. A reference to the book by Gerd Theissen, *The Shadow of the Galilean: The Quest of the Historical Jesus in Narrative Form* (London: SCM, 1987), in which Jesus is never visible.

7. For a discussion of such writings by American visitors, especially Mark Twain's famous satiric travelogue, *The Innocents Abroad, or The New Pilgrim's Progress* (1869), see H. Obenzinger, *American Palestine: Melville, Twain and the Holy Land Mania* (Princeton, N.J.: Princeton University Press, 1999).

8. Benjamin Z. Kedar, *The Changing Land: Between the Jordan and the Sea: Aerial Photographs from 1917 to the Present*, Jerusalem: Yad Izhak Ben-Zwi Press, 1999.
9. Moxnes, "Construction of Galilee," 34–36, 69–70.
10. For the following, see especially several essays on Herodian economy and urbanrural relations in Galilee in Sean Freyne, *Galilee and Gospel*; and D. Oakman, "Models and Archaeology in the Social Interpretation of Jesus," in *Social Scientific Models for Interpreting the Bible*, 102–31.
11. Massey, *Space, Place and Gender*, 168.
12. Harvey, *Condition of Postmodernity*, 226.
13. Peter Richardson, *Herod* (Columbia: University of South Carolina Press, 1996), xiii.
14. Shurmer-Smith and Hannam, *Worlds of Desire, Realms of Power*, 165.
15. See Nagy, Meyers, Meyers, and Weiss, eds., *Sepphoris in Galilee*; and several studies in Edwards and McCollough, eds., *Archaeology and the Galilee*; Reed, *Archaeology and the Galilean Jesus*, 100–138; Richard A. Horsley, *Archaeology, History and Society in Galilee* (Valley Forge, Pa.: Trinity Press International, 1996), 43–65.
16. Cf. W. L. MacDonald, *The Architecture of the Roman Empire*, vol. 2, *An Urban Appraisal* (New Haven, Conn.: Yale University Press, 1986).
17. Tsvika Tsuk, "The Aqueducts to Sepphoris," in *Galilee through the Centuries: Confluence of Cultures*, 161–75.
18. Reed, *Archaeology and the Galilean Jesus*, 62–99; Richard A. Horsley, *Galilee: History, Politics, People* (Valley Forge, Pa.: Trinity Press International, 1995), 158–85.
19. Freyne ("Jesus and the Urban Culture of Galilee," in *Galilee and Gospel*, 196) finds a clash between two worlds, that of the urban centers and that of the rural hinterlands represented in the gospel parables: "day labourers, debt, resentment of absentee landlords, wealthy estate owners with little concern for tenants needs, exploitative stewards of estates, family feuds over inheritance, etc."
20. James F. Strange, "First Century Galilee from Archaeology and from the Texts," in *Archaeology and the Galilee*, 39–48.
21. Sean Freyne, "Town and Country Once More: The Case of Roman Galilee," in *Galilee and Gospel*, 59–72; Douglas Oakman, "Models and Archaeology."
22. Attempts to judge the size of land plots and the possibility to sustain a family indicate that even in Galilee, which was the richest area in Palestine, life was hard, with little safety, for instance, if the crop should fail; Fiensy, *The Social History of Palestine in the Herodian Period*, 92–105.
23. It is difficult to estimate how much the taxes and tithes amounted to, perhaps between 15 and 25 percent, but since the margins were so small, taxes were burdensome; Fiensy, *Social History of Palestine*, 102–4.
24. Hanson, "The Galilean Fishing Economy and the Jesus Tradition."
25. Horsley, *Archaeology, History and Society in Galilee*, 178–85; idem, "Jesus and Galilee: The Contingencies of a Renewal Movement," in *Galilee through the Centuries*, 57–74.
26. The classical study by Robert Redfield (*The Little Community: Viewpoints for the Study of Human Whole* [Chicago: University of Chicago Press], 1955) shows how "the little community" has a number of characteristics that are important for human identity: it is small, it is distinctive, it is homogeneous and self-sufficient.
27. Freyne, "Jesus and the Urban Culture of Galilee."
28. J. D. Crossan and J. L. Reed (*Excavating Jesus* [San Francisco: Harper, 2001], 126–28) have a similar understanding of the social and economic pressure on

households, but regard Jesus' words as directed at peasants who were already dispossessed, and suggests that they only in the later Jesus tradition were understood as words of voluntary dispossession.

29. Eric M. Meyers, "Ancient Synagogues: An Archaeological Introduction," in *Sacred Realm: The Emergence of the Synagogue in the Ancient World* (ed. Steven Fine; New York: Oxford University Press, 1996), 3–20. But see Lee I. Levine, *The Ancient Synagogue* (New Haven, Conn.: Yale University Press, 2000), 42–53. Levine accepts the evidence of gospels about synagogues (maybe too uncritically), but emphasizes the main point that I am arguing, that "the synagogue at this time was first and foremost a communal institution," ibid., 52.

30. Lee I. Levine, "The Sages and the Synagogues in Late Antiquity: The Evidence of the Galilee," in *The Galilee in Late Antiquity* (ed. Lee I. Levine; New York: Jewish Theological Seminary of America, 1992), 201–22.

31. R. A. Horsley, "Synagogues in Galilee and the Gospels," in *Evolution of the Synagogue* (ed. H. Clark Kee and Lynn H. Cohick; Harrisburg, Pa.: Trinity, 1999), 46–69.

32. The last appearance of Jesus in a synagogue was the conflict in the synagogue in Nazareth, Mark 6:1–6; Matt. 13:53–58. Luke has moved this to the beginning of Jesus' career, 4:16–30, but later mentions of visits to synagogues or with synagogue leaders (Luke 6:6–11; 8:41–56) are parallels to narratives that are earlier than Mark 6 and Matt. 13. Later mention of synagogues in all the synoptic gospels refer to criticism of Pharisees and scribes, or to persecutions, e.g., Mark 12:38–39; 13:9.

33. Turner, *Dramas, Fields and Metaphors,* 231–34.

34. This is a question that has not been much discussed in recent historical Jesus studies, and Peter Richardson rightly points to the need for further detailed studies of the areas surrounding Galilee and their history, culture, and social situations; "Enduring Concerns: Desiderata for Future Historical-Jesus Research," in *Whose Historical Jesus?* (ed. W. E. Arnal and M. Desjardins; Studies in Christianity and Judaism 7; Waterloo, Ont.: Wilfred Laurier University Press, 1997), 301.

35. The question can profitably be raised in terms of *localization* of identity as it is being discussed in social anthropology and geography. In an important essay on ethnic groups and boundaries, the anthropologist Fredrik Barth has argued that it is "the ethnic boundary that defines the group, not the cultural stuff it encloses"; *Ethnic Groups and Boundaries* (ed. Fredrik Barth, Oslo: Universitetsforlaget, 1969), 15.

36. Shurmer-Smith and Hannam, *Worlds of Desire,* 125–39.

37. Crossan (*Historical Jesus,* 303–53) emphasizes the combination of meals and exorcism and healings as expressions of the power of the kingdom.

38. H. W. Hoehner (*Herod Antipas,* 197–202) argues that Jesus' withdrawal was to avoid the impression that the kingdom he preached was in competition with Antipas's rule.

39. Reed, *Archaeology and the Galilean Jesus,* 103–14.

40. On the other hand, there are reports from traditional communities in Norway that people did not travel much, not even over what we would consider short distances.

41. See Freyne, "Town and Country Once More: The Case of Roman Galilee," *Galilee and Gospel,* 59–72; and especially Sawicki, *Crossing Galilee.* Sawicki speaks of "counter-strategies of the colonized," and distinguishes between "collaborative adaptation" and "resistive adaptation" (216–21).

42. Cf. A. N. Wilder, *Early Christian Rhetoric: The Language of the Gospel* (New York: Harper & Row, 1964).

43. Scott, *Hear Then the Parable*, 79–202.
44. Reed, *Archaeology and the Galilean Jesus*, 114.
45. William R. Herzog II, *Parables as Subversive Speech: Jesus as Pedagogue of the Oppressed* (Louisville, Ky.: Westminster John Knox, 1994).
46. Ibid., 233–58.
47. Moxnes, *Economy of the Kingdom*, 34–35; based on Sahlins, *Stone Age Economics* (Chicago: Alderdine-Atherton, 1972), 185–276.

Bibliography

Sources:

Apuleius. *The Golden Ass.* Loeb Classical Library. Cambridge, Mass.: Harvard University Press, 1965.

Clement of Alexandria. *Werke.* Edited by O. Stählin. GCS 52. Berlin: Akademie Verlag, 1972.

Jerome. *Commentaire sur S. Matthieu.* Vol. 2. Introduction by E. Bonnard. SC 259. Paris: Éditions du Cerf, 1977.

Justin Martyr. *The First and Second Apologies.* Introduction by L. W. Barnard. New York: Paulist Press, 1997.

Lucianus Samosatensis (Lucian). *Opera Omnia.* 4. London: Heinemann, 1919.

Origen. *Commentaire sur l'Évangile selon Matthieu.* SC 162. Paris: Éditions du Cerf, 1970.

———. *Der Kommentar zum Evangelium nach Mattäaus.* Vol. 2. Edited by H. J. Vogt. Stuttgart: Hierseman, 1990.

Robinson, J. M. *The Nag Hammadi Library in English.* 3. rev. ed. Leiden: Brill, 1988.

Robinson, J. M., P. Hoffmann, and J. S. Kloppenborg, *The Critical Edition of Q.* Hermeneia; Minneapolis: Fortress, 2000.

Tertullian. *Opera.* 2 vols. CCSL 1–2. Turnholt: Brepols, 1954.

Secondary Literature:

Aasgaard, Reidar. '*My Beloved Brothers and Sisters!*': Christian Siblingship in the Apostle. London: Continuum/T. & T. Clark, forthcoming.

Allison, Dale C. *The Jesus Tradition in Q.* Harrisburg, Pa.: Trinity Press International, 1997.

———. *Jesus of Nazareth: Millenarian Prophet.* Minneapolis: Fortress, 1998.

———. "Q 12:51–53 and Mark 9:11–13 and the Messianic Woes." Pages 289–310 in *Authenticating the Words of Jesus.* Edited by B. Chilton and C. A. Evans. NTTS 28:1. Leiden: Brill, 1999.

———. *The Intertextuality of Jesus.* Harrisburg, Pa.: Trinity Press International. 2000.

Anderson, James C. *Roman Architecture and Society.* Baltimore: Johns Hopkins Press, 1987.

Appleby, J., L. Hunt, and M. Jacob. *Telling the Truth about History.* New York: Norton, 1994.

Arnal, W. "Major Episodes in the Biography of Jesus: An Assessment of the Historicity of the Narrative Tradition." *Toronto Journal of Theology* 13 (1997): 201–26.

Auge, Marc. *Non-places: Introduction to an Anthropology of Supermodernity.* London: Verso, 1995.

Avalos, Hector. *Health Care and the Rise of Christianity.* Peabody, Mass.: Hendrickson, 1999.

Baer, Richard A. *Philo's Use of the Categories Male and Female.* ALGHJ 3. Leiden: Brill, 1970.

Balch, David L. *Let Wives Be Submissive: The Domestic Code in 1 Peter.* SBLMS 26. Chico, Calif.: Scholars Press, 1981.

Barth, Fredrik, ed. *Ethnic Groups and Boundaries.* Oslo: Universitetsforlaget, 1969.

Barton, S. C. *Discipleship and Family Ties in Mark and Matthew.* Society for New Testament Studies Monograph Series 80. Cambridge: Cambridge University Press, 1994.

Bassler, J. M. "The Widows' Tale: A Fresh Look at 1 Tim 5:3–16." *JBL* 103 (1984): 23–41.

Bauer, Walter. "Matt 19,12 und die alten Christen." Pages 253–62 in his *Aufsätze und kleine Schriften.* Edited by G. Strecker. 1914 Reprint. Tübingen: Mohr, 1967.

Bauer, W. *A Greek-English Lexicon on the New Testament and Other Early Christian Literature.* Trans. and adaptation of 4th rev. ed. by W. F. Arndt and F. W. Gingrich. 2. rev. ed. by Gingrich and F. W. Danker. Chicago: University of Chicago Press, 1979.

Berkey, Robert F. "*Eggizein, phtanein,* and realized eschatology." *JBL* 82 (1963): 177–87.

Bettini, M. *Anthropology and Roman Culture: Kinship, Time, Images of the Soul.* Baltimore: Johns Hopkins University Press, 1991.

Betz, Hans Dieter. *Galatians. A Commentary on Paul's Letter to the Churches in Galatia.* Philadelphia: Fortress. 1979.

———. *The Sermon on the Mount.* Hermeneia. Minneapolis: Fortress, 1995.

Blackburn, Barry L. "The Miracles of Jesus." Pages 353–94 in *Studying the Historical Jesus.* Edited by B. Chilton and C. A. Evans. NTTS 19. Leiden: Brill, 1994.

Blinzler, Josef. "*Eisin eunochoi.*" *ZNW* 48 (1957): 254–70.

———. "Justinus *Apol.* I 15,4 und Matthäus 19:11–12." Pages 45–55 in *Mélanges Bibliques: En homage au R. P. Beda Rigaux.* Edited by A. Descamps and A. de Halleu. Gembloux: Duculot, 1970.

Bockmuehl, Markus. "'Let the Dead Bury Their Dead' (Matt. 8:22/Luke 9:60)," *JTS* 49 (1998): 553–81.

Borg, Marcus J. *Jesus in Contemporary Scholarship.* Valley Forge, Pa.: Trinity Press International, 1994.

Bornkamm, Günther. *Jesus of Nazareth.* New York: Harper & Row, 1960. Eng. trans. from German original, 1956.

Breytenbach, C. "Mark and Galilee: Text World and Historical World." Pages 75–85 in *Galilee Through the Centuries: Confluence of Cultures.* Edited by Eric M. Meyers, Duke Judaic Studies Series 1, Winona Lake, Ind.: Eisenbrauns, 1999.

Brooks, Stephenson H. *Matthew's Community: The Evidence of His Special Sayings Material.* JSNTSup 16. Sheffield: Sheffield University Press, 1987.

Brown, Peter. "Sorcery, Demons and the Rise of Christianity: From Late Antiquity into the Middle Ages." Pages 119–46 in his *Religion and Society in the Age of St. Augustine.* New York: Harper & Row, 1972.

Brown, Peter. *The Body and Society. Men, Women and Sexual Renunciation in Early Christianity.* New York: Columbia University Press, 1988.

Brown, Raymond E. *The Birth of the Messiah: A Commentary on the Infancy Narratives in Matthew and Luke.* Garden City, N.Y.: Doubleday, 1977.

Brown, Raymond E., et al., eds. *Mary in the New Testament.* Philadelphia: Fortress, 1978.

Bultmann, Rudolf. *The History of the Synoptic Tradition.* Oxford: Blackwell, 1963.

Burckhard, Christoph. "Jesus of Nazareth." Pages 15–72 in *Christian Beginning: Word and Community from Jesus to Post-Apostolic Times.* Edited by J. Becker. Louisville, Ky.: Westminster/John Knox, 1993.

Burrus, Virginia. *"Begotten, not Made": Conceiving Manhood in Late Antiquity.* Stanford, Calif.: Stanford University Press, 2000.

Bynum, C. W. "Women's Stories, Women's Symbols: A Critique of Victor Turner's Theory of Liminality." Pages 105–25 in *Anthropology and the Study of Religion*. Edited by R. L. Moore and F. L. Reynolds. Chicago: Center for the Scientific Study of Religion, 1984.

Carmignac, Jean. "Les dangers de l'eschatologie." *JBL* 17 (1971): 365–90.

———. *Le Mirage de l'Eschatologie: Royauté, Règne et Royaume de Dieu . . . sans Eschatologie*. Paris: Letouzey et Ané, 1979.

Carr, A., and M. Stewart Van Leeuwen, eds. *Religion, Feminism, and the Family*. Louisville, Ky.: Westminster John Knox, 1996.

Casey, Edward S. *Getting Back into Place: Toward a Renewed Understanding of the Place-world*. Bloomington: Indiana University Press, 1993.

———. *The Fate of Place*. Berkeley: University of California Press, 1998.

Catchpole, David. "Q and the 'Friend at Midnight' (Luke xi.5–8/9)." *JTS* n.s. 34 (1983): 407–24.

———. *The Quest for Q*. Edinburgh: T. & T. Clark, 1993.

Charlesworth, James H., ed. *Jesus' Jewishness: Exploring the Place of Jesus within Early Judaism*. New York: Crossroad, 1991.

Charlesworth, James H., and Craig A. Evans, "Jesus in the Agrapha and Apocryphal Gospels." Pages 479–533 in *Studying the Historical Jesus*. Edited by B. Chilton and C. A. Evans. NTTS 19. Leiden: Brill, 1994.

Chilton, Bruce, and C. A. Evans, eds. *Studying the Historical Jesus*. NTTS 19. Leiden: Brill, 1994.

Clark, Elizabeth A. *Reading Renunciation: Asceticism and Scripture in Early Christianity*. Princeton, N.J.: Princeton University Press, 1999.

Clines, David J. A. "*Ecce Vir*, or, Gendering the Son of Man." Pages 352–75 in *Biblical Studies/Cultural Studies*. JSOT Sup 266. Edited by J. Cheryl Exum and S. D. Moore. Sheffield: Sheffield University Press, 1998.

Cohen, S. J. D. "Introduction." Pages 1–8 in *The Jewish Family in Antiquity*. Edited by S. J. D. Cohen. Brown Jewish Studies 289. Atlanta: Scholars Press, 1993.

———, ed. *The Jewish Family in Antiquity*. Brown Jewish Studies 289. Atlanta: Scholars Press, 1993.

Collins, John J. "Marriage, Divorce and Family in Second Temple Judaism." Pages 104–62 in L. G. Perdue, J. Blenkinsopp, J. J. Collins, and C. Meyers. *Families in Ancient Israel*. Louisville, Ky.: Westminster John Knox, 1997.

Corrington, Gail P. "The Defense of the Body and the Discourse of Appetite: Continence and Control in the Greco-Roman World." *Semeia* 57 (1992): 65–74.

Cotter, Wendy J. "Children Sitting in the Agora." *Forum* 5:2 (1989): 63–82.

———. "The Parable of the Mustard Seed and the Leaven: Their Function in the Earliest Stratum of Q." *Toronto Journal of Theology* 8 (1992): 38–51.

Cresswell, Tim. *In Place, out of Place: Geography, Ideology, and Transgression*. Minneapolis: University of Minnesota Press, 1996.

Crossan, John D. *In Parables: The Challenge of the Historical Jesus*. New York: Harper & Row, 1973.

———. "Mark and the Relatives of Jesus." *NovT* 15 (1973): 81–113.

———. *In Fragments: The Aphorisms of Jesus*. San Francisco: Harper & Row, 1983.

———. *The Historical Jesus: The Life of a Mediterranean Jewish Peasant*. San Francisco: Harper, 1991.

Crossan, J. D., and J. L. Reed. *Excavating Jesus*. San Francisco: Harper, 2001.

Dahl, Nils A. "Parables of Growth." *ST* 5 (1951): 132–66.

———. "The Problem of the Historical Jesus." 1953. Reprinted pages 81–111 in his *Jesus the Christ*. Edited by D. H. Juel. Minneapolis: Fortress, 1991.

D'Angelo, Mary Rose. "ABBA and 'Father': Imperial Theology and the Jesus Traditions." *JBL* 111 (1992): 611–30.

Davies, Stevan L. *The Gospel of Thomas and Christian Wisdom.* New York: Seabury Press, 1983.
———. *Jesus the Healer.* New York: Continuum, 1995.
Davies, William David. *The Gospel and the Land: Early Christianity and Jewish Territorial Doctrine.* Berkeley: University of California Press, 1974.
———. *The Territorial Dimension of Judaism.* Minneapolis: Fortress, 1991.
Davies, W. D., and Dale C. Allison. *A Critical and Exegetical Commentary on the Gospel According to Saint Matthew.* 3 vols. Edinburgh: T. & T. Clark, 1988–97.
Destro, A., and M. Pesce, "Kinship, Discipleship, and Movement: An Anthropological Study of John's Gospel." *BibInt* 3 (1995): 266–84.
Dewey, Arthur J. "The Unkindest Cut of All? Matt 19:11–12." *Forum* 8:1–2 (1992): 113–22.
Dodd, C. H. *The Parables of the Kingdom.* Rev. ed. New York: Scribner's, 1961.
Doran, Robert. "The Divinization of Disorder: The Trajectory of Matt 8:20// Luke 9:58// Gos. Thom. 86." Pages 210–19 in *The Future of Early Christianity: Essays in Honor of Helmut Koester.* Edited by Birger A. Pearson. Minneapolis: Fortress, 1991.
Douglas, Mary. *Natural Symbols: Explorations in Cosmology.* With new introduction. New York: Pantheon, 1982.
Duling, D. "Kingdom of God, Kingdom of Heaven: New Testament and Early Christian Interpretation," *ABD* 4 (1992): 62–65.
Duncan, J., and D. Ley, eds. *Place, Culture, Representation.* London: Routledge, 1993.
Edelman, Lee. *Homographesis: Essays in Gay Literature and Cultural Theory.* New York: Routledge, 1994.
Edwards, Douglas R., and C. Thomas McCollough, eds. *Archaeology and the Galilee.* South Florida Studies in the History of Judaism 143. Atlanta: Scholars Press, 1997.
Elliott, John H. *A Home for the Homeless: A Social-Scientific Criticism of 1 Peter, Its Situation and Strategy.* 2d ed. Minneapolis: AugsburgFortress, 1990.
———. *1 Peter.* AB 37B. New York: Doubleday, 2000.
Elliott, J. K., ed. *The Apocryphal Jesus.* Oxford: Oxford University Press, 1996.
Engberg-Pedersen, Troels. "Philo's *De Vita Contemplativa* as a Philosopher's Dream." *Journal for the Study of Judaism in the Persian, Hellenistic and Roman Period* 30 (1999): 40–64.
Fatum, Lone. "Image of God and Glory of Man: Women in the Pauline Congregations." Pages 50–133 in *The Image of God: Gender Models in Judeo-Christian Tradition.* Edited by Kari E. Børresen. Minneapolis: Fortress, 1995.
Fiensy, D. *The Social History of Palestine in the Herodian Period.* Studies in the Bible and Early Christianity 20. Lewiston, N.Y.: Mellen, 1991.
Fischer, M., O. Potchter, and Y. Jacob. "Dwelling Houses in Ancient Israel: Methodological Considerations." *Journal of Roman Archaeology* 11 (1998): 671–78.
Fleddermann, Harry T. "The Demands of Discipleship: Matt 8:19–22 par. Luke 9:57–62." Pages 541–61 in *The Four Gospels: Festschrift Frans Neirynck.* Vol. 1. Edited by F. Van Segbroeck et al. Leuven: Leuven University Press, 1992.
———. *Mark and Q: A Study of the Overlap Texts.* BETL 122. Leuven: Leuven University Press, 1995.
Flusser, David. *Jesus.* In coll. with R. Steven Notley. 2d ed. Jerusalem: Magnes, 1998.
Freyne, Sean. *Galilee from Alexander the Great to Hadrian, 323 B.C E. to 135 C.E.* Wilmington, Del.: M. Glazier: 1980.
———. *Galilee and Gospel: Collected Essays.* WUNT 125. Tübingen, Mohr, 2000.
———. "Town and Country Once More: The Case of Roman Galilee." Pages 59–72 in his *Galilee and Gospel: Collected Essays.* WUNT 125. Tübingen: Mohr, 2000.
Fridrichsen, Anton. *The Problem of Miracle in Early Christianity.* Minneapolis: Augsburg, 1972.
Funk, Robert W. *Jesus as Precursor.* Semeia Suppl. 2. Philadelphia: Fortress, 1975.

Funk, Robert W., and Roy W. Hoover, eds., *The Five Gospels: The Search for the Authentic Words of Jesus*. New York: Macmillan, 1993.

Georgi, D. "The Interest in Life of Jesus Theology as a Paradigm of the Social History of Biblical Criticism." *HTR* 85 (1992): 51–83.

Giddens, A. *Modernity and Self Identity*. Cambridge: Polity Press, 1991.

Gillis, John R. *A World of Their Own Making: Myth, Ritual, and the Quest for Family Values*. Cambridge, Mass.: Harvard University Press, 1996.

Gilmore, D. D. "Introduction: The Shame of Dishonour." Pages 1–21 in *Honour and Shame and the Unity of the Mediterranean*. Edited by D. D. Gilmore. American Anthropological Association Special Publication 22. Washington: American Anthropological Association, 1987.

Goodman, M. *The Ruling Class of Judea: The Origins of the Jewish Revolt against Rome AD 66–70*. Cambridge: Cambridge University Press, 1987.

Goss, R. *Jesus Acted Up: A Gay and Lesbian Manifesto*. San Francisco: Harper, 1993.

Green, Elizabeth. "More Musings on Maleness: The Maleness of Jesus Revisited." *Feminist Theology* 20 (1999): 9–27.

Guijarro, Santiago. "The Family in First-Century Galilee." Pages 42–65 in *Constructing Early Christian Families*. Edited by H. Moxnes. London: Routledge, 1997.

Guijarro Oporto, Santiago. *Fidelidades en conflicto: la ruptura con la familia por causa del discipulado y de la misón en la tradición sinóptica*. Salamanca: Universidad Pontifica, 1998.

Guyot, Peter. *Eunuchen als Sklaven und Freigelassene in der griechisch-römische Antike*. Stuttgarter Beiträge zur Geschichte und Politik 14. Stuttgart: Klett-Cotta, 1980.

Halperin, David M. *Saint-Foucault: Towards a Gay Hagiography*. New York: Oxford University Press, 1995.

Hamerton-Kelly, Robert. *God the Father: Theology and Patriarchy in the Teaching of Jesus*. Philadelphia: Fortress, 1979.

Hanson, K. C. "Kinship." Pages 62–79 in *The Social Sciences and New Testament Interpretation*. Edited by R. L. Rohrbaugh. Peabody, Mass.: Hendrickson, 1996.

———. "The Galilean Fishing Economy and the Jesus Tradition." *BTB* 27 (1997): 99–111.

Hanson, K. C., and Douglas E. Oakman. *Palestine in the Time of Jesus: Social Structures and Social Conflicts*. Minneapolis: Fortress, 1998.

Harnack, Adolf von. *Die Mission und Ausbreitung des Christentums in den ersten drei Jahrhunderten*. 4th ed. Leipzig: J. C. Hinrich, 1924.

Harvey, David. *The Condition of Postmodernity*. Oxford: Blackwell, 1989.

Henten, J. W. van, and A. Brenner. *Families and Family Relations as Represented in Early Judaism and Early Christianities*. Studies in Theology and Religion 2. Leiden: Deo, 2000.

Herzog, William R., II. *Parables as Subversive Speech: Jesus as Pedagogue of the Oppressed*. Louisville, Ky.: Westminster John Knox, 1994.

Hirschfeld, Y. *The Palestinian Dwelling in the Roman-Byzantine Period*. Jerusalem: Franciscan Printing Press, 1995.

Hobsbawm, E. *Primitive Rebels: Studies of Archaic Forms of Social Movements in the 19th and 20th Centuries*. New York: Norton, 1959.

Hock, Ron. *The Infancy Gospels of James and Thomas*. The Scholars Bible 2. Santa Rosa, Calif.: Polebridge, 1995.

Hoehner, Harold W. *Herod Antipas*. SNTSMS 17. Cambridge: Cambridge University Press, 1972.

Hollenbach, Paul W. "Jesus, Demoniacs and Public Authorities: A Socio-Historical Study." *JAAR* 49 (1981): 567–88.

Hörig, Monika. "Dea Syria—Atargatis." *ANRW* II.17.3 (1984): 1537–81.

Horsley, R. A., and J. S. Hanson. *Bandits, Prophets and Messiahs: Popular Movements in the Time of Jesus*. Minneapolis: Winston, 1985.

Horsley, Richard A. *Jesus and the Spiral of Violence: Popular Jewish Resistance in Roman Palestine*. San Francisco: Harper & Row, 1987.

———. *Galilee: History, Politics, People*. Valley Forge, Pa.: Trinity Press International, 1995.

———. *Archaeology, History and Society in Galilee*. Valley Forge, Pa.: Trinity Press International, 1996.

———. "Jesus and Galilee: The Contingencies of a Renewal Movement." Pages 57–74 in *Galilee through the Centuries*. Edited by Eric M. Meyers. Duke Judaic Studies Series 1. Winona Lake, Ind.: Eisenbrauns, 1999.

———. "Synagogues in Galilee and the Gospels." Pages 46–69 in *Evolution of the Synagogue*. Edited by H. Clark Kee and Lynn H. Cohick. Harrisburg, Pa.: Trinity Press International, 1999.

Humphries, Michael L. *Christian Origins and the Language of the Kingdom of God*. Carbondale and Evansville: Southern Illinois University Press, 1999.

Hurtado, L. W. "A Taxonomy of Recent Historical-Jesus Work." Pages 272–95 in *Whose Historical Jesus*. Edited by W. E. Arnal and M. Desjardins. Studies in Christianity and Judaism 7. Waterloo, Ont.: Wilfred Laurier University Press, 1997.

Illich, Ivan. *Gender*. New York: Pantheon, 1982.

Jacobs-Malina, Diane. *Beyond Patriarchy: The Images of Family in Jesus*. New York: Paulist Press, 1993.

Jacobson, Arland D. *The First Gospel: An Introduction to Q*. Sonoma, Calif.: Polebridge, 1992.

———. "Divided Families and Christian Origins." Pages 361–80 in *The Gospel behind the Gospels: Current Studies on Q*. SupNT 75. Edited by Ronald A. Piper. Leiden: Brill, 1995.

———. "Jesus against the Family: The Dissolution of Family Ties in the Gospel Tradition." Pages 189–218 in *From Quest to Q: Festschrift James M. Robinson*. BETL 146. Edited by J. Ma. Asgeirsson, K. de Troyer, and M. W. Meyer. Leuven: Leuven: University Press, 2000.

Jameson, M. "Private Space and the Greek City." Pages 171–95 in *The Greek City from Homer to Alexander*. Edited by O. Murray and S. Price. Oxford: Clarendon House, 1990.

Kedar, Benjamin Z. *The Changing Land: Between the Jordan and the Sea: Aerial Photographs from 1917 to the Present*. Tel Aviv: Yad Izhak Ben-Zwi Press, 1999.

Kelber, Werner H. *The Kingdom in Mark: A New Place and a New Time*. Philadelphia: Fortress, 1974.

Kieffer, R. *Le monde symbolique de Saint Jean*. Paris: Cerf, 1989.

Kingsbury, Jack Dean. "The Verb *anakolouthein* ('to follow') as an Index of Matthew's View of His Community." *JBL* 97 (1978): 56–73.

Klausner, Joseph. *Jesus of Nazareth: His Life, Times and Teaching*. 1925 ed. Reprint, New York: Bloch, 1989.

Kleinmann, A. *Patients and Healers in the Context of Culture*. Berkeley: University of California Press, 1980.

Kloppenborg, John S. "Alms, Debt and Divorce: Jesus' Ethics in Their Mediterranean Context." *TJT* 6 (1990): 182–200.

———. "City and Wasteland: Narrative World and the Beginning of the Sayings Gospel (Q)." *Semeia* 52 (1990): 145–60.

———. *The Formation of Q*. Philadelphia: Fortress, 1987. Reprint, with new preface. Harrisburg, Pa.: Trinity Press International, 1999.

———. *Excavating Q: The History and Setting of the Sayings Gospel*. Edinburgh: T. & T. Clark, 2000.

Kloppenborg Verbin, John S. "Discursive Practices in the Sayings Gospel Q and the Quest of the Historical Jesus." Pages 149–90 in *The Sayings Source Q and the Historical Jesus*. Edited by A. Lindemann. BETL 158. Leuven: Leuven University Press, 2001.

Kodell, Jerome. "The Celibate Logion in Matthew 19:12," *BTB* 8 (1978): 19–23.
Köster, Helmut. *Ancient Christian Gospels*. Philadelphia: Trinity, 1990.
Kraemer, Ross. *Her Share of the Blessings: Women's Religions among Pagans, Jews and Christians in the Greco-Roman World*. New York: Oxford University Press, 1992.
Kruse, H. "Das Reich Satans." *Biblica* 58 (1977): 29–64.
Kuefler, M. *The Manly Eunuch: Masculinity, Gender Ambiguity, and Christian Ideology in Late Antiquity*. Chicago: University of Chicago Press 2001.
Kwok, Pui-Lan. "On Color-Coding Jesus: An Interview with Pui-Lan Kwok." Pages 161–80 in *The Post-Colonial Bible*. Edited by R. S. Sugirtharajah. Sheffield: Sheffield Academic Press, 1998.
Lampe, G. W. H. "Miracles and Early Christian Apologetics." Pages 203–18 in *Miracles: Cambridge Studies in Their Philosophy and History*. Edited by C. F. D. Moule. London: Mowbray, 1965.
Lefebvre, Henri. *The Production of Space*. French original, *La production de l'espace*, 1974. Oxford: Blackwell, 1991.
Levine, Lee I. ed. *The Galilee in Late Antiquity*. New York: Jewish Theological Seminary of America, 1992.
———. "The Sages and the Synagogues in Late Antiquity: The Evidence of the Galilee." Pages 201–22 in *The Galilee in Late Antiquity*. Edited by Lee I. Levine. Cambridge, Mass.: Harvard University Press, 1992.
———. *The Ancient Synagogue*. New Haven, Conn.: Yale University Press, 2000.
Lightfoot, R. H. *Locality and Doctrine in the Gospels*. New York and London: Harper, 1938.
Long, Jaqueline. *Claudian's In Eutropium: Or, How, When and Why to Slander a Eunuch*. Chapel Hill: University of North Carolina Press, 1996.
Luz, Ulrich. *Das Evangelium nach Matthäus*. Evangelish-Katholischer Kommentar zum Neuen Testament 1:1–3. 3 vols. Neukirchen-Vlyn: Neukirchener, 1985–97.
MacDonald, W. L. *The Architecture of the Roman Empire*. Vol. 2, *An Urban Appraisal*. New Haven, Conn.: Yale University Press, 1986.
Malbon, Elisabeth Struthers. "*The Oikia autou:* Mark 2:15 in Context." *NTS* 31 (1985): 282–92.
———. *Narrative Space and Mythic Meaning in Mark*. Sheffield: Sheffield Academic Press, 1991.
Malina, Bruce J. *Christian Origins and Cultural Anthropology*. Atlanta: John Knox Press, 1986.
———. *The Social World of Jesus and the Gospels*. London and New York: Routledge, 1996.
———. "Christ and Time: Swiss or Mediterranean?" Pages 179–214 in his *The Social World of Jesus*.
Malina, Bruce J., and J. H. Neyrey. *Calling Jesus Names: The Social Value of Labels in Matthew*. Sonoma, Calif.: Polebridge. 1988.
Manguel, Alberto, and Gianni Guadalupi. *The Dictionary of Imaginary Places*. Rev. ed. Toronto: Knopf, 1999.
Marjanen, Antti. *The Woman Jesus Loved: Mary Magdalene in the Nag Hammadi Library and Related Documents*. Nag Hammadi and Manichaean Studies 40. Leiden: Brill, 1996.
———. "Women Disciples in the *Gospel of Thomas*." Pages 89–106 in *Thomas at the Crossroads: Essays on the Gospel of Thomas*. Edited by Risto Uro. Edinburgh: T. & T. Clark, 1998.
Marmon, Shaun. *Eunuchs and Sacred Boundaries in Islamic Society*. Oxford: Oxford University Press, 1995.
Massey, Doreen. *Space, Place and Gender*. Cambridge: Polity, 1994.
McArthur, Harvey K. "Son of Mary." *NovT* 15 (1973): 38–58.
McDowell, Linda. "Spatializing Feminism." Pages 31–32 in *Body Space*. Edited by Nancy Duncan. London and New York: Routledge, 1996.

————. *Gender, Identity and Place*. Cambridge: Polity, 1999.

Meeks, Wayne A. "The Image of the Androgyne: Some Uses of a Symbol in Earliest Christianity." *History of Religion* 13 (1974): 165–208.

Meier, John P. *A Marginal Jew: Rethinking the Historical Jesus*. Vols. 1 and 2. New York: Doubleday, 1991–94.

Meyer, Marvin W. "Making Mary Male: The Categories 'Male' and 'Female' in the Gospel of Thomas." *NTS* 31 (1985): 554–70.

Meyers, Eric M. "Ancient Synagogues: An Archaeological Introduction." Pages 3–20 in *Sacred Realm: The Emergence of the Synagogue in the Ancient World*. Edited by Steven Fine. New York: Oxford University Press, 1996.

————. "Jesus and His Galilean Context." Pages 57–66 in *Archaeology and the Galilee*. Edited by Douglas R. Edwards and C. Thomas McCollough. South Florida Studies in the History of Judaism 143. Atlanta: Scholars Press, 1997.

————, ed. *Galilee through the Centuries: Confluence of Cultures*. Duke Judaic Studies Series 1. Winona Lake, Ind.: Eisenbrauns, 1999.

Michaels, J. Ramsey. "The Itinerant Jesus and His Home Town." Pages 177–94 in *Authenticating the Words of Jesus*. NTTS 28:1. Edited by B. Chilton and C. A. Evans. Leiden: Brill, 1990.

Miller, John W. *Jesus at Thirty: A Psychological and Historical Portrait*. Minneapolis: Fortress, 1997.

Miller, Robert J. "Historical Method and the Deeds of Jesus." *Forum* 8 (1992): 5–31.

Moloney, Francis J. "Matthew 19:3–12 and Celibacy. A Redactional and Form Critical Study." *JSNT* 2 (1979): 42–60.

Moore, Stephen D. "Ugly Thoughts: On the Face and Physique of the Historical Jesus." Pages 376–99 in *Biblical Studies/Cultural Studies*. JSOT Sup 266. Edited by J. Cheryl Exum and S. D. Moore. Sheffield: Sheffield University Press, 1998.

Moore, Stephen D., and Janice C. Anderson. "Taking It Like a Man: Masculinities in 4 Maccabees." *JBL* 117 (1998): 249–73.

Moran, W. R. "The Conclusion of the Decalogue (Ex 20,17=Dt 5,21)." *CBQ* 29 (1967): 543–54.

Moretti, F. *Atlas of the European Novel: 1800–1900*. London: Verso, 1999.

Morgan, David. "The Masculinity of Jesus in Popular Religious Art." Pages 251–66 in *Men's Bodies, Men's Gods*. Edited by Björn Krondorfer. New York: New York University Press, 1996.

Moxnes, H. "Honor and Shame." *BTB* 23 (1993): 167–76.

————. "Conventional Values in the Hellenistic World: Masculinity." Pages 263–84 in *Conventional Values in the Hellenistic World*. Edited by Per Bilde et al. Aarhus: Aarhus University Press, 1997.

————, ed. *Constructing Early Christian Families*. London: Routledge, 1997.

————. "What Is Family? Problems in Constructing Early Christian Families." Pages 13–41 in *Constructing Early Christian Families*. Edited by H. Moxnes. London: Routledge, 1997.

————. "The Historical Jesus: From Master Narrative to Cultural Context," *BTB* 28 (1999): 135–49.

————. "The Construction of Galilee as a Place for the Historical Jesus." *BTB* 31 (2001): 26–37, 64–77.

————. "Jesus the Jew: Dilemmas of Interpretation." Pages 83–103 in *Fair Play: Diversity and Conflicts in Early Christianity: Essays in Honour of Heikki Räisänen*. Edited by I. Dunderberg, C. Tuckett, and K. Syreeni; NovTSup 103. Leiden: Brill, 2002.

————. "Jesus from Galilee in an Age of Nationalism." In *Discovering Jesus in Our Place: Contextual Christologies in a Globalised Age*. Edited by S. Stålsett. Madras: ISPCK (forthcoming).

Müller, Klaus W. "König und Vater." Pages 21–43 in *Königsherrschaft Gottes und himmlischer Kult*. Edited by M. Hengel and A. M. Schwemer. WUNT 55. Tübingen: Mohr, 1991.

Murphy-O'Connor, J. "John the Baptist and Jesus: History and Hypotheses." *NTS* 36 (1990): 359–74.

Myre, André. "Jésus avait-il une maison?" Pages 305–19 in *"Où demeures-tu" (Jn 1,38): La maison depuis le monde biblique*. Edited by Jean-Claude Petit. Quebec: Fides. 1994.

Nagy, R. M., C. L. Meyers, E. M. Meyers, and Z. Weiss, eds. *Sepphoris in Galilee: Crosscurrents of Culture*. Winona Lake, Ind.: Eisenbrauns, 1996.

Neyrey, Jerome H. "Loss of Wealth, Loss of Family and Loss of Honour: The Cultural Context of the Original Macarisms in Q." Pages 139–58 in *Modelling Early Christianity*. Edited by Philip F. Esler. London: Routledge, 1995.

———. "Meals, Food, and Table Fellowship." Pages 159–82 in *The Social Sciences and New Testament Interpretation*. Edited by R. L. Rohrbaugh. Peabody, Mass.: Hendrickson, 1996.

———. *Honor and Shame in the Gospel of Matthew*. Louisville, Ky.: Westminster John Knox Press, 1998.

Nock, Arthur Darby. "Eunuchs in Ancient Literature." *ARW* 23 (1925): 25–33. Reprint. Pages 7–15 in his *Essays on Religion and the Ancient World*. Oxford: Clarendon, 1972.

Nonn, T. "Hitting Bottom: Homelessness, Poverty and Masculinities." *Theology & Sexuality* 3 (1995): 11–26.

Oakman, Douglas. "Models and Archaeology in the Social Interpretation of Jesus." Pages 102–31 in *Social Scientific Models for Interpreting the Bible: Essays by the Context Group in Honor of Bruce J. Malina*. Edited by J. J. Pilch. Biblical Interpretation Series 53. Leiden: Brill, 2001.

Obenzinger, H. *American Palestine: Melville, Twain and the Holy Land Mania*. Princeton, N.J.: Princeton University Press, 1999.

Osiek, Carolyn. "The Family in Early Christianity: Family Values Revisited." *CBQ* 58 (1996): 1–24.

Osiek, Carolyn, and D. L. Balch, *Families in the New Testament World*. Louisville, Ky.: Westminster John Knox, 1997.

Owusu, Daniel Addae. "Jesus the African Healer." Master's thesis. Faculty of Theology, University of Oslo, 2001.

Patterson, Stephen J. "Fire and Dissension: Ipsissima Vox Jesu in Q 12:49, 51–53?" *Forum* 5:2 (1989): 121–39.

———. *The Gospel of Thomas and Jesus*. Sonoma, Calif.: Polebridge, 1993.

———. "Wisdom in Q and Thomas." Pages 187–221 in *In Search of Wisdom*. Edited by Leo G. Perdue et al. Louisville, Ky.: Westminster/John Knox, 1993.

———. "Askesis and the Early Jesus Tradition." Pages 49–69 in *Asceticism and the New Testament*. Edited by Leif E. Vaage and V. Wimbush. London and New York: Routledge, 1999.

Perdue, L. G., et al. *Families in Ancient Israel*. Louisville, Ky.: Westminster John Knox, 1997.

———. "The Household, Old Testament Theology, and Contemporary Hermeneutics." Pages 223–57 in L. G. Perdue et al. *Families in Ancient Israel*. Louisville, Ky.: Westminster John Knox, 1997.

Peskowitz, M. "Family/ies in Antiquity: Evidence from Tannaitic Literature and Roman Galilean Architecture." Pages 9–36 in *The Jewish Family in Antiquity*. Edited by S. J. D. Cohen. Brown Jewish Studies 289. Atlanta: Scholars Press, 1993.

Pilch, John J. *Healing in the New Testament: Insights from Medical and Mediterranean Anthropology*. Minneapolis: Fortress, 2000.

Piper, Ronald A. *Wisdom in the Q-Tradition: The Aphoristic Teaching of Jesus.* SNTSMS 61. Cambridge: Cambridge University Press, 1989.

———. "Wealth, Poverty and Subsistence in Q." Pages 219–64 in *From Quest to Q. FS James M. Robinson.* Edited by J. Ma. Asgeirsson, K. de Troyer, and M. W. Meyer. BETL 146. Leuven: Leuven University Press, 2000.

Pitre, B. J. "Blessing the Barren and Warning the Fecund: Jesus' Message for Women Concerning Pregnancy and Childbirth." *JSNT* 81 (2001): 59–80.

Pryor, J. W. "John 4:44 and the *Patris* of Jesus." *CBQ* 49 (1987): 254–63.

———. "Jesus and Family—a Test Case." *Australian Biblical Review* 45 (1997): 56–69.

Räisänen, Hekki. "Exorcisms and the Kingdom: Is Q 11:20 a Saying of the Historical Jesus?" in *Symbols and Strata: Essays on the Sayings Gospel Q.* Edited by Risto Uro. Publications of the Finnish Exegetical Society 65. Göttingen: Vandenhoeck & Ruprecht, 1996.

Redfield, Robert. *The Little Community: Viewpoints for the Study of Human Whole.* Chicago: University of Chicago Press, 1955.

Reed, J. L. *Archaeology and the Galilean Jesus.* Harrisburg, Pa.: Trinity, 2000.

Renan, Ernest. *Vie de Jésus.* Paris: Michel Levy Frères, 1863.

Richard, Louis. "Juvenal et les galles de Cybèle." *Revue de l'Histoire des Religions* 169 (1966): 51–67.

Richardson, Peter. *Herod.* Columbia: University of South Carolina Press, 1996.

———. "Enduring Concerns: Desiderata for Future Historical-Jesus Research." Pages 296–307 in *Whose Historical Jesus?* Edited by W. E. Arnal and M. Desjardins. Studies in Christianity and Judaism 7. Waterloo, Ont.: Wilfred Laurier University Press, 1997.

———. "First Century Houses and Q's Setting." Pages 63–83 in *Christology, Controversy and Community: New Testament Essays in Honour of David R. Catchpole.* Edited by D. Horrell and Chr. M. Tuckett. NovTSup 99. Leiden: Brill, 2000.

Ringose, Kathryn M. "Living in the Shadows. Eunuchs and Gender in Byzantium." Pages 85–109 in *Third Sex, Third Gender.* Edited by G. Herdt. New York: Zone, 1994.

Robbins, Vernon K. "Rhetorical Composition and the Beelzebul Controversy." Pages 161–93 in *Patterns of Persuasion in the Gospels.* Burton L. Mack and Vernon K. Robbins. Sonoma, Calif.: Polebridge, 1989.

Rohrbaugh, Richard L. "A Dysfunctional Family and Its Neighbours (Luke 15:11–32)." Pages 141–64 in *Jesus and His Parables: Interpreting the Parables of Jesus Today.* Edited by V. G. Shillington. Edinburgh: T. & T. Clark, 1997.

Ruether, Rosemary. "What Do the Synoptics Say? The Sexuality of Jesus." *Christianity and Crisis* 38 (1978): 134–37.

Sahlins, Marshall. *Stone Age Economics.* Chicago: Alderdine-Atherton, 1972.

Sanders, E. P. *Jesus and Judaism.* Philadelphia: Fortress, 1985.

———. "Jesus in Historical Context." *Theology Today* 50 (1993): 429–48.

———. "Jesus' Galilee." Pages 3–41 in *Fair Play: Diversity and Conflicts in Early Christianity: Essays in Honour of Heikki Räisänen.* Edited by I. Dunderberg, C. Tuckett, and K. Syreeni. NovTSup 103. Leiden: Brill, 2002.

Sanders, G. "Gallos." *RAG* 8 (1972): 984–1034.

———. "Les galles et le gallat devant l'opinion chrétienne." Pages 1062–91 in *Hommages à Maarten J. Vermaseren.* Vol. 3. Edited by M. B. De Boer and T. A. Edridge. Ètudes preliminaires aux religions orientales dans l'empire Romain 68. Leiden: Brill, 1978.

Satlow, Michael L. "'Try to Be a Man': The Rabbinic Construction of Masculinity." *HTR* 89 (1996): 19–40.

Sawicki, Marianne. *Crossing Galilee: Architectures of Contact in the Occupied Land of Jesus.* Harrisburg, Pa.: Trinity, 2000.

Schaberg, J. *The Illegitimacy of Jesus: A Feminist Theological Interpretation of the Infancy Narratives.* San Francisco: Harper & Row, 1987.

Schama, Simon. *Landscape and Memory.* London: HarperCollins, 1995.

Schepelern, Wilhelm. *Der Montanismus und die Phrygische Kulte.* Tübingen: Mohr, 1929.

Schleiermacher, F. *The Life of Jesus.* Edited and with introduction by J.C. Verheyden. Philadelphia: Fortress, 1975.

Scholz, Piotr O. *Der ermannte Eros.* Düsseldorf: Artemis & Winkler, 1997.

Schröter, Jens. *Erinnerung an Jesu Worte: Studien zur Rezeption der Logionüberlieferung in Markus, Q und Thomas.* WMANT 76. Neukirchen-Vluyn: Neukirchener, 1997.

Schüssler Fiorenza, Elisabeth. *Jesus: Miriam's Child, Sophia's Prophet.* New York: Continumm, 1994.

———. *Jesus and the Politics of Interpretation.* New York: Continuum, 2000.

Schweitzer, Albert. *The Quest of the Historical Jesus.* 1st complete ed. Edited by J. Bowden. Minneapolis: Fortress, 2001. Translation of *Geschichte der Leben-Jesu-Forschung.* Tübingen: Mohr, 1906, 1913, 1950.

Scott, Bernard Brandon. *Hear Then the Parable: A Commentary on the Parables of Jesus.* Minneapolis: Fortress, 1989.

Segovia, Fernando F., and Mary Ann Tolbert, eds. *Readings from This Place.* Vol. 1, *Social Location and Biblical Interpretation in the United States.* Vol. 2, *Social Location and Biblical Interpretation in Global Perspective.* Minneapolis: Fortress, 1995.

Seim, Turid Karlsen. *The Double Message: Patterns of Gender in Luke and Acts.* Nashville: Abingdon Press, 1994.

———. "Children of the Resurrection: Perspectives on Angelic Asceticism in Luke-Acts." Pages 115–25 in *Asceticism and the New Testament.* Edited by Leif E. Vaage and V. Wimbush. London and New York: Routledge, 1999.

Shields, Rob. *Places on the Margin: Alternative Geographies of Modernity.* London and New York: Routledge, 1991.

Shurmer-Smith, Pamela, and Kevin Hannam. *Worlds of Desire, Realms of Power: A Cultural Geography.* London: Edward Arnold, 1994.

Smith, Jonathan Z. "Towards Interpreting Demonic Powers in Hellenistic and Roman Antiquity." *ANRW* II 16.1 (1978), 425–39.

———. *Map Is Not Territory.* Chicago: University of Chicago Press, 1978. Reprinted, 1993.

———. *To Take Place.* Chicago: University of Chicago Press, 1992.

Smith, Mahlon H. "No Place for a Son of Man." *Forum* 4:2 (1988): 83–107.

———. "Kinship Is Relative: Mark 3:31–35 and Parallels." *Forum* 6:1 (1990): 80–94.

Smith, Morton. *Jesus the Magician.* New York: Harper & Row, 1978.

Sobrino, Jon. *Jesus the Liberator: A Historical-Theological Reading of Jesus of Nazareth.* Maryknoll, N.Y.: Orbis, 1993.

Soja, Edward W. *Postmodern Geographies: The Reassertion of Space in Critical Social Theory.* London: Verso, 1989.

Sparke, Matthew. "Displacing the Field in Fieldwork: Masculinity, Metaphor and Space." Pages 212–33 in *Bodyspace: Destabilizing Geographies of Gender and Sexuality.* Edited by N. Duncan. London: Routledge, 1996.

Stager, L. E. "The Archaeology of the Family in Ancient Israel." *BASOR* 260 (1985): 1–36.

Staumbaugh, John E. *The Ancient Roman City.* Baltimore: Johns Hopkins Press, 1988.

Stegemann, E. W., and W. Stegemann. *The Jesus Movement: A Social History of Its First Century.* Edinburgh: T. & T. Clark, 1999.

Stein, Robert H. "Luke 14:26 and the Question of Authenticity." *Forum* 5:2 (1989): 187–92.

Strange, James F. "First Century Galilee from Archaeology and from the Texts." Pages 39–48 in *Archaeology and the Galilee.* Edited by Douglas R. Edwards and C. Thomas McCollough. South Florida Studies in the History of Judaism 143. Atlanta: Scholars Press, 1997.

Taussig, Michael. *Shamanism, Colonialism, and the Wild Man: A Study in Terror and Healing.* Chicago: University of Chicago Press, 1986.

Theissen, Gerd. *The Miracle Stories of Early Christian Tradition.* Philadelphia: Fortress, 1983.

———. *The Shadow of the Galilean: The Quest of the Historical Jesus in Narrative Form.* London: SCM, 1987.

———. "We Have Left Everything . . ." (Mark 10:28): Discipleship and Social Uprooting in the Jewish-Palestinian Society of the First Century." Pages 60–93 in his *Social Reality and the Early Christians.* Minneapolis: Fortress, 1992.

———. *Social Reality and the Early Christians.* Minneapolis: Fortress, 1992.

Theissen, Gerd, and A. Merz. *The Historical Jesus: A Comprehensive Guide.* London: SCM, 1998.

Thomas, Garth. "Magna Mater and Attis." *ANRW* II.17.3 (1984): 1500–1535.

Thompson, Marianne Meyer. *The Promise of the Father.* Louisville, Ky.: Westminster John Knox, 2000.

Tolbert, Mary Ann. "Asceticism and Mark's Gospel." Pages 29–48 in *Asceticism and the New Testament.* Edited by Leif E. Vaage and V. Wimbush. London and New York: Routledge, 1999.

Tougher, Shaun F. "Byzantine Eunuchs: An Overview, with Special Reference to Their Creation and Origin." Pages 168–84 in *Women, Men and Eunuchs: Gender in Byzantium.* Edited by L. James. London: Routledge, 1997.

Trible, Phillis. "Review of R. Hamerton-Kelly, *God the Father.*" *Theology Today* 37 (1980): 118.

Tsuk, Tsvika. "The Aqueducts to Sepphoris." Pages 161–75 in *Galilee through the Centuries: Confluence of Cultures.* Edited by Eric M. Meyers. Duke Judaic Studies Series 1. Winona Lake, Ind.: Eisenbrauns, 1999.

Tuckett, Chr. *Q and the History of Early Christianity.* Edinburgh: T. & T. Clark, 1996.

Turner, Victor W. *Dramas, Fields and Metaphors: Symbolic Action in Human Society.* Ithaca, N.Y.: Cornell University Press, 1974.

Uro, Risto. "Apocalyptic Symbolism and Social Identity in Q." Pages 67–118 in *Symbols and Strata: Essays on the Sayings Gospel Q.* Edited by Risto Uro. Publications of the Finnish Exegetical Society 65. Göttingen: Vandenhoeck & Ruprecht, 1996.

———. "Asceticism and Anti-Familial Language in the *Gospel of Thomas.*" Pages 216–34 in *Constructing Early Christian Families.* Edited by H. Moxnes. London: Routledge, 1997.

———, ed. *Thomas at the Crossroads: Essays on the Gospel of Thomas.* Edinburgh: T. & T. Clark, 1998.

———. "Is *Thomas* an Encratite Gospel?" Pages 140–62 in *Thomas at the Crossroads: Essays on the Gospel of Thomas.* Edited by Risto Uro. Edinburgh: T. & T. Clark, 1998.

Vaage, Leif E. "Q 1 and the Historical Jesus: Some Peculiar Sayings (7:33–34; 9:57–58, 59–60; 14:26–27)." *Forum* 5:2 (1989): 159–76.

———. "The Son of Man Saying in Q: Stratigraphical Location and Significance." *Semeia* 55 (1991): 103–29.

———. "Like Dogs Barking: Cynic *parresia* and Shameless Action." *Semeia* 57 (1992): 25–39.

———. *Galilean Upstarts: Jesus' First Followers according to Q.* Valley Forge, Pa.: Trinity Press International, 1994.

Valantasis, Richard. "Constructions of Power in Asceticism." *JAAR* 63 (1995): 775–821.

———. "A Theory of the Social Function of Asceticism." Pages 544–52 in *Asceticism.* Edited by V. Wimbush and R. Valantasis. New York: Oxford University Press, 1995.

———. *The Gospel of Thomas.* London: Routledge, 1997.

Vale, Ruth. "Literary Sources in Archaeological Description: The Case of Galilee, Galilees and Galileans." *JSJ* 18 (1987): 209–26.

van der Horst, P. W. "'The Finger of God': Miscellaneous Notes on Luke 11:20 and Its *Umwelt.*" Pages 89–103 in *Sayings of Jesus: Canonical and Non-Canonical: Essays in Honour of T. Baarda.* Edited by W. L. Petersen, J. S. Vos and H. J. de Jone. NovTSup 89. Leiden: Brill, 1997.

Vermaseren, M. J. *Corpus Cultus Cybelae Attidisque (CCCA)* Vol. 1. *Asia Minor.* Leiden: Brill, 1987.

Vermes, Geza. *Jesus the Jew: A Historian's Reading of the Gospels.* London: Collins, 1973: Reprint, Philadelphia: Fortress, 1981.

———. *The Religion of Jesus the Jew.* London: SCM Press, 1993.

Viviano, B. T. "The Historical Jesus in the Doubly Attested Sayings: An Experiment." *RB* 103 (1996): 367–410.

Wainewright, E. "The Gospel of Matthew." Pages 635–77 in *Searching the Scriptures.* Vol. 2, *A Feminist Commentary.* Edited by E. Schüssler Fiorenza. New York: Crossroad, 1994.

Wallace-Hadrill, Andrew. "The Social Structure of the Roman House." *Papers of the British School at Rome* 56 (1988): 43–97.

Weiss, Johannes. *Jesus' Proclamation of the Kingdom of God.* Translated, edited, and with introduction by R. H. Hiers and D. L. Holland. Philadelphia: Fortress, 1971. Trans. of *Die Predigt Jesu vom Reiche Gottes.* Göttingen: Vandenhoeck & Ruprecht, 1892.

Wilder, A. N. *Early Christian Rhetoric: The Language of the Gospel.* New York: Harper & Row, 1964.

Willis, W., ed. *The Kingdom of God in 20th-Century Interpretation.* Peabody, Mass.: Hendrickson, 1987.

Young, Steve. "Being a Man: The Pursuit of Manliness in the Shepherd of Hermas." *JECS* 2 (1994): 237–55.

INDEX OF SCRIPTURE
AND ANCIENT SOURCES

INDEX OF AUTHORS

INDEX OF SUBJECTS